BASKETBALL
(AND OTHER THINGS)

A COLLECTION OF QUESTIONS ASKED, ANSWERED, ILLUSTRATED

SHEA
SERRANO

WITH ILLUSTRATIONS BY
ARTURO
TORRES

ABRAMS IMAGE, NEW YORK

TABLE OF CONTENTS

AN INTRODUCTION, BY WAY OF ELEVEN QUESTIONS

1. Are you really going to just answer questions for the introduction to your book?
Yes.

2. Why? Why do that?
It just makes sense to me to do it that way. The entire book is a bunch of different questions getting answered. I think the introduction should be the same.

3. Will you tell me a little about the book?
Sure. The book has 33 chapters. Each chapter is a different basketball question that, as I just mentioned, gets answered. And they're not traditional, normal, regular questions. They're not things like, "Was Larry Bird better than Magic Johnson?" or whatever. They're new questions. Questions that you've (hopefully) not seen before or thought about before. That's what the book is.

Oh, also: The questions are not related to each other, and what I mean when I say that is the book isn't a thing that has to move front to back. It doesn't flow from one chapter to the next like the way a regular book would. In most cases, you don't have to read one chapter to read a chapter that comes after it. You can jump in wherever.

Oh, another also: There's a lot of art in here, and also some charts. That part doesn't really need to be explained, though.

4. Is the book all NBA-related stuff?
Pretty much, yes. There are two chapters that are about pickup basketball, and there's one chapter that's about an NBA player who's not an NBA player anymore, and there's a section about basketball players from TV shows and movies, but other than that, yes, it's all NBA-related stuff.

5. What did you mean in your answer to the third question when you said, "In most cases, you don't have to read one chapter to read a chapter that comes after it"? Why the "in most cases"?

Well, some of the questions ended up requiring answers that were way longer than I was anticipating, and so I just took them and, say, rather than having a single chapter that was 6,000 words, I'd take it and break it into two chapters that were 3,000 words. So there are some double chapters in here and even a couple of triple chapters, which is truly dumb.

6. I read your other book, *The Rap Year Book*, and when I got to the end of it I realized that you'd tricked me into reading a book that was secretly the history of rap. Is this one going to be like that? Is this book secretly the history of basketball?
No. It's not that. It's definitely not that. I mean, yes, there's lots of information in here that, after you've read it, you're going to be like, "Whoa, I know a lot about basketball now," but that's not the point of the book.

7. Okay, so what's the point of this book then? Does it have a bigger idea hidden away inside of it that I won't realize until I'm done reading it?
It does, yes. I'm not going to tell you what it is, though.

8. Since it's a basketball book, am I going to have to know a lot about stats, or learn a lot about stats?
There are stats that get mentioned in the book, definitely. Mostly, it's just regular stuff (points per game, blocks per game, things like that), but there are some spots that reference advanced stats to help prove a point or strengthen a point. Here's a quick summary for you:

- **Player Efficiency Rating (PER):** This one uses a calculation of all the pieces of the traditional box score to tell us how efficient a player is. The average NBA player has a PER of 15. All-Star players are usually around, or above, 20. League MVPs tend to hover near 27.5. Anything above 30 is exceptional. The highest-ever PER was 1963 Wilt Chamberlain (31.82).
- **Box Plus/Minus (BPM):** This is a box score–based measurement that estimates a player's performance relative to the league average, and it's expressed on a Per 100 Possessions basis. What that means is, okay, if a player has a BPM of 5, that means he is 5 points better than an average player over 100 pos-

sessions. Anything above 8 is very good and anything in double-digits is unquestionable. The highest-ever BPM was 2017 Russell Westbrook (15.6).

- **Value Over Replacement Player (VORP):** This converts BPM into an estimate of each player's overall contribution to the team. So basically it tells us how valuable a player is versus replacing that player with someone else, or a "replacement player," in this case defined as "a minimum salary player not in a rotation." Same as BPM, anything above 8 is very good and anything in double-digits is unquestionable. The highest-ever VORP was 2017 Russell Westbrook (12.4).

- **Win Shares (WS):** This is an estimate of the number of team wins a player is responsible for on his team during a particular season. If you add up all the Win Shares on a team, it'll equal up to somewhere near however many games that team won that season. Anything near 15 typically means an MVP-caliber season. 1972 Kareem Abdul-Jabbar had the highest WS ever at 25.37.

Now, one of two things just happened in that stats section above. Either you started reading it and were like, "Wow, this is interesting." Or you started reading it and were like, "Nah, fuck this," and then skipped it. If you're in that second group, all you need to know is that whenever a stat gets mentioned somewhere, high numbers are good and low numbers are bad.

9. The phrase "(AND OTHER THINGS)" that appears in the title of this book—what does it mean?
It means that, on occasion, some of the basketball conversations in here will go sideways for a second. The reason I did it that way is because that's how talking about basketball works for me, which means that's how writing about basketball works for me. I don't think in my life I have ever had a conversation about basketball that traveled in a perfectly straight line. (I suspect it works that same way for a lot of people.) The talks always kind of veer off in different directions, touching on this thing or that thing along the way, before arriving at the conclusion. So, when I was writing the book, I wanted to be careful to keep that feeling intact, and that spirit intact. It just felt natural.

10. You mentioned earlier that this isn't a history book. Was there a cut-off point in time that you decided on?
What I did is I just traveled backward to 1980, the season that Larry Bird and Magic Johnson entered the league, which was the birth of the modern NBA, and then I walked forward from there. There are tiny pieces and footnotes that reference points and events and people from before then, but all of the bigger thoughts and questions and ideas are built up around people and things from 1980 forward.

11. Why did you ask Reggie Miller to write the foreword?
I grew up in San Antonio, and so the Spurs were of course my favorite basketball team growing up and still are my favorite basketball team now. Reggie, though—Reggie was the first basketball player I ever loved. I remember watching him play a game on TV in middle school in the mid-90s and just being absolutely in awe. He was doing all of the things I thought were cool (shooting threes, talking shit, shoving people, etc.), and when you're 13, 14, 15 years old, the only stuff that matters to you is stuff that's cool, you know what I'm saying? He was a king to me; a basketball lord, of sorts.

I watched Reggie without fail for a good decade after I found him, all the way up until his retirement in 2005. His last game was a loss to the Pistons in the playoffs. In the final seconds, Pacers coach Rick Carlisle called a timeout so he could take Reggie out so the crowd could cheer for him. Reggie walked toward the bench and raised his hand and everyone was just glowing with love and it was this very touching, very moving scene. And right when it was about to end, Larry Brown, who was coaching the Pistons, called a timeout, too, and the only reason he did was so everyone could keep cheering for Reggie. The camera cut to the crowd and it was person after person after person in tears. Even after all these years, it remains the only time I ever cried while watching someone's final game.

I didn't know in that moment I'd eventually write a book about basketball and that Reggie would write the foreword for it, but I did know I was going to carry Reggie in my heart forever, and that basketball meant more to me than I'd allowed myself to realize.

FOREWORD
BY REGGIE MILLER

I have a memory from before I was in the league that I think about to this day. I hope I'm right on the dates here. This was in 1986. It was a Sunday and it was during the playoffs. I woke up that morning—this must've been my junior or senior year at UCLA. I remember waking up and getting ready to watch the CBS game. It was between Chicago and Boston. It was the game when Jordan scored 63; the one where he went crazy; the famous game.

I remember just lying in bed watching it. By that point I felt like I was going to be drafted—or, I was *assuming* I was going to be drafted. You're never totally sure that you're going to be in the NBA until you're actually in the NBA, but I definitely thought I could play there. So there's that connection there between me and the NBA because I know—or, I hope—I'm going to be a part of it soon. And I'm watching the game and I'm shaking my head. I'm looking at Michael Jordan and, I mean, Jordan was playing at such a high level. I was like, "I can't believe what I'm witnessing." It was like one-on-five. He was just two steps faster than everyone on the court. And I'm thinking, "How is this humanly possible?" I had played against him in a pickup game once or twice at UCLA during the summer, and I'd also met him when he and my sister both won the Naismith Award. So I'm watching him and I'm like, "I . . . I know I guarded him better than that. This is unbelievable what I'm watching."

Usually you watch a game and you come in and out and you're doing other things. But that game I remember just being fixated on the TV. That's one of the games that always stood out to me because he was playing like he just wasn't from this world, if that makes any kind of sense. My friends were going to eat, they were trying to go out. They were asking me to go with them. And I was like, "What? No. Go. Leave me alone. Just go." I couldn't take my eyes off the TV. I've seen so many games. I've watched so many great players. But it was something about that game, about that performance.

I think part of it was of course because of how great he was playing, but also another part was how I was feeling about becoming a part of that world. It was this really overwhelming feeling of knowing. It felt good. It felt surreal. I'll never forget that.

▶

During my four years at UCLA, every summer in the men's gym we played these pickup games. They weren't just normal pickup games, though. Our UCLA team, we stayed together and we played on one team, okay. And we were good. But there were all these pros that would come through and play, too. Magic was always there and he had a team. Isiah Thomas and Mark Aguirre would be there and they'd have a team. Kiki VanDe-Weghe would have a team. And there was a team of overseas players. Larry was there. Michael showed up a couple times. Everyone came through, because during the summer everyone was in LA.

So we had all these different teams, with all these different pros and we all played round robin on two courts. It was absolutely the best basketball I had ever seen. I mean, it was Magic and Kareem and all those guys unscripted, uninterrupted. Everyone was just flowing. Think about that. Think about being 20 years old and you're playing pickup basketball with Magic Johnson, with Larry Bird, with Michael, with Kareem. That's what we were doing. Two and a half to three months out of the year that's what we were doing. It was pure.

▶

There's something to be said of those moments where you're on the bus or you're on the plane or you're in the locker room with your team and you're just laughing and vibing off one another. Just being in the back of the bus with the LaSalle Thompsons, the Mark Jacksons, the Vern Flemings, the Herb Williamses, the Chuck Persons—it's an incredible experience. That's a part of the NBA that a lot of people never get to see so I guess maybe that's what makes those memories feel so special; they belong to so few people.

I remember being on the bus in the back during my rookie year and it was our first road trip. I'm 22 years old and Clint Richardson—I remember this story so vividly—he pulled me aside. This was when he was in his last year in the league or close to his last year, I believe. He pulled me aside and he said, "Look, be yourself. Don't be a follower. Be a leader. You don't have to dress like everyone else. Be unique in this league." That sounds like real general or basic advice, but to hear it from a veteran when you're a rookie, that's a big thing. It's a big moment. It was a real big moment for me.

John Long, who was my mentor my rookie year, he was 31 at the time and I was 22. He was the shooting guard. I only started one game that season. He started all the other games. And before every game we would sit down and we would watch tape of the opposing guard and we would talk about how we were going to guard him. And for a guy that'd been in the league for as long as he had—he was there for, like, a decade before I got there—for him to sit down with a rookie who was going to take his spot eventually and teach me what the NBA was, it was incredible. "Reg, you can't talk to Alvin Robertson." "Reg, this is how we're gonna guard Ricky Pierce." "Reg, you see how Randy Wittman is using the screen here? Look at his arms. You wanna knock his arms down and lock and go on this one." "Reg, when you play Ron Harper you're gonna wanna play physical with him. But be smart. You're gonna hold him with your left hand and keep your right hand up because the ref is right behind you and he's looking at your right hand." It was those lessons that were invaluable as a rookie. And more than that, it is those things that I remember the most.

The shots are great, you know. Hitting big shots against the Knicks and the Nets and the Sixers and the Celtics and the Bulls; those were great. Those are the things everyone talks about, the things everyone asks about. But it's those little lessons I learned from John Long, from Byron Scott, who came to our team in the mid-'90s and really made us feel like we could win in the playoffs, from anyone who sat down and just talked in private, those are the special moments. It's those things that I'll remember and always look back on so fondly.

▶

During the first lockout year, I got cast in a small part in *Gang Related*, a movie starring Jim Belushi and Tupac. It was shot out in LA and my whole scene was . . . I think I was a hotdog vendor. That was my part. But I was playing Reggie Miller as a hotdog vendor because of the lockout. And the whole scene with Jim Belushi was like, "Oh, God. It must really be hard out here for you right now, Reggie." And I was supposed to be like, "Well, I gotta find extra money doing something." That was the whole thing. It was real short. But still, it was just so cool to be on set. And then when Tupac showed up, it was like he just took the whole set to another level. His voice—that voice alone would just get you hyped for every take, every scene. And he and I would talk and he was a big basketball fan so we had that instant connection over our love of the game of basketball.

Of the four sports, I think it's easiest for basketball to become absorbed into other parts of pop culture because think about it: A lot of times people aren't going out to play a casual game of baseball. It's not a thing you can just jump up and do. Everyone's gotta have a glove, there's gotta be a big field. And with football, it takes a lot of people to play a game. Basketball, though, you don't really need much beyond a ball and something to throw it in. You can play it one-on-one, two-on-two, three-on-three. It's just an easy game to access. Plus, the players are in jerseys and shorts. You can see them. They're very recognizable. A football player has to wear a helmet all the time. Baseball players have hats on and their uniforms also feel a little more official. Basketball, to me, it just feels more accessible. It feels more available.

Go back to grade school: Other than playing on the monkey bars, what was everyone doing? You could always find a bunch of kids playing basketball on the blacktop. So whether you played or just watched, we all grew up with it. Somehow it just becomes a part of everything. Of music, of movies, of television. Even when it isn't the main focal point of what's happening, it's there somewhere. Maybe in the background or even behind the background. It's there. Basketball is always there.

WHAT YEAR WAS
MICHAEL JORDAN THE BEST
VERSION OF MICHAEL JORDAN?

Let's you and I concede a point. Let's you and I agree that Michael Jordan, generally regarded as the greatest basketball player of all time, is exactly that: the greatest basketball player of all time.

Perhaps you don't believe that, and if you don't, then that's fine.[1] Perhaps you think it's Kareem Abdul-Jabbar, who was an excellent player for longer than anyone else ever was an excellent player.[2] Or perhaps you think it's Wilt Chamberlain, who once averaged more than 50 points and 25 rebounds for an entire season, which is all the way unbelievable. Or perhaps you think it's Greg Oden, the first-ever number-one NBA draft pick to have a picture of his penis posted to the Internet. Maybe there's a chance you think it's Magic Johnson (the best ever at controlling the flow of a game), LeBron James (the best ever at being great at all the positions), Tim Duncan (the best ever at being the love of my life, and also some basketball things). All of those are fine choices.[3] And if one of those (or anyone else) is your pick for greatest ever, let's pretend, at least for the duration of this chapter, that you, like me, think it's Jordan.

That being so, here's the question: If Michael Jordan is the greatest basketball player of all time, then what year was it that Michael Jordan was the best version of Michael Jordan? When was the greatest basketball player of all time at his absolute greatest?

▶

To figure out what season Michael Jordan was the best version of Michael Jordan, we have to look at four different things.

- The box score stats—specifically, his points, rebounds, assists, blocks, and steals averages. Rather than take straight game averages, though, let's do it based on per 100 possessions, which helps to evap-orate away most variations that might otherwise pop up because of changes in playing time or game pace.
- The advanced stats I explained in the introduction—Player Efficiency Rating, Box Plus/Minus, Value Over Replacement Player, Win Shares.
- His playoffs performance each season, which, at least in a certain measure, is generally more important than regular season performance.
- Any additional or extenuating factors that might've affected a season's arc, or even a single game's arc, like: The time he put up 38-7-5 in Game 5 of the 1997 NBA Finals when he had the flu, which remains iconic.[4] Or the time when at the end of a game against the Nuggets in 1991 he shot a free throw with his eyes closed just to needle then-rookie Dikembe Mutombo, which remains cool. Or the time during a game against the Jazz in 1987 when a Jazz fan sitting near courtside shouted at him to pick on someone his own size after he'd dunked on John Stockton (6'1"), to which Jordan responded by dunking over the nearly 7-foot-tall Mel Turpin on the next possession and then shouting "Is that big enough?" at the fan, which remains hilarious.

Jordan played 13 seasons with the Bulls. That means there are 13 versions of Michael Jordan for us to pick from.[5] However, one of those was the season he returned from his first retirement (1995 Jordan), and not including the playoffs, he only played 17 games that year, so we can eliminate that one. That leaves us with 12 different versions of Michael Jordan. Of those, one Jordan was Great, two Jordans were Very Great, six Jordans were Very, Very, Great, two Jordans were Very, Very, Very Great, and one Jordan was The Greatest. They're arranged here by ascending greatness.

---

1. It's actually not fine.
2. Hall of Fame inductee; six-time NBA champion; six-time League MVP; ten-time All-NBA First Team; five-time All-NBA Second Team; five-time All-Defensive First Team; six-time All-Defensive Second Team; nineteen-time All-Star.
3. They're not.
4. It also remains maybe a lie. In 2013, Tim Grover, Jordan's longtime trainer, told Henry Abbott of ESPN's *TrueHoop* that Jordan was intentionally food poisoned by the pizza place they'd ordered pizza from the night before Game 5.
5. None of his Wizards seasons are even close to anything he did with the Bulls, so they're out.

THE GREAT MICHAEL JORDAN(S)

SEASON:	1985–86
ADVANCED STATS:	WS: 1.5; BPM: 4.7; VORP: 0.8; PER: 27.5
PER 100 POSSESSIONS:	43.5 points, 6.8 rebounds, 5.7 assists, 2.2 blocks, 3.9 steals
TEAM PLAYOFFS SUCCESS:	Lost to the Celtics in the first round (3–0)

Three significant things happen this year. First, Jordan breaks his foot three games into the season. (It's the only big injury he had during his career.) Second, he returns in the middle of March, helps the Bulls get into the playoffs, then averages 43.7 points per game,[6] one of those games being his famed 63 points in Boston Garden. And third, after the 63-point game, Larry Bird sums up Jordan's performance by saying, "I think he's God disguised as Michael Jordan." If Larry Bird calls you God, it ain't that far away from God calling you God, you know what I'm saying?

THE VERY GREAT MICHAEL JORDAN(S)

SEASON:	1984–85
ADVANCED STATS:	WS:14.0; BPM:8.2; VORP:8.1; PER:25.8
PER 100 POSSESSIONS:	35.5 points, 8.2 rebounds, 7.4 assists, 1.1 blocks, 3.0 steals
TEAM PLAYOFFS SUCCESS:	Lost to the Bucks in the first round (3–1)
AWARDS:	Rookie of the Year

Jordan's first season in the league was wildly successful. Regarding rookies, his 14.0 Win Shares are still the eighth-most ever (by comparison, Kobe Bryant's WS his rookie year was 1.8; LeBron tallied 5.1), his per game scoring average is the seventh highest (28.2), and his

VORP is the highest ever. So it was for sure obvious that Jordan was going to be special, because by most accounts he already was when he arrived. But he wasn't anywhere near what he eventually became.

SEASON:	1996–97
ADVANCED STATS:	WS: 18.3; BPM: 6.7; VORP: 6.8; PER: 27.8
PER 100 POSSESSIONS:	41.8 points, 8.3 rebounds, 6.0 assists, 0.8 blocks, 2.4 steals
TEAM PLAYOFFS SUCCESS:	Beat the Bullets (3–0), then the Hawks (4–1), then the Heat (4–1), then the Jazz to win the title (4–2)
AWARDS:	Finals MVP

A very great year and season that gets pulled into a singular version of itself by the gravity of The Flu Game.

THE VERY, VERY GREAT MICHAEL JORDAN(S)

SEASON:	1986–87
ADVANCED STATS:	WS: 16.9; BPM: 8.6; VORP: 8.8; PER: 29.8
PER 100 POSSESSIONS:	46.4 points, 6.6 rebounds, 5.8 assists, 1.9 blocks, 3.6 steals
TEAM PLAYOFFS SUCCESS:	Lost to the Celtics in the first round (3-0)

Jordan begins to truly start flexing. He wins his first of ten career scoring titles, doing so by averaging 37.1 points per game.[7] He also leads the entire league in PER, WS, and VORP. (This is also the year that *RoboCop*, *Predator*, *Lethal Weapon*, and *The Running Man* came out.) (It doesn't have anything to do with Jordan, but it just seems like a thing I should mention.)

SEASON:	1989–90
ADVANCED STATS:	WS: 19.0; BPM: 10.6; VORP: 10.1; PER: 31.2
PER 100 POSSESSIONS:	42.7 points, 8.8 rebounds, 8.1 assists, 0.8 blocks, 3.5 steals
TEAM PLAYOFFS SUCCESS:	Beat the Bucks (3–1), then the 76ers (4–1), then lost to the Pistons in the Conference Finals (4–3)

Big playoff success here,[8] both for his Bulls (one game within making the Finals) and for himself (his 36.7 points per game in the 1990 playoffs is still the most in NBA history by a player in a playoff run of 15+ games). The Bulls end up getting obliterated in Game 7 in the Conference Finals against the Pistons, but it's hardly Jordan's fault (he puts up 31 points, 8 rebounds, 9 assists; Pippen, who suffered a migraine before the game, puts up 2 points, 4 rebounds, 2 assists, and 2-4-2 sounds less like a basketball stat and more like a middle-school soccer team's record).

SEASON:	1991–92
ADVANCED STATS:	WS: 17.7; BPM: 8.6; VORP: 8.3; PER: 27.7
PER 100 POSSESSIONS:	39.4 points, 8.4 rebounds, 8.0 assists, 1.2 blocks, 3.0 steals
TEAM PLAYOFFS SUCCESS:	Beat the Heat (3–0), then the Knicks (4–3), then the Cavs (4–2), then the Trail Blazers to win the title (4–2)
AWARDS:	League MVP, Finals MVP

Another MVP. Another title. The Bulls win 67 games during this season, fourth-most in league history as of 2016. Add in bonus credits here because (a) at this point in his career, it's only the second time he plays in a Game 7 (the Knicks clobbered their way there), and he ends up fucking bodying everyone in it (46 points, 6 rebounds, 4 assists, 2 steals, 3 blocks); (b) this is the year he undresses poor Clyde Drexler in the Finals; and (c) it's also the year he gives us the iconic Jordan Shrug. All important and essential moments for Jordan.

SEASON:	1995–96
ADVANCED STATS:	WS: 20.4; BPM: 8.6; VORP: 8.3; PER 29.4
PER 100 POSSESSIONS:	42.5 points, 9.3 rebounds, 6.0 assists, 0.7 blocks, 3.1 steals
TEAM PLAYOFFS SUCCESS:	Beat the Heat (3–0), then the Knicks (4–1), then the Magic (4–0), then the Seattle Supersonics to win the title (4–2)
AWARDS:	League MVP, Finals MVP, All-Star Game MVP

This was the first full season Jordan played since his rookie year where he didn't lead the league in VORP, but it's also the 72-win year, so those two things cancel each other out if you want to pick nits about his stats.

---

6. Still an NBA record as I write this.

7. The highest season scoring average he'd ever notch. It's also the only time someone who wasn't Wilt Chamberlain broke 37. Wilt averaged 50.3 in 1962, 44.8 in 1963, 38.3 in 1961, and 37.6 in 1960. Wilt was not fucking around.

8. Not coincidentally, also his first year with Phil Jackson as head coach, and also-also the first time Scottie Pippen is an All-Star.

SEASON:	1990-91
ADVANCED STATS:	WS: 20.3; BPM: 10.8; VORP: 9.8; PER: 31.6
PER 100 POSSESSIONS:	42.7 points, 8.1 rebounds, 7.5 assists, 1.4 blocks, 3.7 steals
TEAM PLAYOFFS SUCCESS:	Beat the Knicks (3-0), then the 76ers (4-1), then the Pistons (4-0), then the Lakers to win the title (4-1)
AWARDS:	League MVP, Finals MVP

Wins his second MVP trophy. Beats Patrick Ewing and the Knicks, Charles Barkley and the 76ers, Isiah Thomas and the Pistons, and Magic Johnson and the Lakers to win his first-ever NBA championship,[9] averaging a just plain goofy 31 points and 11 assists in the Finals, a thing that's even more impressive when you realize that he'd never averaged more than 10 assists in a postseason. I think it was right around this time when most everyone else in the league was like, "Well, fuck."

SEASON:	1997-98
ADVANCED STATS:	WS: 15.8; BPM: 4.6; VORP: 5.3; PER: 25.2
PER 100 POSSESSIONS:	40.0 points, 8.1 rebounds, 4.8 assists, 0.8 blocks, 2.4 steals
TEAM PLAYOFFS SUCCESS:	Beat the Nets (3-0), then the Hornets (4-1), then the Pacers (4-3), then the Jazz to win the title (4-2)
AWARDS:	League MVP, Finals MVP, All-Star Game MVP

Here's the last minute of Michael Jordan's career as a Chicago Bull, played at the end of Game 6 of the NBA Finals, a series the Bulls were leading 3–2 against the Jazz (and playing in Utah):

- **0:59:** Swishes two free throws to tie the game 83–83. Jordan has 41.
- **0:42:** John Stockton hits a three to put the Jazz up 86–83.
- [Chicago Timeout]
- **0:41:** Jordan receives the inbounds pass from Scottie Pippen at almost the midcourt logo.
- **0:37:** Jordan stutter-steps, then drives by Bryon Russell, who is attempting to guard him. Jordan lays it up over Antoine Carr to make it 86–85, Jazz. Jordan has 43.
- **0:36:** Stockton brings the ball up court.
- **0:22:** Stockton passes the ball to Karl Malone in the post.
- **0:21:** Jordan, who'd been guarding Jeff Hornacek, sneaks around the back and slaps the ball away from Malone, then steals it.
- **0:17:** Jordan dribbles up the court, and he does not call timeout, nor does Phil Jackson, because both of them know what's about to happen next, as does everybody in the arena, because by 1998 they'd been watching Jordan slit the throats of his opponents for nearly a decade and a half.
- **0:12:** Jordan, at the left corner of the three-point line, waits. Dribbles.
- **0:11:** Jordan waits. Dribbles.
- **0:10:** Jordan waits. Dribbles.
- **0:09:** Jordan waits. Dribbles.
- **0:08:** Jordan attacks, dribbling toward the top of the key.
- **0:07:** Jordan stops, crossover dribbles, discards Bryon Russell, shoots.
- **0:06:** Cash. Bulls lead 87–86. Jordan has 45 points.[10]
- **0:05:** Bob Costas: "That may have been—who knows what will unfold in the next several months—

---

9. This is such a great list of bodies to collect on your way to winning a ring; all Hall of Famers, all listed in the NBA's 50 Greatest Players of All Time.

10. A weird aside: 45 is the number he chose to wear when he returned from his first retirement because he said 23 was the last number his father saw him wear before he was murdered.

but that may have been the last shot Michael Jordan will ever take in the NBA."

- **0:02:** Stockton misses a three.
- **0:00:** Jordan wins his sixth NBA championship.

1998 Jordan is not the most statistically dominant Jordan, but he is the one who is the most theatrical. In a large-scale one-on-one Jordans-Only tournament, I fully expect him to figure out a way to beat the eight Jordans he beat here.[11]

THE VERY, VERY, VERY GREAT MICHAEL JORDAN(S)

SEASON:	1987-88
ADVANCED STATS:	WS: 21.2; BPM: 12.2; VORP: 11.8; PER 31.7
PER 100 POSSESSION:	43.6 points, 6.8 rebounds, 7.4 assists, 2.0 blocks, 3.9 steals
TEAM PLAYOFFS SUCCESS:	Beat the Cavs (3-2), then lost to the Pistons (4-1)
AWARDS:	League MVP, Defensive Player of the Year, All-Star Game MVP

Terror. His VORP and BPM were the highest ever measured up to that point. His PER was the best ever of everyone in the NBA's history who wasn't Wilt Chamberlain. He won his first League MVP. He also won Defensive Player of the Year. He also won All-Star Game MVP, too, just because he felt like it. Through 2016, it's still the only season a player had 100+ blocks and 250+ steals.

SEASON:	1988-89
ADVANCED STATS:	WS: 19.8; BPM: 12.6; VORP: 12.0; PER: 31.1
PER 100 POSSESSIONS:	40.0 points, 9.9 rebounds, 9.9 assists, 1.0 block, 3.6 steals
TEAM PLAYOFFS SUCCESS:	Beat the Cavs (3-2), then beat the Knicks (4-2), then lost to the Pistons (4-2)

Somehow even better than 1988 Jordan, mostly due to the fact that he has the most efficient shooting season of his career.[12] He becomes the first player since Oscar Robertson to average 30-8-8. And maybe most importantly, this is the year he hits a massively important shot in the playoffs ("The Shot" to beat Cleveland in an elimination Game 5). 1989 was the birth of Bloodthirsty Jordan.[13]

THE GREATEST VERSION OF MICHAEL JORDAN OF ALL

SEASON:	1992-93
ADVANCED STATS:	WS: 17.2; BPM: 9.5; VORP: 8.9; PER: 29.7
PER 100 POSSESSION:	43.0 points, 8.8 rebounds, 7.2 assists, 1.0 blocks, 3.7 steals
TEAM PLAYOFFS SUCCESS:	Beat the Hawks (3-0), then the Cavs (4-0), then the Knicks (4-2), then the Suns to win the title (4-2)
AWARDS:	Finals MVP

---

11. If you want to swap him out with 1991 Jordan, I understand.
12. He had a .614 true shooting percentage, which measures two-point shots, three-point shots, and free throws together. Bonus: He had the best rebounding and assists seasons of his career here, too.
13. Bonus: His playoffs BPM of 12.8 in 1989 was the best by any player since Kareem in 1977.

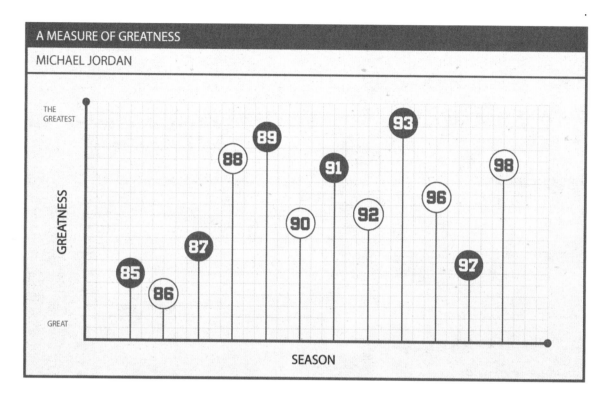

A MEASURE OF GREATNESS

MICHAEL JORDAN

The Alpha Jordan. The greatest version of the greatest player. Just think on these three things, which really encapsulate all that Michael Jordan is, was, and would become.

1. The Bulls are down 0–2 to the Knicks in the Eastern Conference Finals, a thing that is doubly troubling because the Knicks have homecourt advantage and then triply troubling because the Knicks had managed to take the Bulls to seven games the year before, so it was clear they weren't super afraid of them. The Bulls should've lost that series. They really should've. But they didn't. It didn't even go to a Game 7. They won the next four games, the last three of which showed us a Jordan that was fully formed and unstoppable (54 points in Game 4, 29 points and 14 assists in Game 5, then 25 points and 9 assists to close it out).

2. In the Finals, Jordan averaged 41 points per game against the Suns, and 46.1 points per 100 posses-sions in the whole playoffs, the highest he ever had during a championship run and second in his career only to his 1986 God Disguised as Michael Jordan series, but it's even more impressive than that performance because that was 3 games long and this was 19 games long.

3. Jordan's total points for the 1993 playoffs: 666.

God Jordan was a great version of him. Devil Jordan was the greatest, though.

WHO'S YOUR FRANKENPLAYER
MADE OUT OF?

An aside: *The intro to this chapter is a recollection of an event that happened over 25 years ago. I'm going to write it without researching or fact-checking anything beforehand. When I'm done, I'll go back and add footnotes to it to show what parts I got correct and what parts I got wrong.*

I vaguely remember accidentally watching a movie when I was in elementary school called *Frankenhooker*. I don't think it was pornography,[1] but there was definitely nudity in it.[2] The premise of the movie was: A guy's girlfriend[3] gets run over by a lawn mower[4] and chopped into pieces. He is too brokenhearted to accept the loss, so he comes up with a plan: He plots to kill several prostitutes[5] and use their body parts to rebuild his girlfriend.[6] He goes to where all the prostitutes hang out, arranges to have them come to his house[7] for a sex party,[8] then chops them all up.[9] After that, he stitches all the appropriate parts together, hooks the corpse puzzle up to a machine, uses a thunderstorm to jolt her full of electricity, then she comes to life like how it happened with Dr. Frankenstein and his monster.[10] That's the movie. It was wildly inappropriate for a child to watch,[11] but I'm glad that I did because now a retelling of it serves as the intro for this chapter, which is a thing where the goal is to take a bunch of different parts of different basketball players and stitch them together and make a Frankenplayer.

▶

This is mostly a fun exercise, but there are still a couple of rules that need to be followed.

- **THE MICHAEL JORDAN RULE:** You are only allowed to pick a player for a category once. So, say, if you decide you want to have World B. Free's jump shot for the Jump Shot category, that means you can't use him for the Hair category or Name category. This rule exists mostly to just prevent you from saying something like, "Give me Steph Curry's jumper and then divide all the rest of the categories up between Michael Jordan and LeBron James."

- **THE SKIP 2 MY LOU RULE:** For a player to be eligible to be included in the Frankenplayer, he has to have played at least 10 games in the NBA. (Skip 2 My Lou is the streetball alter ego of Rafer Alston, who played in the NBA for 11 years.)

- **THE PEAK PLAYER RULE:** This one is less a rule and more of a general guideline, but: If a player is chosen for a particular category, you can assume it's meant as When He Was At His Peak. In cases where a specific year is necessary, it'll be noted.

▶

Several of the categories are things where you can take just a straight measurement and not need much else beyond that, so let's burn through those first. For Vertical Leap, give me Zach LaVine, a two-time Slam Dunk contest champion who recorded a 46-inch vertical in 2014. For Hands, it'd probably be best to just go

---

1. Correct. Not pornography.
2. Very correct.
3. Incorrect. She was the guy's fiancée.
4. Correct. Note: The lawn mower was a gift for the guy's father. What's more, the guy, who's very smart but who's kind of a loser, had rigged the lawn mower so that it would operate via remote control. The fiancée was showing the dad how it worked when she accidentally remote controlled it right TF over herself.
5. Correct.
6. Half-correct: He's going to rebuild his fiancée.
7. Incorrect. He has them go to a motel.
8. Incorrect. He tells them they'll be participating in a beauty pageant for his brother.
9. Incorrect. He actually came up with a very deadly version of cocaine. He decided he couldn't go through with killing them and was planning to leave, but then one of the prostitutes found the death cocaine and so they all started doing it. Somehow, it caused them to explode. Exploding prostitutes seems like a thing you wouldn't forget, but I did.
10. All correct. And I should mention here that he'd kept a few of her parts after they'd gotten scattered around by the lawn mower, the most important of which was her head.
11. Very correct.

with a pair of the biggest, so I'm taking small forward Giannis Antetokounmpo's, whose hands measure a foot in length from the tip of the thumb to the tip of the pinky. For First-Step Speed, let's go with Stephon Marbury, mostly because I remember reading a 2005 profile of point guard Steve Nash by Chuck Klosterman where the explosiveness of Stephon Marbury, who was then a point guard with the Suns, was described as "physically palpable when he blows past people; it feels like wind." And for End-To-End Speed, let's go with 2009 Toney Douglas, who ran the ¾ court sprint time at the NBA Draft Combine in 3.03 seconds, which is the fastest on record.[12]

NAME

This is a critical category. If we're building a basketball megapower player, he needs to have a basketball megapower name. "Stromile Swift" is great, but not intimidating enough. "Detlef Schrempf" has always been a personal favorite of mine, but I can admit that it doesn't have the class or regality of a "World B. Free" or even "Metta World Peace." "Fat Lever" and "Frank Brickowski" are the reverse of what we're looking for, as are "Mookie Blaylock" and "Bimbo Coles." "Tree Rollins" is good, but sounds a little too immobile to be perfect. "Sleepy Floyd" is cool, but maybe a little too cool, if that makes sense. "Speedy Claxton" is fun, but ultimately it sounds like something you'd call a chubby child. "Jamario Moon" is a solid possibility, and certainly in the class with "Magic Johnson." "Chauncey Billups" is secretly a great name, too. None of them is the best one, though. Because the best name belongs to God Shammgod, a streetball legend who played 20 games with the Washington Wizards during the 1998 season. He gets the nod here.

HAIR

Four ways to go here. You can go Beautiful Pristine, and pick someone whose hair was iconic in a classic way, like Allen Iverson's cornrows or Artis Gilmore's Afro and muttonchops. You can go Time Capsule Pristine, and pick someone whose hair was iconic in an era-specific way, like when Anthony Mason got "Knicks" shaved into the side of his head in the '90s or when Bill Walton had an unkempt hippie ponytail in the '70s. You can go Awful Pristine, and pick someone whose hair was iconic in the ugliest way possible, like when Drew Gooden had all of his head bald save for a tiny square at the nape of his neck or any time Dennis Rodman did anything after 1993. Or you can go Aging Man Pristine, and go with someone whose hair was iconic in a very pragmatic way, like Clyde Drexler when he was very surely going bald in 1992 or Nate Thurmond when his hairline was at the back of his head in 1975. I'm going Nate Thurmond. I want my Frankenplayer to look like a dockworker from the '70s.

VISION

Give me Jason Kidd's vision here. Jason Kidd saw angles and eventualities better than anyone I've ever watched play basketball. The best was during a Nets–Knicks game in the early 2000s when, after tapping the ball away from Knicks point guard Howard Eisley to force a steal, Kidd picked it up, threw it up ahead of a Knicks player toward Lucious Harris, but did so low enough and with enough side-spin on it that the spin caused the ball to shoot left after hitting the ground, in effect bending around the defender. It was like Angelina Jolie bending the bullet path in *Wanted*, except but real life.

FOREHEAD[13]

Paul George from the Pacers has an especially tidy forehead. I'll take his from any year, makes no difference. (Having a tidy forehead is only a weird thing to notice until you've noticed it, after which it becomes impossible to notice anything else.) (Damian Lillard also has a nice forehead, so if George's is already spoken for then Lillard's is fine.)

---

12. To be clear: Two guys have run it faster: Jereme Richmond in 2011 and Marcus Thornton in 2015 both ran it in 3.02 seconds. Neither of them made the NBA, though, so they're out. It should also be noted that a lot of the top tier drafts elect not to do some of the Draft Combine drills, the sprint being one of them. But for comparison: John Wall, regularly considered one of the fastest current-era players, ran it in 3.14.
13. This section is assuming we've ended up deciding against the Nate Thurmond hair.

CHIN

Early in the 1985 season, the Celtics and the Sixers played each other. During the game, Dr. J and Larry Bird got into a fight, only it was a fight in half the sense of the word, because Moses Malone and Charles Barkley, then teammates of Dr. J, held Bird while Dr. J fired off three solid shots to the jaw. Somehow, Larry Bird did not die, or even get knocked out, or even get knocked down. Larry Bird's chin is made of adamantium.

SHOULDERS

2010 Dwight Howard's shoulders looked like bowling balls.

ARM MUSCULATURE

You could go 1992 David Robinson. Or maybe 2004 Ben Wallace. Either of those would be fine selections, for sure. I think I want 2007 Andre Iguodala's arms, though.

WINGSPAN

Manute Bol had a wingspan of 8'6", if you can even believe that. Easy pick here.

PENIS

There are three ways to handle the penis situation.[14] The first is you say that you'll choose Wilt Chamberlain's penis because it's the most infamous NBA penis (in his 1991 book, *A View from Above*, Wilt claimed that he'd slept with 20,000 different women in his life). His penis was probably very durable. The second is that you lean the opposite direction, and you say that you'll choose A.C. Green's penis, who remained a virgin for the duration of his NBA career (1985–2001). His penis was probably very pristine. The third is that you go in blind and just choose a penis that's never been in the news but you assume would be attractive (Serge Ibaka, or maybe J.J. Redick). I think I go pristine. It has to be A.C. Green here.

FINISHING IN THE LANE ABILITY

Beginning in 2013, the NBA began tracking "drives," which get defined as "any touch that starts at least 20 feet from the hoop and is dribbled within 10 feet of the hoop and excludes fast breaks." From then to 2016, Steph Curry had the highest field goal percentage at 54.0 percent.[15] Under him is Tony Parker at 53.3 percent. And then third is Goran Dragic. I'm tempted to pick Dragic here because his name sounds almost like Dragon, and I'm inclined to always lean toward the guy named Dragon in any situation.[16] But I'm stepping over him to get to Parker for this category. He gets the pick over Curry because (1) Steph has the added benefit of guys charging at him hard to get him off the three-point line, which makes it at least a tad easier for him to get to the rim than for Parker, who has never been a three-point threat,[17] and (2) since the NBA began keeping tabs on this in 2013, that means an In-His-Prime Steph is getting measured against a Too-Old Tony Parker. So give me 2006[18] Tony Parker.[19]

SHOOTING ABILITY

This one needs to be broken up into three different subcategories: Catch and Shoot, Come off the Pick and Shoot, and Pull-Up off the Dribble and Shoot. Give me 2015 Klay Thompson for Catch and Shoot.[20] Give me 1998 Reggie Miller for Come off the Pick and Shoot.[21] Give me 2016 Steph Curry[22] for Pull-Up off the Dribble and Shoot. If it can only be one, though, then I suppose it has to be Steph, who, if you mush all of those subcategories into one, his cumulative score is probably the highest.

THE ABILITY TO PROTECT THE PAINT

Give me the 1994 version of Hakeem Olajuwon. He averaged four blocks per game over the course of the playoffs that year. There are players who averaged more blocks per game over the course of a season than that,[23] but I'll generally take what someone does in the playoffs over what someone does during the regular season. And to be sure, there are even a handful who averaged more blocks per game over a playoff run,[24] but nobody ever averaged higher than that WHILE winning a championship. So give me Hakeem.

Let's finish with a bunch of quick ones:

Give me Shaquille O'Neal's power around the rim, Richard Hamilton's endurance, Brandon Knight's willingness to step in front of a train,[25] Dirk Nowitzki's one-footed fadeaway,[26] Jason Williams's flair, Gary Payton's trash-talking ability, Kawhi Leonard's on-the-ball defense, Jerry Stackhouse's affinity for on-court fistfights, Charles Oakley's toughness, Bill Laimbeer's smirk, John Stockton's sturdiness with the ball, Michael Jordan's ability to recognize what needs to happen during a game and also his ability to do it, anybody but Kobe Bryant's nickname, Anfernee Hardaway's lankiness, Dominique Wilkins's ferocity during dunks, LeBron James's doeverythingness, Wilt Chamberlain's rebounding ability, Kareem Abdul-Jabbar's scoring consistency, Scottie Pippen's nose, Russell Westbrook's pettiness, Shawn Kemp's celebrations, Bill Russell's rings, Charles Barkley's readiness to throw someone through a window, Isiah Thomas's nasty streak, David Robinson's divinity, Kevin McHale's low post game, Patrick Ewing's mustache, Kirk Hinrich's accessories, Chris Paul's inner anger, DeMarcus Cousins's outer anger, Tim Duncan's in-game demeanor, and J.R. Smith's postgame demeanor.

   Take all those pieces, stitch them together, and there you go: that's my Frankenplayer.

---

14. If somebody ever actually did make an X-rated version of *Frankenhooker*, this sentence would probably be in it.

15. This particular leaderboard is only considering players 6'3" and under with at least 600 field goal attempts off drives over that time frame.

16. I am very excited for the Dragan Bender era.

17. He's a career 32 percent shooter from there.

18. Since 2000, no short player (6'3" or under) has made more shots at the basket in a season than Tony Parker did during the 2006 season (330). Second is Russell Westbrook (324 in 2016). Third is Stephon Marbury (308 in 2002). Fourth is Allen Iverson (298 in 2005).

19. Rod Strickland, a fireball point guard who played in the league for 17 seasons, shot 64.4 percent at the rim during his last five seasons. I have absolutely no problem with swapping Parker out for Strickland, if need be.

20. My favorite record in the NBA is Klay Thompson scoring 37 points in the third quarter of a January game against the Kings in 2015. He shot 100 percent from the field and free throw line, including 9/9 from three (it could've been 10/10 but a foul was called on his 10th before he shot it). And he didn't even take his first shot until the 9:44 mark, which means he averaged nearly 4 points a minute. I've watched the highlight video of that quarter at least 40 times. It's never not impressive.

21. That's the year he shoved Jordan to get free for the game-winning three in Game 4 of the Eastern Conference Finals.

22. The greatest shooting season for any player of all time.

23. Mark Eaton, a 7'4" mountain who played for the Jazz for 11 seasons, averaged 5.56 blocks per game during the 1985 season. That's the highest of all time.

24. Mark Eaton averaged 5.8 blocks per game for the Jazz during their 1985 playoff run (it only lasted 5 games). Manute Bol did the same thing over the same number of games for the Bullets during their 1986 run.

25. Or in front of DeAndre Jordan.

26. Taking it over Kareem's sky hook and Tim Hardaway's crossover.

This is a broader/trickier/sneakier question to try and answer than maybe you're thinking. There are just so many subcategories that you can get sucked into, or caught up in, or transfixed by, or some combination of all three of those things, and so what happens is you end up answering it without really answering it, or answering it with qualifiers, which is the same as not really answering it. I mean:

- Should THE GREATEST DUNKER be the one who turned the dunk[1] from a high percentage shot into graceful artistry? The first guy who seemed less like he was jumping and more like he was writing poetry, or conducting a symphony, or making abstract art, or making love? If yes, then it's Julius Erving, a man who played basketball with such poise and intoxicating coolness that he was allowed to become a fake doctor[2] because of it.
- Should THE GREATEST DUNKER be the one who was the most aggressively athletic and intimidating? The one who dunked it the way a great white shark attacks a seal? The one who dunked it so demonstrably that you were absolutely sure he was going to be awarded more than the traditional two points for it? The one who, when he planted his two feet into the hardwood for liftoff, launched himself upward with so much force that it felt like he for sure had to have just committed a felony against the ground? Because then it's Dominique Wilkins.[3]
- Should someone be considered THE GREATEST DUNKER simply because he was the one who dunked it the most often (Shaquille O'Neal[4])? Or the one who was the first to ever do it in a game (Jack Inglis did a version of it in the 1910s,[5] and Joe Fortenberry is said to have done the first real dunk in a real game in 1936)? Or the one who revolutionized the act by turning it from a statement play into a personal brand, which is what Michael Jordan did.
- Should THE GREATEST DUNKER be the one who dominated an NBA Dunk Contest? Or maybe one who used the best prop during a Dunk Contest? Blake Griffin jumped over the hood of a Kia and dunked it during the 2011 NBA Dunk Contest while a choir stood at halfcourt and sang R. Kelly's "I Believe I Can Fly." At the 2009 Dunk Contest, Dwight Howard went into an actual phone booth he'd had brought to the arena, came out wearing a Superman cape, then dunked it on a goal that was 12 feet tall. Gerald Green, a sinewy grasshopper with bionic legs, had a teammate climb up a ladder at the 2008 NBA Dunk Contest, balance a birthday cupcake on the back of the rim, stick a candle in it, light the candle, climb off the ladder, then throw a bounce alley-oop pass. Green ran up, jumped, caught the ball on his way to the rim, paused in midair, BLEW OUT THE FUCKING CANDLE, then dunked it.
- Should THE GREATEST DUNKER be the one with the best nickname (Darryl Dawkins calling himself

---

1. Did you know it wasn't until 1972 that the term "slam dunk" started to become popularized? It was Lakers announcer Chick Hearn who did it. Before then, mostly it was called a "dunk shot," and that's just about the corniest shit I can think of.
2. Darrell Griffith, a 6'4" shooting guard who played with the Jazz from 1980 to 1991, was also a fake doctor (Dr. Dunkenstein). I think the only fake position higher than fake doctor in the NBA is fake king, a position held by LeBron James. Lower than fake king and fake doctor is Fred "The Mayor" Hoiberg. And lower than everyone is Brian Cardinal, "The Janitor." Man, imagine you work your whole life to make it to the NBA and you finally get there and someone hits you with "The Janitor" as a nickname.
3. My personal favorite dunker. I watched Dominique dunk on Larry Bird so hard one time that—hand to God—Larry Bird's eyeballs exploded in his own skull.
4. From the 2001 season to the 2005 season, Shaq dunked it 1,190 times. That's the most of any player over any five-year stretch since they started recording that stat. For perspective: Shaq had 219 dunks in the 2001 season alone. The next closest person was David Robinson. He had 114. (A fun aside: Shaq's dunks over that five-year stretch were more than Scottie Pippen had in his entire 17-year career. He finished with 1,116 dunks.)
5. At the time, basketball courts didn't look like what they look like now. Many of them had cages around them, and hoops were attached to poles at the gates. Inglis climbed up on the cage, received a pass from a teammate, then dropped the ball down into the goal from the gate on some Vega from *Street Fighter II Championship Edition* shit. I'm super sad that I wasn't alive in 1910 to see it, but I'm also pretty happy I wasn't alive in 1910 on account of me not being white so it probably wouldn't have been that great of a time for me.

"Chocolate Thunder,"[6] obviously)? Or the one who was so dominant at dunking that a rule change was set in place (dunking was banned for nine seasons in the NCAA because a bunch of older white men were mad that Lew Alcindor was dunking on the heads of a bunch of younger white men)? Or maybe THE GREATEST DUNKER should be the one who was so perfectly built for dunking on people and then celebrating his own excellence afterward that even his opponents couldn't do much of anything besides congratulate him for it, and of course I'm talking about the time that Shawn Kemp dunked on Chris Gatling and Gatling responded by nodding his head and dapping up Kemp, which is just about the most ludicrous thing. If someone dunks on me in front of 17,000 people, all that means is there are 17,000 witnesses for the police to talk to when they show up and start trying to find out why I hit someone in the back of the head with a folding chair during a timeout.

• Should THE GREATEST DUNKER be someone who's had an all-time great in-game dunk? Something like Jordan's And-One dunk over Patrick Ewing in the 1991 playoffs? Or Dr. J hitting Michael Cooper with the Rock the Baby cradle dunk in 1983? Or Shawn Kemp exorcising Alton Lister's soul from his body in the 1992 playoffs? Or Darryl Dawkins breaking a backboard any of the times he broke a backboard? Or Blake Griffin jumping up to the 7'1" Timofey Mozgov's neck and then throwing the ball down into the rim rather than dunking it in 2010?

No. THE GREATEST DUNKER shouldn't be any one of those things. THE GREATEST DUNKER needs to be *all* of those things.

Vince Carter is THE GREATEST DUNKER in the history of the NBA.

▶

The first person I ever saw dunk in real life was a man named Cricket. That wasn't his real name, of course, but one thing I know is if you ever meet anyone nicknamed after a bug, you definitely do not ever ask that person his or her real name. So I didn't. Nobody did. He was Cricket. We called him Cricket.

Cricket was an unimpressive fellow. He was short. He wasn't very handsome. He wasn't very cool. He wasn't very much of anything, really. I kept hearing about him at this park that I played at; kept hearing about some guy who nobody ever explained gravity to, some guy who was just running around dunking on everyone, apparently. But I also kept hearing he was 5'8" or 5'9", and so I couldn't allow myself to believe the stories. *That's only an inch taller than me,* I told myself. *There's no way someone an inch taller than me is doing anything close to what these people are saying,* I told myself.

I think I probably went four or five months of hearing about Cricket before I happened into him. It was at a gym on Lackland Air Force Base when I saw him. I think I was in ninth or tenth grade, and my friends and I would occasionally play there if we were able to finagle a pass from someone because it was walking distance from our houses. We'd been there for a bit that one day and we were just sort of waiting our turn to play, talking shit or whatever. And during the game that preceded ours, one of the guys I was with leaned over and was like, "Ay, I think that's Cricket right there," and he pointed to for sure the last person I was expecting him to point to. I responded with something close to "Get the fuck outta here," to which he replied, "I'm serious." Maybe three, four, five minutes later, there wasn't any doubt anymore.

What happened was an errant jumper banged off the back of the rim and ricocheted out toward the three-point line. Cricket snatched it out of the air, then sprinted toward the other end of the court before anyone on either team had realized what was happening. He was running full speed. He picked up the ball near the free throw line, lobbed it up at the backboard, springboard-

---

6. Stevie Wonder gave Dawkins the name "Chocolate Thunder." Stevie would regularly attend games. He had a guy who would sit with him and tell him what was happening in the game. That's probably the most beautiful thing I ever heard. Basketball is such a dope sport that even blind men watch it.

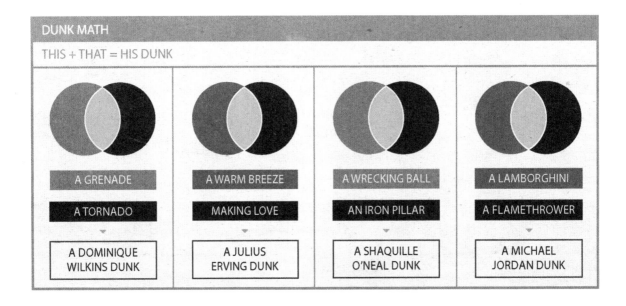

DUNK MATH

THIS + THAT = HIS DUNK

A GRENADE	A WARM BREEZE	A WRECKING BALL	A LAMBORGHINI
A TORNADO	MAKING LOVE	AN IRON PILLAR	A FLAMETHROWER
A DOMINIQUE WILKINS DUNK	A JULIUS ERVING DUNK	A SHAQUILLE O'NEAL DUNK	A MICHAEL JORDAN DUNK

ed up into the atmosphere, caught the ball off the rebound, then ultra-mega-dunked it. It was legit the most amazing thing I'd ever seen on a basketball court that I actually played on in real life. I couldn't move. I couldn't talk. I couldn't do anything. Nobody could. We were transfixed.

I know that sounds silly, but look, my friends and I, we were all short, unathletic Mexican kids. Most of the other people we hung out with and played basketball with were, too. We were all doing good just to touch the backboard. None of us had ever seen anyone dunk in person. And it would've been one thing if Cricket was this overpowering superhuman who you could just look at and say, "Oh yeah, that guy is something special." But Cricket wasn't that. Cricket wasn't special. Cricket was one of us. And so when he dunked—dude. Okay, imagine you walked outside and saw a sasquatch skateboarding down your street. That's what this felt like watching it happen. It was total shock and surprise.

But so Cricket threw the ball up, caught it off the bounce off the backboard, dunked it, and that was that. He turned into a beam of light and stardust and disappeared and nobody ever saw him again. Sometimes I think about that day and I get real happy and also real

sad. I've never dunked it on a regulation goal in my life. I've never even touched the rim. Dunking was something hallowed, something incredible. And Cricket could do it. I wonder where Cricket is. I wonder what he's doing right now. I hope it's something special. I'm sure it's not. He probably works at AutoZone or something like that. (I learned months later that Cricket's name was Gerald. I hope his AutoZone name tag says that and not "Cricket.")

▶

Vince Carter is THE GREATEST DUNKER in the history of the NBA. I'll go through each of the categories from earlier because he fits in all of them, and he fits near the top of the discussion of each.

- **ARTISTRY:** Regarding dunking, there are only three NBA superstars who have ever been as captivating as they are graceful as they are athletically beautiful. Dr. J was the first. Jordan came next. And then it's Vince. Others have obviously been fantastic. Kobe has a string of Oh My God dunks you can pull up on YouTube, but they're almost always buoyed by another bit (generally someone in the frame getting dunked on). LeBron is a gorgeous basketball player but he's more bull than eagle in the lane. Tracy

McGrady dunked like he was a sonnet that'd come to life. Blake is a masher. Larry Nance was secretly elite, but a tad too waifish.[7] Clyde never exhibited that creativity. Spud Webb and Nate Robinson are spark plugs and worthy of your admiration but just too small for the conversation. So again I say: The three at the top here are Dr. J, Jordan, and Vince. Everyone else is tussling underneath them.

- **AGGRESSIVELY ATHLETIC:** (Please see Dunk Contest below.)
- **PERSONAL BRAND:** No basketball player made greater use of the dunk-as-brand movement than Michael Jordan (it's literally his logo). And no player will ever get as close to being as complete a player while also prominently featuring the dunk as a tool. LeBron is the closest we've come. And I'll give you one guess who it is that bridges the gap between those two.
- **DUNK CONTEST:** The 1988 Dunk Contest is the unquestioned best Dunk Contest of all time.[8] But Vince Carter's performance at the 2000 NBA Dunk Contest is the single most impressive Dunk Contest performance that's ever been. He was so good in it that he took the dormant, lifeless franchise (there was no Dunk Contest in 1998 or 1999) and turned it into a marquee event again. He was doing things nobody'd ever seen before, and in ways nobody thought were possible. He did a 360-degree wind-mill, which is easy to type but is a thing maybe 15 people on the entire planet can do. After that, he did a 180-degree windmill from behind the backboard and used just three steps to gather momentum, an ath-letic feat akin to Tom Brady throwing a 70-yard pass while lying on the ground. He caught a bounce pass in the air and then took it between his legs, dunked it, then pointed up at God and I'm sure God was up there in heaven like, "What the fuck did I just see???" because that's what everyone who was watching it said. He did one dunk where he put his arm all the way in the rim and then hung from his elbow and nobody knew what to do or say. It was mesmerizing.

- **NICKNAME/CELEBRATION:** He's got the Vinsanity nickname and that one's okay, and he's got Air Canada from when he played with Toronto and that one's fun, but he's also got the Half Man, Half Amazing nickname, and "Half Man, Half Amazing" really is a Hall of Fame nickname. For celebrations, he had the aforementioned God Point[9] at the 2000 Dunk Contest, but he also had the more heralded "It's Over, It's Over" celebration. A lesser celebrated but equally personally gratifying one was when he dunked it after returning from a knee injury, then paused for a second to look down, dust his knee off so as to say it's fine, and then jogged back down the court.
- **IN-GAME DUNK:** Yes. YES. He literally jumped over a human who was 7'2" tall. And he did it in a game. It happened at the 2000 Olympics in the USA's game against France. It was the second half, the USA was up by 15 with the ball. Gary Payton missed a layup, a Frenchman nabbed the rebound and then tried a doofy no-look outlet pass. Vince stole it just a little outside the three-point line, took three dribbles at the rim, gathered himself, and then jumped over Frederic Weis, a name few people knew and now one that nobody will forget. Nobody had done it before. Nobody's done it since. The French even gave it a name: *Le dunk de la mort*, which translates to "The Dunk of Death." It's the greatest, most impressive in-game dunk in basketball history. That's not hyper-bole.

Just think on it like a scale score. No other dunker scores as high as Carter does in as many categories as Carter does. If you approach it that way, then it's easy to see:

Vince Carter is THE GREATEST DUNKER in the history of the NBA.

---

7. His son, Larry Nance Jr., is in the league as I write this and he is already shaping up to be a wonderful dunker.
8. If we're talking about just straight-up dunking, then the best dunk contest was 2016's.
9. Dirk Nowitzki re-created this at the 2015 All-Star Game after catching an alley-oop and dunking it while his tippy toes were just barely off the ground. It was a great moment.

WHAT'S THE ORDER OF THE
FIRST ROUND OF THE FICTIONAL

This is a simple thing because the argument prompt here is a straight arrow: What's the draft order of the first round of the Fictional Basketball Player Draft? That's it. That's all. Which fictional person goes in what fictional spot if you take all of the fictional basketball players and put them in a big fictional room and have a big fictional draft? That's what this chapter is. Simple.

That said, there *are* four rules, so let's start there.

· **RULE NO. 1:** This will operate the same as the first round of the NBA Draft, in that there will be 30 picks, but it will also not be like the first round of the NBA Draft, in that in this version there aren't any teams making the picks; we're just assigning spots. Also, there's no second round. Also, it goes from the 30th pick to the 1st pick rather than 1st to 30th. Also, there's no rule against drafting cartoon characters. Or children. Or animals.

· **RULE NO. 2:** Fictional basketball players portrayed by real NBA players are eligible to be drafted, but real NBA players who portray themselves in movies or TV shows are not eligible. Ex: In 1993, Shaq appeared as himself in the music mockumentary *CB4*. A year later, he was in *Blue Chips* as the all-world center Neon Boudeaux. *Blue Chips* Neon is eligible to be drafted but *CB4* Shaq isn't. This serves as a counterweight to prevent this from becoming an actual NBA draft by just cheat-dipping into movies where a bunch of players had quick cameos (*Space Jam*, *Forget Paris*, etc.).

· **RULE NO. 3:** Rick Fox isn't allowed to participate in any capacity. There's no real reason for this rule other than pettiness. In all actuality, his character from the HBO prison drama *Oz*, a superstar-NBA-player-turned-felon named Jackson Vahue, would've probably gone very high in the draft. It's just that I don't like Rick Fox, is all. So he ain't invited.

· **RULE NO. 4:** If a player from a movie is good because of some version of magic or mysticism (Calvin Cambridge from *Like Mike*, Scott Howard from *Teen Wolf*, Brian from *Thunderstruck*, etc.), then that player will be considered for the draft when they were experiencing the greatest version of their magical powers. Not even if he or she ended up losing them in the movie or TV show.

Now, the draft:

> **NO. 30 PICK:** Derek Vinyard, *American History X*
> **HEIGHT:** 6'0" **WEIGHT:** approximately 175 pounds **POSITION:** point guard
> **MOST MEMORABLE ON-COURT MOMENT:** Winning a race war.

The most surprising thing with Vinyard wasn't just that he was good at basketball, which, to be sure, *was* fairly surprising because I've never been in a situation where we were short a player for a game and thought, "Man, I wish there was a nazi around so he could fill in this last spot." No, the most surprising thing isn't that Vinyard WAS good, it's the WAY that he was good.

A recap of the basketball scene in *AHX*: An obese white supremacist named Seth gets goaded into betting $100 on a pickup basketball game he's playing in. This is troublesome for a number of reasons,[1] the most pressing of which being that Seth doesn't have the $100 he just bet. He wanders over to the bleachers to his nazi support group and begs them to front the money. Nobody believes in him so nobody gives it to him. Instead, Derek, who's been sitting and watching the game, says, "I'll take care of this," then removes his sweatshirt (to reveal a large swastika tattooed on his chest) and wanders out onto the court. He brokers a deal with the other players there: He'll take all the white guys on his team, all the black guys will form the other team, and they'll play out the rest of the game that way. In lieu of money, though, they're going to play for territory now: The losing race has to leave the courts and isn't allowed to play there anymore. Everyone

---

1. He weighs nearly 400 pounds, he's very clearly not any good at basketball, etc.

agrees to the terms, and so the game starts. And that's where it gets surprising.

Before Vinyard joins the game, the camera shows a shot of him watching everyone play. And during that shot he makes a comment about how one of the black players is being too showy for his tastes. But so when Derek's scene starts and he's actually playing in the game, I was 100 percent expecting him to be on his Only Fundamentals shit. But on the very first play, he receives a pass, pump fakes a shot, drives into the lane, and then throws an unnecessary behind-the-back pass to a guy for a dunk. On the second play, he brings the ball up the court, dribbles through his legs, does another pump fake, then drives into the lane again and goes behind the back to himself this time as he lays it up. And then on the third play, he intercepts an errant pass, charges down the court fast as he can, and then, all alone, all alone where a layup would've been just fine or, even more in character, a two-handed set shot,[2] he jumps up and does a reverse two-handed dunk. I'd assumed before the game Vinyard was going to be John Stockton. Turns out, he's the white Allen Iverson.

So, yes, it'd be risky bringing a reformed skinhead into the locker room. But, given the way he was able to completely control the game despite playing (a) basically 5-on-4 (Seth was useless) and (b) in an extremely pressure-filled situation, it's probably worth a shot to take him with the 30th pick.[3] So here we are: starting the Fictional Basketball Player Draft by picking a nazi.

> **NO. 29 PICK:** Jim Carroll, *The Basketball Diaries*
> **HEIGHT:** 6'0" **WEIGHT:** approximately 150 pounds **POSITION:** point guard
> **MOST MEMORABLE ON-COURT MOMENT:** Hanging on a rim during a thunderstorm yelling at the universe because being a teenager is hard.

To be clear, I'm talking about Jim when he wasn't on drugs. That's the version who gets drafted 29th.

> **NO. 28 PICK:** Jamal Jefferies, *Juwanna Mann*
> **HEIGHT:** 6'1" **WEIGHT:** approximately 175 pounds **POSITION:** shooting guard
> **MOST MEMORABLE ON-COURT MOMENT:** Dunking it with such ferocity that (s)he shatters a backboard.

Jamal gets kicked out of the UBA (this particular movie's version of the NBA) and, because he wants to keep playing basketball, decides to dress up as a woman and play in the women's professional league. That sort of (misguided) dedication is enough to work his way into being the 28th selection, which is impressive, for sure, but maybe less so than it sounds when you see that the 27th pick isn't even a human.

> **NO. 27 PICK:** Buddy, *Air Bud*
> **HEIGHT:** approximately 22" **WEIGHT:** approximately 70 pounds **POSITION:** dog
> **MOST MEMORABLE ON-COURT MOMENT:** Literally any time he did anything close to playing basketball because he's a goddamn dog.

Let me just mention two things here:

1. As I'm writing this, the opening line on the *Air Bud* Wikipedia page is, "The film opens with an abusive, alcoholic clown . . ." and I'll take just a second to remind you that *Air Bud* is a Disney movie about a dog who plays basketball alongside children.

2. Buddy is[4] a dog, so maybe you're wondering how he gets drafted above three actual people here. To that I would just remind you that he's likely the most athletically gifted animal of all time, which is no small feat. He dominates in basketball (*Air Bud*), football (*Air Bud: Golden Receiver*), soccer (*Air Bud: World Pup*), baseball

---

2. Nazis fucking love two-handed set shots, I would guess.
3. The Bulls drafted Jimmy Butler with the 30th pick in 2011. His and Derek's games are comparable, really.

LEGACY

AIR BUD'S INCOMPARABLE RUN OF MULTI-SPORT DOMINANCE

- **1997** AIR BUD LEARNS TO PLAY BASKETBALL. HE HELPS A TEAM WIN A TITLE.
- **1998** AIR BUD LEARNS TO PLAY FOOTBALL. HE HELPS A TEAM WIN A TITLE.
- **2000** AIR BUD LEARNS TO PLAY SOCCER. HE HELPS A TEAM WIN A TITLE.
- **2002** AIR BUD LEARNS TO PLAY BASEBALL. HE HELPS A TEAM WIN A TITLE.
- **2003** AIR BUD LEARNS TO PLAY VOLLEYBALL. HE HELPS A TEAM WIN A TITLE.

(*Air Bud: Seventh Inning Fetch*[5]), and volleyball (*Air Bud: Spikes Back*). He's the fucking Bo Jackson of the animal kingdom.

> **NO. 26 PICK:** Jim Halpert, *The Office*
> **HEIGHT:** 6'3" **WEIGHT:** approximately 190 pounds **POSITION:** small forward
> **MOST MEMORABLE ON-COURT MOMENT:** Giving a Michael Jordan shrug to another man's fiancée after scoring a basket.

There's only six minutes of footage of Jim Halpert playing basketball in all nine seasons of *The Office*, but look at how he stuffed that tiny amount of time with ample evidence that he is better at basketball than a nazi, a drug addict, a man pretending to be a woman, and a dog. He:

- Starts the game by offering to guard Roy, rumored to

be the opposing team's best player (and, not coincidentally, fiancé to Pam, whom Jim is secretly in love with).
- Dives out of bounds to save a loose ball; what's more, he shows the wherewithal to knock it ahead to a teammate (Michael Scott) for a layup (he misses it).
- Performs a behind-the-back evasive dribble maneuver so mesmerizing that Pam forgets she is engaged to Roy and reflexively cheers for Jim.
- Sets an off-the-ball pick hearty enough to get Dwight a wide-open jumper, and let's be sure and point out here that Jim spent no small amount of his nonbasketball life needling Dwight, so the fact that he'd actively work to get him an easy bucket isn't just a testament to his basketball IQ but also to his dedication to winning.
- Demands to guard Roy again after Michael proves himself incapable of doing it.

- Gets his nose busted open by Roy while playing defense, then immediately retaliates on offense by taking Roy down low, banging on him a bit, then dropping a fadeaway jumper over him.
- Steals the ball from Roy in the open court then drives it in for a layup.
- Takes Roy in the paint again on offense, this time planting a very firm elbow into Roy's chest, one he delivers with such poetic fury that it knocks Roy to the ground.

So in that six-minute stretch we see Jim display fearlessness, tenacity, intelligence, savvy, a firm allegiance to team, assertiveness, toughness, and a willingness to obliterate a man in front of the woman that man's supposed to marry. Jim Halpert is a winner.

NO. 25 PICK: Mifundo, *The Air Up There*
HEIGHT: 6'9" **WEIGHT:** approximately 220 pounds **POSITION:** power forward
MOST MEMORABLE ON-COURT MOMENT: Nearly winning an intertribal championship that could've topsy-turvied the African mining ecosystem.

I imagine you figured if anyone was going to be drafted from *The Air Up There*, it was going to be Saleh, basketball star of the movie, prince of the Winabi tribe, and the future of St. Joe's basketball. And that makes sense because the most exhilarating moment of *TAUT* is when Saleh hits Mifundo, his towering archrival, with the Jimmy Dolan Shake and Bake move[6] and then mega slam dunks it at the buzzer to win THE BIG GAME. But what gets forgotten is that Mifundo was basically wrecking all of Saleh's shit all before then. (His team carried a double-digit lead for almost all of the contest, and they were even up seven with just under two minutes left before Saleh's brother checked in and saved everything.) Mifundo was legit a bigger, stronger, more polished version[7] of what Saleh was supposed to be. He gobbles up Saleh's spot here, just like he gobbled up Saleh in the low post.[8]

NO. 24 PICK: John Tucker, *John Tucker Must Die*
HEIGHT: 5'10" **WEIGHT:** approximately 180 pounds **POSITION:** point guard
MOST MEMORABLE ON-COURT MOMENT: Flip dunk in a thong.

He literally did a flip dunk during practice just because he felt like showing off. That's incredible. I mean, we're talking about unprecedented athleticism here. Not just in basketball, but in all of history. You have to have something like a 75-inch vertical to flip dunk if you're 5'10". In comparison, Jason Richardson, one of the greatest modern-day leapers in the NBA, has a recorded vertical of just over 46 inches. That alone makes Tucker a steal at the 24th pick. Factor in the fact that he was also such a charming and effervescent leader that he convinced all the other players on his high school basketball team to wear thongs, and all of a sudden maybe we should be talking about how he should've landed way, way, way higher up.

---

4. "Was" is a better word here. Buddy died in 1998. A thing that'll somehow make you feel even worse: He was the same dog who was in Full House. Michelle Tanner's dog is dead. ⊗
5. This is a perfect movie title.
6. The Jimmy Dolan Shake and Bake move is an overly complicated string of instructions that ends with the offensive player tossing the ball between the defender's legs. It takes nearly 30 seconds start to finish. That's six seconds longer than the length of the shot clock in the NBA.
7. Some of the blame here has to fall to his coach, Jimmy Dolan, played by Kevin Bacon. His most inspired bit of coaching during the championship game was to clap his hands very aggressively and shout, "Guard him, guard him, guard him!"
8. Mifundo is played by Ilo Mutombo, Dikembe Mutombo's older brother. Ilo played four years at the University of Southern Indiana. By the end of his playing career there he was the school's all-time leading rebounder and their second leading scorer.

WHAT'S THE ORDER OF THE
FIRST ROUND OF THE FICTIONAL
BASKETBALL PLAYER DRAFT?

PART 2

...continued

> **NO. 23 PICK:** Jimmy Chitwood, *Hoosiers*
> **HEIGHT:** approximately 6'0" **WEIGHT:** approxi-
>   mately 160 pounds **POSITION:** guard
> **MOST MEMORABLE ON-COURT MOMENT:** Hitting
>   a shot at the buzzer to win the 1952
>   Indiana State Championship.

Before writing each one of the blurbs for these Fictional Basketball Player Draft chapters, I rewatched the movie (or shows) that featured the player I was going to write about. Mostly, I was watching trying to scout the player, and that's what I'd intended to do here, too. But you know what I ended up wondering about when I sat through *Hoosiers* again? Do you think Jimmy Chitwood, the mysterious but charming hero,[1] was a racist? I don't ask that because of anything that happens in the movie; nothing overt ever happens that would lead me to believe so. I just ask because of the context. The movie's set from 1951 to 1952, and also mostly everything takes place in rural Indiana. In 1950, Indiana was 95.5 percent white. And it was in 1949 that the Indiana School Desegregation Act was passed. It just seems pretty impossible that Chitwood could've been raised as a progressive, you know what I'm saying?

> **NO. 22 PICK:** Monica Wright, *Love & Basketball*
>   (or Quincy McCall, *Love & Basketball*)
> **HEIGHT:** 5'7" (or 5'10") **WEIGHT:** approxi-
>   mately 130 pounds (or approximately
>   175 pounds) **POSITION:** point guard
> **MOST MEMORABLE ON-COURT MOMENT:** Winning
>   a one-on-one matchup against Quincy
>   McCall in college (or winning a one-
>   on-one matchup against Monica Wright
>   after college).

Do you remember the scene where Monica and Quincy were in college and deeply in love and it was great and beautiful and they played that game of one-on-one in his dorm room and each time someone scored a point the other person would have to take a piece of clothing off? Okay, there was a part during the game where Monica was trying to stop Quincy from scoring, and to do so she simply grabbed him by the penis. He dropped the ball, she picked it up, then she scored. If in the universe this draft exists in you're allowed to grab people in the junk, then Monica gets picked in this draft spot. That's just a super strong defensive move.[2] My best hope is that each time after she does it, she wags her finger in front of the person's genitals like how Dikembe Mutombo would wag his finger in a guy's face after he blocked his shot.

If that's not the case, though, then give me Quincy McCall in this spot. (Note: It has to be the Quincy McCall from before he found out his dad cheated on his mom, though. That's when he was still happy playing basketball. After he found out about the infidelity, his whole essence turned jagged and pointy.)

> **NO. 21 PICK:** Dr. Christopher Turk, *Scrubs*
> **HEIGHT:** 6'0" **WEIGHT:** approximately 195
>   pounds **POSITION:** shooting guard
> **MOST MEMORABLE ON-COURT MOMENT:** It was ac-
>   tually an off-the-court moment. Turk
>   found some face paint and he was
>   supposed to throw it away but instead
>   he painted his head like a basketball
>   and then J.D. dribbled him.

Good size, good strength, good agility. Plus, he was so in love with basketball he was willing to play pickup games in the front parking lot and drop-off area of Sacred Heart Hospital. Double plus, he was such a

---

1. Jimmy ends up hitting the game winner at the buzzer to win the state championship for his team. It's based on a real thing that happened, only in the real-life version, the player was named Bobby Plump, a decidedly less cool name than Jimmy Chitwood. Also, Plump's shot won his team the 1954 title. In the movie, Chitwood's shot wins them the 1952 title.
2. Draymond Green nearly won a title for the Golden State Warriors in 2016 by attacking wieners.

devoted teammate that one time he laid down in the middle of a busy street with J.D. after J.D. knocked himself unconscious during shootaround because he didn't want any of the other players to know J.D. had knocked himself out.

> **NO. 20 PICK:** Danny Valdessecchi, *Blind Dating*
> **HEIGHT:** 6'0" **WEIGHT:** approximately 175 pounds **POSITION:** point guard
> **MOST MEMORABLE ON-COURT MOMENT:** Winning a game of H-O-R-S-E for $$$ against some people hoping to take advantage of his being blind.

This one is a very risky gamble. On the one hand, Danny's blind, and being blind makes it just about impossible to be a professional basketball player. In fact, the one scene we see of Danny isn't even of an actual game: It's him playing H-O-R-S-E against a guy. He makes every shot he takes during the competition, sure, but again, it's H-O-R-S-E. There's no defense, there's no crowd, there's no anything. He basically just gets to stand there, sonar in on where the goal is, and then chuck a shot up there.

On the other hand, we find out early in the movie that Danny is about to start going to law school, which means in a few years he'll be a blind lawyer, which means there's a tiny, tiny, tiny chance he's the new Daredevil, and fuck you if you think I'm missing out on a chance to draft Daredevil.[3] (More Daredevil evidence: There's a part in the movie where Danny slides down a two-story-high stair rail and then when he lands, his buddy catches him to slow his momentum down, and when he catches Danny he says, "That's it. I am convinced. You are the Batman." That's the sort of foreshadowing that accompanies lots of superhero stories.)

> **NO. 19 PICK:** Lewis Scott, *Celtic Pride*
> **HEIGHT:** 6'2" **WEIGHT:** approximately 190 pounds **POSITION:** shooting guard
> **MOST MEMORABLE ON-COURT MOMENT:** Winning an NBA Finals Game 7 on the road in Boston.

Lewis Scott is the star of a team playing in the NBA Finals here, which means that this isn't an especially daring pick. But, I mean, a blind guy just got drafted. I need a safe bet.

> **NO. 18 PICK:** Calvin Cambridge, *Like Mike*
> **HEIGHT:** approximately 4'6" **WEIGHT:** approximately 85 pounds **POSITION:** point guard
> **MOST MEMORABLE ON-COURT MOMENT:** Throwing an alley-oop to himself off the backboard and dunking it from the free throw line.

An orphan finds a pair of shoes that possibly belonged to Michael Jordan. He gets shocked by electricity. Then he averages 25 points per game in the NBA. Sign me the fuck up.

> **NO. 17 PICK:** Clarence Withers, *Semi-Pro*
> **HEIGHT:** 5'10" **WEIGHT:** approximately 160 pounds **POSITION:** guard
> **MOST MEMORABLE ON-COURT MOMENT:** Executing the first-ever alley-oop.

Mostly because of André 3000's verse on 2007's "Walk It Out (Remix)," which is still absolutely perfect and pristine.[4]

---

3. To be clear, I'm talking about Netflix *Daredevil*, not Ben Affleck *Daredevil*.
4. "Your white tee, well, to me, look like a nightgown / Make your mama proud, take that thing two sizes down / Then you'll look like the man that you are, or what you could be."

NO. 16 PICK: David 8, *Prometheus*
HEIGHT: 6'0" WEIGHT: approximately 174
    pounds POSITION: robot
MOST MEMORABLE ON-COURT MOMENT: Swishing
    a 29-foot hook shot while riding a
    bicycle.

David is a robot that looks like a human and talks like a psycho.[5] Granted, we have very little footage of him actually playing basketball. Really, the closest we get is a scene where we see him alone on a dark court shooting a hook shot from several feet beyond the three-point line while riding a bicycle.[6] I would argue that that's plenty reason to draft him, though. I mean, granted, he won't be allowed on a bicycle during the game, but I figure riding a bike and shooting a hook shot from 29 feet away isn't any more difficult than running and shooting a hook shot from 29 feet away. If anything, doing it without a bike makes it easier. You pair him up with someone who sets good screens and that shit is a wrap, homie. He's averaging 30 a game, easy. So he could get drafted at the 16th spot off the strength of that prospect alone.

Here's the thing, though. I suspect he's going to be just a very good all-around player, too. As evidence, I'll point you toward the promo commercial that was running on the Internet when *Prometheus* was in theaters. It was this pretend commercial advertising David 8 as a purchasable thing for people and the whole commercial was basically just a narrator asking David four separate questions and David answering them.

Q1: What can you do, David?

David: I can do almost anything that could possibly be asked of me. I can assist your employees. I can make your organization more efficient. I can carry out directives that my human counterparts might find . . . distressing or unethical. I can blend in with your workforce effortlessly.

[This is exactly what I'd want a guy to say to me if I was interviewing him to be on my team, because it sounds a lot like he's interested only in the betterment of the team, but it also sounds a lot like he wouldn't mind cracking someone in the back of the head with a pipe if I asked him to.]

Q2: David, what do you think about?

David: I think about anything. Children playing. Angels. The universe. Robots.

[I can't say for certain, but this would be my guess for the answer Tim Duncan gave when Gregg Popovich asked him this question after the Spurs drafted him in 1997.]

Q3: David, what makes you sad?

David: War. Poverty. Cruelty. Unnecessary violence. I understand human emotions, although I do not feel them myself. This allows me to be more efficient and capable.

[Perfect.]

Q4: Is there anything you would like to say, David?

David: I would like to express gratitude to those who created me.

[Bang.]

NO. 15 PICK: Steve Urkel, *Family Matters*
HEIGHT: 5'10" WEIGHT: approximately 150
    pounds POSITION: guard
MOST MEMORABLE ON-COURT MOMENT: Being
    allowed to play.

The hapless, helpless, hopeless Steve Urkel was the water boy for his high school basketball team, the lowly Vanderbilt Muskrats. In a game where they were down by 22 points with seven minutes left in the fourth quarter and the coach was left with no other options,[7] he subbed Steve in. And then he sat and watched in awe as Urkel fucking DESTROYED the other team.

It was like if someone put a pair of suspenders on Chris Paul. His most impressive stretch came in the last minute of the game, which makes sense because that's always the time when champions reserve their seats in Valhalla. The Muskrats were down five and on defense. Steve stole the ball, charged down the court, then threw a perfect alley-oop pass off the backboard to the trailing big man. On the very next play, he helped force another steal, then dropped off a behind-the-back pass for a wide-open layup. With six or so seconds left and his team down one—and make no mistake, by this point they were absolutely "Steve Urkel's team"—he executed a devastating step back move to free space up between him and his defender, then he raised up and let fly a gorgeous 20-footer. There was never a doubt. The ball never even considered touching the rim. It barely considered touching the net. The buzzer went off as the ball swished through, giving the Muskrats a one-point win. Then he went home and didn't have sex with Laura Winslow.

> **NO. 14 PICK:** Lucas Scott, *One Tree Hill*
> **HEIGHT:** 6'0" **WEIGHT:** approximately 165 pounds **POSITION:** guard
> **MOST MEMORABLE ON-COURT MOMENT:** Defeating his estranged half brother, Nathan, in a high-stakes game of one-on-one.

Nathan, Lucas's half brother, had what was for sure the more successful basketball career (he actually ended up making it into the league proper, while Lucas's career was derailed because of heart complications). But he gets bumped here for Lucas for two reasons, one of which is obvious and the second of which is (possibly) less so:

1. NATHAN LOST TO LUCAS WHEN THEY PLAYED ONE-ON-ONE. This is the obvious one. They played each other. Lucas won. Lucas was the better player. And since we're allowing draftees to keep their magic powers or whatever when they have them, I'm gonna go ahead and allow Lucas to keep the good version of his heart. So there you go. That solves that.

2. NATHAN DIDN'T HAVE THE RIGHT DISPOSITION FOR STARDOM. I know this one might sound incorrect, what with him mostly being a selfishly successful person and also given that he was basically built up to be a basketball star by his father from birth, but I just don't think he was nearly petty enough or vindictive enough. I mean, he pawed at the idea of it, like the way he prodded Lucas about being an unwanted, unnecessary human early in the series, or the way he shot that no-look free throw to win the game against

Oak Lake and his then-nemesis Damien West. But that was all just surface stuff.

He eventually came around to loving Lucas. And when he finally had a chance to be his absolute pettiest—in that father/son game, playing for a chance to beat his loathsome dad in front of everyone, which was his dad's worst fear—he welched.

The play: After having demolished the dads for almost the entire game, the scorekeeper announced he was going to make the ending more exciting by making it a Next Basket Wins thing, which, FYI, seems wildly unfair. But so the sons had possession and Nathan had the ball and drove in for the game-winning layup, only except instead of getting the layup he got clobbered by his dad, who put two forearms into Nathan's chest, crashing him to the floor. "I couldn't give you the winning bucket, Nathan," he tells him. Nathan gets up, they reset the offense, then he turns the ball over on purpose. The dads come down and toss the ball to Nathan's dad in the post. Nathan offers up a freebie layup, explaining, "You don't deserve my best game, dad," and then, "You know what? If you wanna win so bad, go ahead. I'll give it to you." Then he moves out of the way. His dad, a real winner, looks at him in disbelief, then scores the layup. The team of fathers wins. Afterward, Nathan tells him, "You didn't beat me, dad. You never will." And I guess that was supposed to be a more devastating, more righteous blow, but FUCK THAT SHIT.

I don't want righteousness. I don't want dignity. The Second Place Hall of Fame is littered with virtuous people and their loser morals. Give me a murderer. Give me the trophy. Give me the guy who's gonna make a bet to play one-on-one against a guy and the loser has to quit the basketball team, then he beats the guy, then he makes him stay on the team anyway out of spite, which is what Lucas did on the very first episode of season one. Give me Lucas Scott over Nathan.[8]

---

5. The best kind of robot, if you ask me.
6. Robots play basketball weird.
7. He'd lost all but four of his players to injuries or fouls, and openly contemplated letting the team get disqualified rather than play Urkel. It was Eddie Winslow who convinced him to put Steve in.
8. Also, Lucas is way hotter than Nathan. That's important to me.

WHAT'S THE ORDER OF THE
FIRST ROUND OF THE FICTIONAL

... continued

> **NO. 13 PICK:** Kyle Lee Watson, *Above the Rim*
> **HEIGHT:** 5'10" **WEIGHT:** approximately 165
>   pounds **POSITION:** point guard
> **MOST MEMORABLE ON-COURT MOMENT:** Getting
>   dismantled in a game of one-on-one
>   against Thomas "Shep" Sheppard.

(He's tied with the no. 12 pick.)

> **NO. 12 PICK:** Scott Howard, *Teen Wolf*
> **HEIGHT:** 5'4" **WEIGHT:** approximately 122
>   pounds **POSITION:** guard
> **MOST MEMORABLE ON-COURT MOMENT:** Making two
>   free throws with no time left on the
>   clock to lift his team, the Beavers,
>   over their rivals, the Dragons.

FYI: I don't want the *Teen Wolf* version of Scott Howard. I want the human version of Scott Howard. Teen Wolf was certainly the more exhilarating player, what with his dunks and Harlem Globetrotter dribbling exhibitions, and also he was a fucking wolf playing basketball. But Human Scott was the superior player.

This is Teen Wolf's stat line from that first game he played in (which was the only game we got to see him play for more than a little bit): 8/8 on shot attempts, one rebound, two blocks,[1] one steal, and one assist. This is Human Scott's stat line from the last game he played in: 5/6 on shot attempts, 4/4 on free throws (including the two that won the game that he shot alone because he was fouled at the buzzer), six assists, and two steals. I'd probably seen *Teen Wolf* a good 15, 20 times and hadn't realized Human Scott was better until I sat down and watched it specifically to write this blurb because that's when I wrote the stats down. Stats are dope. Stats defeated a werewolf.

(All that said, I am absolutely okay with the *Teen Wolf* version of Scott Howard showing up to the draft.)

> **NO. 11 PICK:** Will Smith, *The Fresh Prince*
>   *of Bel-Air*
> **HEIGHT:** 6'2" **WEIGHT:** approximately 180
>   pounds **POSITION:** guard
> **MOST MEMORABLE ON-COURT MOMENT:** Demolishing
>   Isiah Thomas in a game of one-on-one.[2]

Smith, who averaged 61.5 points per game over the two games he's shown playing during his high school basketball career, was an overwhelming offensive presence on the court.[3] Here is literally the first thing he did in his first game: He was set up to do the beginning-of-the-game jump ball, the ref threw the ball up, then Will jumped, then rather than tap it to one of his useless teammates he simply grabbed the ball out of the air,[4] then shot it WHILE HE WAS STILL IN THE AIR. What's more: HE DID THAT SHIT FROM HALF COURT. It's one of the four or five most impressive basketball shots in the fictional basketball universe.[5] He had a massive ego and an affinity for kissing cheerleaders during games, but the potential for having that sort of firepower on your team makes him worth the risk.[6]

---

1. It's very likely that he only had one block, as it appears they use the same clip of him blocking someone in the game montage twice.
2. In a dream sequence, BTW.
3. Really, the only person who ever stopped him from scoring was Carlton, and the only reason he was able to do so was that Will never expected him to try because they were on the same team.
4. Absolutely illegal.
5. It goes: 1. Snake Plissken's full-court buzzer beater to save his life in *Escape from L.A.*; 2. John Tucker's flip dunk; 3. Hancock shooting it on an outside goal from several hundred feet away; 4. Will Smith's jump ball jumper; 5. Jordan's stretch dunk; 6. Billy Hoyle's hook shot from half court to get Gloria on *Jeopardy!*; 7. David 8's hook shot three while riding a bicycle; 8. Hoops McCann shooting that thing through the little metal hoop on top of the thing on the boat at the end of *One Crazy Summer*.
6. Kobe Bryant was drafted 13th and also went straight from high school to the pros. I'm figuring (hoping) Will's pro career is going to look a lot like Kobe's.

> **NO. 10 PICK:** Jesus Shuttlesworth, *He Got Game*
> **HEIGHT:** 6'5" **WEIGHT:** approximately 205
>   pounds **POSITION:** guard
> **MOST MEMORABLE ON-COURT MOMENT:** Snatching
>   the alpha-dominance from his dad
>   during a game of one-on-one.

In March of 2015, I wrote a thing about fictional basketball players with Jason Concepcion for *Grantland*. In the article, Jason made an incredibly salient point about Jesus Shuttlesworth that has remained with me to this day. He said, "How good is Jesus Shuttlesworth? So good that the GOVERNOR of NEW YORK STATE has Jesus's father sprung from Attica, WHERE HE IS SERVING TIME FOR KILLING JESUS'S MOTHER, in the hope that he can convince Jesus to attend Big State University, the governor's alma mater." If you're so brilliant a player that government officials are releasing convicted murderers as a response to your basketball existence, you're sliding into the top ten every single time.

> **NO. 9 PICK:** Moses Guthrie, *The Fish That
>   Saved Pittsburgh*
> **HEIGHT:** 6'7" **WEIGHT:** approximately 209
>   pounds **POSITION:** guard
> **MOST MEMORABLE ON-COURT MOMENT:** Any time he
>   did anything on the court because
>   Dr. J is walking poetry.

My favorite thing about this movie is that there's a part where a woman is crying and expressing concern about a person and Moses Guthrie, star player of the Pittsburgh Pisces[7] (played by Dr. J), responds to the situation by saying, "Come with me," and then he takes her to a basketball court and makes her watch him play basketball in street clothes by himself for three minutes.[8] Moses is not that great of a therapist, I don't think.

> **NO. 8 PICK:** Lola Bunny, *Space Jam*
> **HEIGHT:** 3'2" **WEIGHT:** approximately 35
>   pounds **POSITION:** guard[9]
> **MOST MEMORABLE ON-COURT MOMENT:** Running up
>   a defender's face, jumping off it,
>   then dunking.

Two things here:

1. Lola mostly just gets mushed into the Sex Icon role in *Space Jam*, which is weird because it's a movie for children,[10] but she's a phenomenal basketball player. She's fast, she's aggressive, she has unquestionable dribbling skills and an overwhelming vertical (during a one-on-one match against Bugs Bunny she dunks it easily, despite barely being 3 feet tall). Best case scenario she ends up being a championship-caliber point guard; worst case scenario she ends up being the new Reggie Jackson. If this draft weren't so guard heavy, she'd be closer to the third or fourth spot.

2. Lola Bunny is the first non-human I was ever attracted to. Others on that list: Blue, the main raptor from *Jurassic World*; Neytiri from *Avatar*; Roxanne from *A Goofy Movie*; and the cartoon fox version of *Robin Hood*.

> **NO. 7 PICK:** Snake Plissken, *Escape from L.A.*
> **HEIGHT:** 5'11" **WEIGHT:** approximately 175
>   pounds **POSITION:** guard
> **MOST MEMORABLE ON-COURT MOMENT:** Making a
>   full court shot under threat of
>   death for a miss.

A very short summary of *Escape from L.A.*: Snake Plissken, a rugged and handsome and amoral but moral

---

7. The premise of *The Fish That Saved Pittsburgh* is the team decides to put together a group of players who are all Pisces.
8. My second favorite thing is in the trailer where the narrator says, "Take an Indian, a preacher, a midget, a magician, a hip deejay, an Arab, an astrologer, and a great big kid and what have you got? It's fish fever."
9. During the player introductions of the game, she's introduced as a small forward, but there's no way I'm putting anyone who's only 3'2" in that position.
10. There's a part where she talks to Bugs Bunny and then his whole body turns rigid. I think that's secretly supposed to signify an erection. Bugs Bunny is more sexually aggressive than I'd realized as a child.

man, gets sent into an apocalyptic future version of L.A. by the government to retrieve an important thing from a bad person. There you go. That's the movie.

The basketball part: The bad person, a Peruvian terrorist named Cuervo, captures Snake. And so since he has Snake, he decides to kill him, but because Cuervo has flair and charisma, he decides to do so in an aggressively charming way.

He has Snake stand at the center of a regulation-size basketball court. The court is fenced in and the fence is surrounded by 20 or so people with guns. Cuervo tells Snake he has to complete a basketball challenge. Cuervo says he's going to turn on a 10-second shot clock. Snake has to take the ball and make a shot at the goal on the far right. If he makes it, the clock will reset, and he will have 10 more seconds to make another basket in the goal on the opposite end of the court. And he has to do it over and over and over again, alternating goals each time, the shot clock being reset each time. If he can score 10 points under these rules, he gets to live and he gets to leave.[11] If he misses a shot, though, he'll be shot. If the shot clock goes before he gets a shot up, he'll be shot. And so there you go. Those are the stakes.

Cuervo turns the shot clock on and Snake takes off toward the goal on the right side of the court. He gets there in time for a layup before the buzzer sounds. (Two points.) As the ball falls through the hoop, though, he bobbles it. The misplay eats up two seconds on the new shot clock. He doesn't have enough time to make it all the way to the other goal for a layup so he settles for a 15-footer. He makes it. (Four points.) He grabs the ball and starts running back toward the other goal, this time only making it to the three-point line. He throws up a three as the buzzer sounds. It's good. (Six points.) By the time he retrieves the ball, he's down to five or so seconds, so he has to heave up a shot from half court at the other goal. Improbably, it rattles in. (Eight points.) He fetches the ball for his last shot, but there are only two seconds left once he's chased it down. He looks at the clock. He looks at the goal. He looks at Cuervo. He looks at death. He's approximately 90 feet from the hoop he has to shoot it in. So, with literally his life at stake, he chucks up a baseball pass toward the basket.

Everything is quiet. Time stops moving forward. The world stops spinning so as to not disrupt the path of the ball. It's flying, it's flying, it's flying. And then, miraculously, it's in. Plissken doesn't even celebrate.

Under the greatest pressure and in the most impossible basketball spot of everyone else on this list, Snake Plissken was unfazed. He shot 100 percent from the field and did that shit in a leather onesie. Nobody's ever been as clutch.

NO. 6 PICK: Sidney Deane, *White Men Can't Jump*
HEIGHT: 5'9" **WEIGHT:** approximately 180 pounds **POSITION:** guard
MOST MEMORABLE ON-COURT MOMENT: Getting hustled by Billy Hoyle out of $62 in a shooting contest.

(He's tied with the no. 5 pick.)

NO. 5 PICK: Billy Hoyle, *White Men Can't Jump*
HEIGHT: 5'9" **WEIGHT:** approximately 170 pounds **POSITION:** guard
MOST MEMORABLE ON-COURT MOMENT: Hustling Sidney Deane out of $62 in a shooting contest.

These guys are the second best fictional basketball playing duo if you're only counting basketball skill (and the first best duo if you're including things outside of basketball skill, like performances in the movie and how interesting or not interesting their existences are).

The only way Billy sneaks ahead of him here in the draft is because his only real weakness was that he would get ultra offended any time anyone made fun of him for not being able to dunk, and that was a very real weakness because it flustered him entirely. By the end of the movie, though, he was able to dunk, so there you go.

NO. 4 PICK: Shep, *Above the Rim*
HEIGHT: 6'3" **WEIGHT:** approximately 185 pounds **POSITION:** guard
MOST MEMORABLE ON-COURT MOMENT: Scoring 34 points in less than three minutes while wearing corduroy pants.

Championship game.

Against his murderous, murdering brother's murder team of murderers.

Where no foul is hard enough to get ejected.

Playing in corduroy pants and a long sleeve shirt.

14/14 from the field.

10/10 on threes.

Team down one with nine seconds left.

Steals the ball.

Throws an alley-oop from behind the three-point line for the game-winning dunk.

All over a 2:34 stretch.

Beautiful.

NO. 3 PICK: Butch McRae, *Blue Chips*
HEIGHT: 6'7" **WEIGHT:** approximately 197 pounds **POSITION:** guard
MOST MEMORABLE ON-COURT MOMENT: Throwing the pass that led to Neon Boudeaux getting a game-winning dunk to help his college team beat Indiana, then the number-one-ranked team in the country.

(He's tied with the no. 2 pick.)

NO. 2 PICK: Neon Boudeaux, *Blue Chips*
HEIGHT: 7'1" **WEIGHT:** approximately 325 pounds **POSITION:** center
MOST MEMORABLE ON-COURT MOMENT: Getting a game-winning dunk to help his college team beat Indiana, then the number-one-ranked team in the country.

These guys are the first best fictional basketball playing duo if you're only counting basketball skill (and the least best duo if you're including things outside of basketball skill, like performances in the movie and how interesting or not interesting their existences are).

Neon edges out Butch, an all-world guard, on account of how few big guys there are in this draft. They really are at a premium. If you've got the second pick, it has to be Neon. And if you've got the first pick, it has to be . . .

NO . 1 PICK: Elliot Richards, *Bedazzled*
HEIGHT: 7'6" **WEIGHT:** approximately 290 pounds **POSITION:** center
MOST MEMORABLE ON-COURT MOMENT: Dunking it from well beyond the three-point line.

The undeniable, impossible-to-pass-up, absolutely-has-to-get-chosen, guaranteed-Hall-of-Famer-and-potentially-greatest-of-all-time first pick. His stat line from the game they show him playing in in *Bedazzled* is so absurd that it feels like too much even for a fake player: 104 points, 45 rebounds, 32 assists, 37 steals, and 28 blocks. He dunked it from the three-point line. He shot 40-footers like they were 5-footers and he shot 30-footers without even looking at the rim. He sweat a lot, and he was exceptionally dumb, and he had a teeny tiny penis,[12] but no matter. Championships abound.

---

11. Each basket will be worth two points, regardless of the distance Snake shoots it from. Cuervo is decidedly anti-three-pointers, which is maybe the most surprising part of the future.

12. The plot of *Bedazzled* is a guy makes a deal with the devil (played by Elizabeth Hurley) where he trades his soul for seven wishes, one of which he uses to become an NBA megastar version of himself. Every wish she grants him ends up having some terrible thing attached to it, though, and so when she turned him into an NBA All-Star, she also gave him a super small penis. He immediately traded away his stardom and fortune to get back into his normal body and his normal penis. Men are dumb.

The next 2,900 or so words are about NBA players who are remembered for the wrong reasons, which is to say a reason opposite of what (I imagine) they'd hoped they'd become remembered for when they entered the league. Before that, though, a short thing about the person who is the inspiration for this chapter:

A name I will never forget is Matthew Stiegler. (That's not the actual name of the guy, but I don't want to use his real name because the things I am going to say about him in the next few paragraphs are mostly embarrassing.)

I met Matthew in middle school, somewhere between the middle of sixth grade and the first part of seventh grade. He was a nice enough kid—sweet, polite, unathletic but still confident enough to have signed up for the basketball team[1]—but spent, I would guess, somewhere around 40 percent of his middle school life getting picked on. He was not too short and he was not too tall and he was not too skinny and he was not overweight and his head was not a weird shape and his body didn't stink. None of those things were the reason(s) he was picked on. The reason he was picked on: His teeth were incredibly, unbelievably, unstoppably, inconceivably yellow.

It didn't look real, how yellow they were. It looked like if when he was a toddler someone showed him how to brush his teeth and he was just like, "Nah, I'm never, ever gonna do that," and then he really and actually never, ever did that. It looked like if all of his teeth had been replaced with lemon Starbursts®. You know how in X-Men movies there's usually a scene set at the school Charles Xavier runs and there are a bunch of kid mutants running around in the background? Matthew Stiegler looked like he could be one of those background kid mutants, except nobody knew what his superpower was yet, only that it definitely had some-

thing to do with how yellow his teeth were. It was bizarre. I think maybe a big part of it was that he had braces so maybe everything looked worse than it actually was. I don't know. I just know that, for all of the time that I knew him and of him, that was the only part of his existence that anyone seemed concerned with.

Mind you, there's a happy ending to this story— Matt ended up getting his braces off during the summer leading into ninth grade, and so I guess they cleaned his teeth with one of those power washers you use to clean concrete because when he showed up for school that year they were beautifully white and straight—but it doesn't matter. For the rest of my life, and for the rest of the lives of my loser circle of friends from middle school, the first and only thing any of us will think about when someone says the name "Matthew Stiegler" will be his bright, bright, bright yellow teeth.

But so a similar fate has befallen handfuls and handfuls of NBA players. They have, despite being otherwise interesting and layered and nuanced and complex humans, become remembered for the wrong reason(s). I'm going to run through a bunch of them from here going forward, and I'll for sure explain what bad reason or thing it is that most often gets associated with a particular player's name, but I'm also going to include at least one good thing about the person, too, because I enjoy a good redemption story. The good things will be within parentheses and bolded at the end of each player's description.

Also, two tiny guidelines here: (1) I'm not including anyone who only gets remembered because he was a bust. That sort of thing isn't interesting. (And to be clear, a bust CAN appear in here somewhere in this chapter [like, say, Robert "Tractor" Traylor is in here], but it won't be because he was a bust, it'll be for a different reason [Traylor battled weight problems his whole career; it's generally the first thing people bring

---

1. I say "signed up" rather than "tried out" because the district had some policy in place for middle schools that made it so that anyone who signed up to play sports was automatically on the team. The year I was on the seventh-grade team we had near 30 players. There was a first string, second string, third string, fourth string, fifth string, and sixth string. Another rule the district had was that everyone on the team had to play before halftime, which meant that the coach would wait until there was a minute or so to play, then insert all the third-, fourth-, fifth-, and sixth-string kids into the game for a few seconds each between dead balls. It was the saddest parade.

up when they talk about him, if they happen to be talking about him]). (2) It's the same as the first rule, except this time for injuries. If you only get remembered because of your injury, then you're out. If you had an injury but get remembered for something else, then you're in. Example: Jay Williams, drafted in 2002, was injured in a very bad motorcycle accident in 2003. That's what NBA people remember him for. He's out. On the other hand, Jayson Williams, drafted in 1990, broke his leg during a game in 1999 and never played NBA basketball again. People don't really remember him for that, though. They remember him for accidentally killing his driver with a shotgun after it went off while Williams was playing with it. So he's in.

BAD.
Players remembered for bad reasons.

- Danny Ferry: He was caught saying racist things about Luol Deng during a phone call discussing his potential as a free-agent signing. (**1989 National Player of the Year in college.**)[2]
- Kermit Washington: He threw a punch so monstrous and perfectly timed during a basketball fight in 1977 that it nearly killed Rudy Tomjanovich.[3] (**He was an All-Star in 1980.**)
- Gilbert Arenas: He was a three-time All-Star, a three-time All-NBA pick, a wonderfully fun basketball weirdo, and also one time he scored 60 points against Kobe and the Lakers in 2006. AND YET, mostly the thing he'll be remembered for is bringing a gun into the locker room following a confrontation with one of his teammates. (**I already listed, like, four good things about him.**)
- Latrell Sprewell: His whole entire basketball identity got washed away after he choked his coach, P.J. Carlesimo, during a practice session in 1997.[4] (**Led the Knicks to the Finals in 1999.**)

BAD (BUT ACTUALLY GOOD).
Players remembered for bad reasons (that are actually good reasons).

- Chris Childs: In 2000, Childs punched Kobe Bryant in the face twice during an on-court fight. This, to me, is like saying, "In 2000, Childs discovered the cure for Alzheimer's," or, "In 2000, Childs pulled to safety several women and children from a burning building." Fighting is bad. You shouldn't do it and I don't recommend it. But I love Chris Childs for this basketball moment. (**He's perfect.**)
- JaVale McGee: Perhaps the unintentionally silliest, most accident-prone player of the last decade. I love him. (**Led the NBA in Block Percentage in 2011.**)
- Frank Brickowski: His name was Frank Brickowski. (**His name was fucking Frank Brickowski. Far as I'm concerned, he should've had it legally changed to Fucking Frank Brickowski.**)
- Vernon Maxwell: Crazy. (**He was crazy.**)[5]
- Chris Dudley: During a game in 1999 between the Knicks and the Lakers, Chris Dudley was attempting to guard Shaquille O'Neal. Shaq backed Dudley down to near the rim, spun, then dunked all of the meaning out of Dudley's life. Dudley went tumbling into the courtside cameramen and -women. He immediately jumped up, grabbed the basketball, and then fucking chucked it at Shaq as Shaq was jogging back down the court. I am 100 percent in favor of people throwing things at other people when they get mad at them. (**The fifth-best offensive rebounding percentage in NBA history, behind just Dennis Rodman, Moses Malone, Larry Smith, and Jeff Foster.**)[6]

WEIRD BODY.
They got weird bodies.

- Manute Bol: The real-life Enderman from Minecraft. (**Has the second-highest Blocks Per Game average in NBA history.**)

- Bryant Reeves: Like if a John Deere tractor shot 70 percent from the free throw line. (**Averaged 15.2 points per game and also 7.8 rebounds per game for his first three NBA seasons.**)
- Popeye Jones: Face. (**Led the NBA in offensive rebounds in 1995.**)
- Muggsy Bogues: Tiny. (**From 1989 to 1995, only John Stockton had more assists.**)
- Oliver Miller: I'm a big, big fan of chunky or overweight NBA players. I like it a bunch.[7] I like the dichotomy, probably. (**He one time put up 32 points, 13 rebounds, and 5 blocks in a game in 1993.**)

WEIRD (NOT BODY-RELATED).
They got weird things that aren't body-related.

- Chris Andersen: Tattoos. Lots of tattoos. So many tattoos. (**Led the NBA in Block Percentage in 2010.**)
- Delonte West: Delonte gets two. (1) In 2009, he was arrested while driving a motorcycle with a bag that was filled with guns and ammo.[8] (2) There's been an often-circulated rumor that the cause of the demise of the first generation of LeBron's Cavaliers was due to Delonte having slept with LeBron's mother. It has never been proven (or even addressed in any sort of way, really), which has only helped its legend grow. (**He was third on the 2009 Cavs in VORP.**)

- Kelvin Cato: Cato arrived to the Rockets as part of the trade that sent Scottie Pippen to Portland for the 2000 season. He wasn't terribly good while he was in Portland (he averaged less than four points per game while there), but the Rockets still eventually signed him to a six-year, $42,000,000 contract extension. The seasons that followed were mostly a bust. In 2002, E.S.G., a Houston-famous rapper, rapped the line "Tell Kelvin Cato we want our money back" in a song called "This Is For My." The Rockets traded Cato that next season. (**He was eighth in the NBA in Defensive Box Plus Minus in 2004.**)[9]
- Greg Oden: I saw his penis[10] on the Internet.[11] (**Shot 63 percent from the free throw WITH HIS OFF HAND for a year at Ohio State because he was recovering from torn ligaments in his right wrist.**)
- Andrei Kirilenko: A story broke in 2006 about how Kirilenko's wife, a Russian pop star named Masha Lopatova, allowed him to cheat on her one time every year. She told the *Salt Lake Tribune*: "If I tell my child, 'No pizza, no pizza, no pizza,' what does he want more than anything? Pizza!" (**He had three games with at least five points, rebounds, assists, blocks, and steals in his career. Only Hakeem Olajuwon had more.**)
- Metta World Peace: Changed his name from Ron Artest (a decent name) to Metta World Peace (a name that sounds less like a person's name and

---

2. This does not cancel out the racism thing, in case you were wondering.
3. "His skull was dislocated and spinal fluid was leaking from his brain." —ABC News
4. Sprewell was suspended for 68 games for the incident. Sprewell, who thought the punishment was excessive, told *60 Minutes*, "I wasn't choking him that hard. I mean, he could breathe." It's not funny, but it's funny, you know what I'm saying?
5. See Chapter 12.
6. This list started off strong, and then it just turned to paper by the end.
7. If we're making a list of The 10 Best-at-Being-Chunky Chunky NBA Players, then it's Miller first and then Late-in-His-Career Shawn Kemp, Late-in-His-Career Shaq, Glen Davis, Old Derrick Coleman, Regular Boris Diaw, Postsurgery Sean May, Jerome James and Eddy Curry (they both played for the Knicks at the same time, which is just wonderful), and Raymond Felton (my favorite fat point guard).
8. The original story was that it was a guitar case full of guns like he was in *Desperado*, but he said in a 2011 interview that it was just a regular bag.
9. My researcher sent me this stat. When he sent it, I said, "Thanks," but what I thought was, "What the fuck?"
10. The way I know Greg Oden is a nice person is when he was asked about why he'd taken the photo, he said he'd done so because "When a girl sends me 100 pictures, I have to send something back every now and then. I'm not an asshole."
11. It's important to note that this was in 2010, and so NBA player penises being on the Internet was still a decent-size news story. (Conversely, in 2016 Draymond Green's penis ended up on the Internet one afternoon and by the next morning nobody was even talking about it anymore.) Also, remember that Oden was the first pick in his draft, which makes it all even heavier. David Robinson was the first pick in his draft. Imagine if his penis had ended up on the Internet somewhere. Or Shaq's. Or Tim Duncan's. Or Yao Ming's.

more like the name of an awareness rally on a college campus somewhere). **(The 2004 Defensive Player of the Year.)**

- Shawn Kemp: Kids. Lots of kids. So many kids. **(Six-time All-Star.)**

SAD.
Players I only really remember for sad reasons.

- Eddie Griffin: He was killed when he drove his car through a railroad crossing barrier and then it was hit by a train. **(The 2001 Freshman of the Year in college.)**
- Malik Sealy: He was killed in a car crash when a drunk driver smashed into his car. **(His jersey was retired by the Timberwolves.)**
- Reggie Lewis: His heart stopped working during an off-season practice. **(He's one of only two Celtics to have had his jersey retired without winning a championship.)**
- Dražen Petrović: He died in a car crash in Germany during the off-season. **(Often credited with helping to globally expand the NBA.)**
- Len Bias: He was chosen second in the 1986 draft by the Boston Celtics, who'd just won the NBA championship. His draft day was June 17th. On June 19th, he died of a cocaine overdose. **(The ACC Player of the Year twice.)**

JORDAN'S SCROLL.
Players whose spirits were collected by Michael Jordan.

- Sam Bowie: I will never for the rest of my life forget that Bowie was drafted second in the 1984 draft, and the only reason I will never forget that is because Michael Jordan was drafted third in that same draft.[12] **(Jerry Tarkanian tells a great story in his book, *Runnin' Rebel*, about how he knew he'd lost out on recruiting Bowie when Bowie was spotted driving a Cadillac.)**[13]
- Bryon Russell: Of all the antagonists that Jordan stared down during his career, it's Bryon Russell who exists now as the figurehead for that particular cohort, as it was Russell against whom Jordan hit his only ever game-winning buzzer beat in the Finals, and then Russell again when Jordan hit the game-winning and series-winning shot at the end of Game 6 of the 1998 Finals. When Jordan gave his Hall of Fame speech in 2009, Russell sat in the stands, looking decidedly uncomfortable as Jordan lobbed grenades at him.[14] **(He played 628 games for the Jazz, the eighth most in franchise history.)**
- Craig Ehlo: The guy on the other end of The Shot. **(Ehlo scored 24 points that night and he had a sprained ankle while doing it.)**
- Barkley/Ewing/Malone: This is an unfair categorization for these three players. They of course had big, bright, substantial careers that are remembered for much more than being on the losing end of a Jordan face-off. It's just that I can't help but blow dirt in Karl Malone's eyes any chance I get.[15]

---

12. How's this for bad luck: The Blazers could've drafted Bob McAdoo in 1972, Larry Bird in 1978, Michael Jordan in 1984, and Kevin Durant in 2007.
13. "If he's driving a Cadillac, he's going to [play for] Kentucky, and we're not going to get him."
14. This is how I know that Bryon Russell is a better sport than me. There's no way I'd have lasted more than one, maybe two jabs from Jordan before standing up, shouting something like, "You know what, Mike? Fuck you and fuck your tiny mustache," and then leaving.
15. I don't like Karl Malone, sure, but I would never deny that he was a marvelous basketball player (albeit, not when he was most needed to be). Here's a question, though, and I thought about it when I was going through all the draft picks from all the years: The Knicks chose Patrick Ewing with their number-one pick in the 1985 draft. It was a good decision and a smart decision. THAT SAID, Karl Malone was the 13th pick in that same draft. Do you think that, if given the chance to go back in time and make their pick again knowing the way both of their careers played out, the Knicks would still choose Ewing? Or would they choose Malone this time?

DECISIONS

BAD DRAFT PICKS FROM 1993 TO 2016, WITH A BETTER PLAYER STILL AVAILABLE IN PARENTHESES

1993	PHI	SHAWN BRADLEY (PENNY HARDAWAY)	2005	ATL	MARVIN WILLIAMS (CHRIS PAUL)
1994	MIN	SHARONE WRIGHT (EDDIE JONES)	2006	CHA	ADAM MORRISON (J.J. REDICK)
1995	GSW	JOE SMITH (KEVIN GARNETT)	2007	POR	GREG ODEN (KEVIN DURANT)
1996	GSW	TODD FULLER (KOBE BRYANT)	2008	MIN	O.J. MAYO (RUSSELL WESTBROOK)
1997	VAN	ANTONIO DANIELS (TRACY MCGRADY)	2009	MEM	HASHEEM THABEET (STEPH CURRY)
1998	LAC	MICHAEL OLOWOKANDI (DIRK NOWITZKI)	2010	NJN	EVAN TURNER (DEMARCUS COUSINS)
1999	TOR	JONATHAN BENDER (SHAWN MARION)	2011	MIN	DERRICK WILLIAMS (KAWHI LEONARD)
2000	LAC	DARIUS MILES (JAMAL CRAWFORD)	2012	CLE	DION WAITERS (DAMIAN LILLARD)
2001	WAS	KWAME BROWN (PAU GASOL)	2013	CHA	CODY ZELLER (GIANNIS ANTETOKOUNMPO)
2002	CLE	DAJUAN WAGNER (AMAR'E STOUDEMIRE)	2014	OKC	MITCH MCGARY (CLINT CAPELA)
2003	DET	DARKO MILIČIĆ (DWYANE WADE)	2015	PHI	JAHLIL OKAFOR (KRISTAPS PORZINGIS)
2004	TOR	RAFAEL ARAÚJO (ANDRE IGUODALA)	2016	PHX	DRAGAN BENDER (THON MAKER)

- Kwame Brown: Jordan, working as the president of basketball operations and minority owner for the Washington Wizards in 2001, chose Kwame Brown, a high schooler, as the number-one pick in the 2001 draft. Then Jordan set out on, in a manner of speaking, destroying him.[16] (**One time he allegedly swiped a guy's birthday cake from him and then threw it at him. This one isn't "good" so much as it is "weird."**)

OH, SHIT. *THAT* GUY?
Players you don't remember, but actually you do.

- Frédéric Weis: "You know Frédéric Weis?" No. "Sure you do." I really don't. "He's that 7-foot-tall French guy that Vince Carter jumped over in the Olympics."

Oh, shit. *That* guy.[17] (**France's leading rebounder at the 2000 Olympics, where France won the silver medal.**)
- Rick Rickert: "You know Rick Rickert?" No. "Sure you do." I really don't. "You remember that story from, like, 2004 about Kevin Garnett getting so mad during a practice that he punched a guy on his team?" Yeah. "Well . . ." Oh, shit. *That* guy. (**A Big Ten Freshman of the Year in college.**)
- Tyronn Lue: "You know Tyronn Lue?" No. "Sure you do." I really don't. "Remember when Allen Iverson stepped over that guy during the 2001 Finals?" Yeah. "Well . . ." Oh, shit. *That* guy.[18] (**He had cornrows.**)
- Timofey Mozgov: "You know Timofey Mozgov?" No. "Sure you do." I really don't. "You remember that game in 2010 when Blake Griffin dunk-murdered a guy?" Yeah. "Well . . ." Oh, shit. *That* guy.

(The second-leading scorer for the Cavs in the 2015 NBA Finals.)

- Alton Lister: "You know Alton Lister?" No. "Sure you do." I really don't. "You remember when Shawn Kemp dunked on that one guy so hard that it knocked him off his feet and then Kemp double-pointed at him as he lay on the ground?" Yeah. "Well . . ." Oh, shit. *That* guy. (Received an MVP vote in 1983.)

CHOKE.

Players remembered for choking, which is to say missing a shot or messing up in a way that would relay that it was the stress of the situation that resulted in the miss or mess-up rather than just missing or messing up otherwise.[19]

- Nick Anderson: See Chapter 20. (The second leading scorer in Magic history.)
- Michael Ruffin: I love this one. Ruffin's Wizards were up three against the Raptors with just 3.8 seconds left in the game. The Raptors were inbounding from full court because they were out of timeouts. Anthony Parker threw a desperation pass toward the Raptors' side of the court. Ruffin tipped the ball and then even stole it, but rather than hold on to it, he tossed it into the air in celebration. There was too much time left, though, and so rather than the buzzer go off as the ball harmlessly fell back toward the court, it got there with enough time for a Raptors player (Mo Peterson)

to catch it and shoot a three at the buzzer to send the game into overtime. (His NBA 2K player looked exactly like the real-life version of him.)

- Charles Smith: Game 5. 1993 Eastern Conference Finals. Knicks vs. Bulls. Knicks down one. Smith gathers the ball under the rim. His first layup is blocked. His second layup gets stripped out of his hands before he can get it past his waist. His third layup is blocked. His fourth layup is blocked. Bulls win. (Had a 52-point game in 1990.)
- The 1994 SuperSonics: They were the number-one seed in the Western Conference that season and then lost in the first round of the playoffs to the eighth-seeded Nuggets. These guys get shoved into this category only because of the way Nuggets center Dikembe Mutombo fell to the ground in tears while holding the ball after the Nuggets won the series in overtime in Game 5 in Seattle. If he doesn't do that, if he doesn't have that moment, the '94 Sonics would've just vanished into history forever. Instead, they live in infamy. (They won 63 games that year.)

---

16. In Michael Leahy's 2005 book, *When Nothing Else Matters: Michael Jordan's Last Comeback,* Leahy describes in longform all the different ways Jordan mentally attacked Brown. It's kind of devastating. (Of course, it must be said that in 2010 Kwame signed a one-year deal with Jordan's Charlotte Bobcats team, so maybe it wasn't as bad as it'd always been made to look. After signing with the Bobcats, Kwame told the press, "We're always going to be linked. I might as well come here, right?")

17. The American version of Frédéric Weis: Shawn Bradley. He was a 7'6" version of one of the air sock things they put in the front of car lots, except teams put him in front of rims. A lot of people dunked on him, but nobody dunked on him the way Tracy McGrady dunked on him. Tracy McGrady dunked on him so hard one time during the playoffs in 2005 that the energy force from the dunk knocked the ears off Bradley's head, which, truth be told, was probably for the best because then at least he couldn't hear everyone laughing at him.

18. Tyronn Lue won an NBA championship as a player and he also won one as an NBA coach. And STILL his name is always first going to be attached to The Step Over. Allen Iverson was such a monumental basketball player that his gravity in history is strong enough to pull the rings off a guy's fingers.

19. Here's a clarification, and I'll use Kobe as my example—that way I can say a nice thing about him since I said a mean thing about him earlier: Kobe Bryant has missed plenty of shots, and he also missed plenty of BIG shots. That said, Kobe Bryant has never once in his career choked. He has never missed a shot because he was nervous; he has only, simply, missed a shot, which is not the same thing.

There was a moment in Game 3 of the 2016 NBA Finals where LeBron James tipped what was supposed to be a pass from Steph Curry to Draymond Green back and up into the air. It happened with just under three minutes left in the third quarter, right near the three-point line, and I feel like that's not a coincidence. I feel like it was supposed to happen at exactly right then because 3 (minutes left) + 3 (rd quarter) + 3 (point line) = 9, and nine is the precise number of universal substances and elements in Hindu philosophy,[1] and also the number nine in Chinese culture is the number most often associated with the dragon,[2] and also nine is the number of days it takes an anvil to fall from Heaven to Earth in Greek mythology. And all of those things are LeBron James, or spiritual extension(s) of LeBron James, and sometimes I just get so fucking excited that the universe does things like that.[3] But I bring up the play right now because of what happened afterward, because it's important. So:

LeBron deflected the pass and he and Steph both chased after the ball. LeBron got there first, and as he was gathering the ball, Steph bumped him just enough to semi-wobble LeBron's legs underneath him. LeBron momentarily went down on all fours, but managed to keep dribbling while in a push-up position because LeBron is a Cirque du Soleil performer, I think.

LeBron got up, then whipped a pass ahead to Kyrie, who by that point had gotten out fast enough on the play to create a 2-on-1 fast break. Kyrie didn't even bother to try and dribble because he knew LeBron's mega-gravity would've fucked everything off, so Kyrie just chucked the ball up at the rim, but not near the rim, or even anywhere near the area that was near the rim. He threw that shit out of the stadium. He threw that shit out of the city limits. They played Game 3 on Wednesday, June 8. Kyrie threw the ball to Tuesday, June 7.

No matter, though.

Because LeBron jumped, and he jumped with the sort of force where you could literally see the newtons he was exerting like how sometimes you can see heat coming up off the road in the summer; the sort of force that if you watch the replay more than twice your kneecaps'll split in two from the stress of even seeing it; the sort of force that should've pushed the Earth off its orbital path and, if not that, then at least cratered its surface.

But so LeBron jumped . . . and then he reached back in time . . . and then he collected the ball in one hand . . . and then he aimed a warhead at the rim . . . and then he electro-ultra-hydro dunked it. And I promise you that when I watched it I legit felt a profound sadness in my body because I realized in real-time I would only ever live an underwhelming life in comparison to what I'd just watched.

Before the dunk, the score was Cleveland 77 and Golden State Warriors 59. After the dunk, the score was Cleveland 79 and Golden State Warriors 59. That struck me as unfair then and still strikes me as unfair now and it will strike me as unfair for the foreseeable future. There should be no scenario where what LeBron James did right then in that moment should be of equal value to, say, a 1992 Brad Daugherty jump shot, which has no artistry, or a 2015 Matthew Dellavedova runner, which has negative artistry. Artistry should be accounted for, as should negative artistry, because that's one of the best parts of basketball.

So let's do that. Let's fix the value of some shots.

▶

A 1980S ADRIAN DANTLEY THREE-POINTER WAS WORTH THREE POINTS BUT IT SHOULD'VE BEEN WORTH: Seven points. // The three-point line didn't show up in the NBA until the 1980 season. Dantley shot all of two three-pointers that season (he

1. Specifically, it's Vaisheshika philosophy: Earth, Water, Air, Fire, Ether, Time, Space, Soul, and Mind.
2. A symbol of magic and power.
3. Bonus: LeBron wore the number 9 at the 2004 Olympics.

missed both). He shot seven in 1981 (and made two), three in 1982 (made one), then was like, "You know what? Fuck three-pointers" in 1983 and shot zero. The most he ever attempted in a season was 11,[4] and here's where I'll tell you that J. R. Smith, who's roughly the same size as Dantley was and also plays the same position that Dantley played,[5] shot 12 three-pointers IN A SINGLE QUARTER on two separate occasions.[6] Anyway, but so the point is: Adrian Dantley making a three was a big thing. It should've been treated as such.[7]

We can extend this valuation to any player who shot (or shoots) less than a dozen three-pointers in any season.

A 1985 PURVIS SHORT [JUMPER/LAYUP/DUNK/FREE THROW] IS WORTH:

Double whatever the actual value of the shot was. // Two things here: (1) I wonder what a newborn baby boy has to look like for a mother or father to look at him and say, "Purvis. This baby is a *Purvis*." (2) Living a life as a "Purvis" has to be harder than living a life as a "Tom" or a "John" or whatever, so I'm doubling all of his points as retribution for the purvisication of his existence. Doing so means we get a two-season stretch where Purvis Short averaged over 50 points per game (1985, 1986) and also two games where he broke Wilt Chamberlain's scoring record (the 59 points he put up during a game against the Nets in the 1984 season becomes 118 points and the 57 points he put up against the Spurs in the 1983 season becomes 114 points). Welcome to the Hall of Fame, Purvis.[8]

This valuation gets extended to just two other players because only two other players have ever had names as unfortunate as "Purvis Short": Fennis Dembo, who suited up for 31 with the world champion Pistons in 1989, and Uwe Blab, who played for three different teams during a five-year bid in the league (1986–90). Both of those guys get their points doubled.

Bonus: Anyone who has (or had) an unfortunate nickname that gets used (or was used) in lieu of his legal name can receive a 10 percent increase in point valuation (free throws become 1.1, two-pointers become 2.2, threes become 3.3). That means we get point boosts for Fat Lever[9] (sounds like a euphemism for a large penis), Pooh Richardson[10] (too close to Poop Richardson), and Bimbo Coles[11] (I suppose Bimbo Coles is better than Idiot Coles, or Doofus Coles, though only slightly). That's it. Spud Webb is a cool name. So is Sleepy Floyd. So is Muggsy Bogues. Those guys don't get anything.

A 1990 BUCK WILLIAMS[12] 10-FOOTER WAS WORTH TWO POINTS BUT IT SHOULD'VE BEEN WORTH:

Three points. // Any player who plays in goggles gets an automatic 50 percent increase in value to any shot he makes. That means two-pointers are worth three points, three-pointers are worth 4.5 points, and free throws are worth 1.5 points apiece.

---

4. It was in 1986. He made one, which puts his average that season at around 9 percent, which isn't very good, if you were wondering.
5. Or at least one of the same positions.
6. Denver at Chicago, February 22, 2008; Detroit at Denver, March 12, 2011.
7. Here's a neat Adrian Dantley stat: As I'm writing this book, there have been 41 20,000-point scorers. Adrian Dantley is on the list, and his 61.7% True Shooting percentage is the highest among them. So despite not being that great at three-pointers, he's the most efficient big-time scorer in NBA history.
8. Purvis had a brother who played in the NBA. His name was Eugene Short. He didn't go by "Eugene," though. He went by "Gene." HIS NAME WAS GENE SHORT.
9. Real name: Lafayette. (Bonus: There was a player in the '70s named Roland Morris whose nickname was Fatty.)
10. Real name: Jerome.
11. Real name: Vernell.
12. Buck Williams was a 6'8" power forward. He played for the Nets from 1982 to 1989, but I only ever associate him with the Blazers (he played with them from 1990 to 1996). I wish more people were nicknamed Buck. Buck is such a dope nickname. I'm a big fan of any first nickname that rhymes with a curse word. (It's not too well known, but "Buck" was also an early nickname for Magic Johnson. An article in the *New York Times* from 1987 says it was given to him as a shortened version of "Young Buck," a nickname he'd been given when he was a rookie on account of how much energy he had.)

We can extend this valuation as an across-the-board increase to anyone who wore goggles during a game because I respect goggles very much.[13] They're the most sophisticated basketball accessory.

(Horace Grant was, and will forever remain, the Alpha Basketball Goggle Wearer. Nobody was fucking with him goggle-wise. Some of my other favorite goggle wearers: Hakeem Olajuwon briefly wore them in 1991 after getting elbowed in the face by Bill Cartwright so hard that it broke his eye socket. Kareem Abdul-Jabbar started wearing them after suffering a couple of scratched corneas and also some weird disease where his eyes started to dry out.[14] James Worthy[15] started wearing them after an eye injury in 1985. Reggie Miller wore them for a bit after he had his eye socket broken in 1996. Amar'e Stoudemire wore them for the rest of his career after suffering a detached retina in 2009. And my favorite one: Tony Parker wore them temporarily after a shard of glass scratched his eye during a fight in a New York nightclub between Drake and Chris Brown, which is just about the most Tony Parker way of all to suffer an eye injury.)

A 1992 JOHN STOCKTON LAYUP WAS WORTH TWO POINTS BUT IT SHOULD'VE BEEN WORTH:
Five points. // John Stockton's playing height was listed as 6'1". That's six inches shorter than the height of the average player,[16] and roughly 10 inches shorter than most of the dinosaurs plodding around near the rim. As such, considerations have to be made for anyone under 6'2" who is skilled enough and deft enough to score a layup (let's say that a layup is any shot that occurs within 5 feet of the rim that isn't a dunk). So let's add 150 percent valuation increase to every layup by a player under 6'2". Added bonus: Anyone who is 6'1" and under and white who dunks it in a game gets a million points.

A 1997 BILL WENNINGTON LAYUP WAS WORTH TWO POINTS BUT IT SHOULD'VE BEEN WORTH:
Zero points. // This is the opposite of the John Stockton blurb. Bill Wennington was a 7-foot-tall cement truck.[17] Layups are not okay when you're 7 feet tall. Dunk it.

That's your job. That's what you need to do when you get the ball near the rim. If you don't, then you get penalized.

We can extend this valuation to anyone who's 7 feet tall or taller, because shooting a layup when you're 7 feet tall or taller has got to be the most unimpressive shit of all.[18]

A 2002 GARY PAYTON ASSIST WAS WORTH ZERO POINTS BUT IT SHOULD'VE BEEN WORTH:
One point. // I know that assists aren't worth points, and that's fine. In just about every case, they shouldn't be worth points. But sometimes they should be.[19] Like the time Gary Payton threw a (completely unnecessary) between-the-legs jump pass to Shawn Kemp at half court that ended up leading to a dunk. Or the time Gary Payton caught a three-quarters court pass and then, rather than turn around and lay it up, he simply passed it backward between his legs to a teammate who dunked it. Or the time Gary Payton chased down an errant pass on a fast break, jumping out of bounds to retrieve the ball, snatching it with his talons, then throwing it back in bounds between his legs to a teammate for a layup. (There's no official stat for it, but I gotta assume Gary Payton led the league in the between-the-legs assists.)

I chose 2002 here because that's the season he averaged the most assists of his career (nine per game), but we can stretch the valuation out to cover his entire career: Give Gary (and only Gary) one point for every one of his assists for the entirety of his career.

A 2008 ANTOINE WALKER THREE-POINTER WAS WORTH THREE POINTS BUT IT SHOULD'VE BEEN WORTH: $1.7 million each. // There's no point valuation adjustment here. This is more important than that. This is a bank account adjustment. Antoine Walker filed bankruptcy in 2010 despite having earned well over $100 million during his career. So if we take the 61 threes he made in 2008, which was the last year of his career, and we give him $1.7 million for each one, then he'll get most of that back.

This valuation, like the one above about Payton, is only applicable to Walker. And Allen Iverson, too. Let's give him his money back also.

A 2014 RAY ALLEN THREE-POINTER IS WORTH THREE POINTS BUT IT SHOULD'VE BEEN WORTH: One point. // Congratulations to the San Antonio Spurs on winning the 2013 NBA Championship in Game 6.[20]

A 2016 KYRIE IRVING CROSSOVER-TO-MID-RANGE JUMPER IS WORTH TWO POINTS BUT IT SHOULD BE WORTH: six points. // It's exactly three times as exciting as his regular midrange jumper so it should be worth exactly three times as much. Also, this one gets an incremental multiplier built into it based on the number of times he's done it in a row. What I mean is, okay, so say he hits two crossover-to-midrange jumpers in a row. The first one is worth six points, but the second one gets double the point allotment because performing a crossover-to-midrange jumper twice in a row is very, very difficult and also very, very dope (so that second one would be worth 12 points). If he does it three times in a row then he gets triple the points (18), four times in a row equals quadruple the points (24), and so on and so forth. Can you even picture how fucking live a stadium would get if Kyrie hit a 24-pointer in a big playoff game?

We can extend this valuation to any of the premier ball handlers in history because it only works in their hands. You can't be fumbling around with the ball and shit. It doesn't look nearly as cool.

13. A quick aside from an article I wrote for *Grantland* in 2014: In 2014, I was coaching a seventh-grade basketball team. There was a kid on there nicknamed Glue (he was a very good defender, so that's why we called him Glue). Early in the season, Glue missed practice the day before one of our games because his dad was taking him to get new glasses (which he was very excited about), along with pre-scription goggles to wear when he played basketball (which he was less enthusiastic about). Glue showed up on game day with both, but chose to wear his glasses during pregame walk-throughs. I asked him about his goggles. He said they were in his locker. I asked him why they weren't on his face. He said he was gonna put them on for the game, that he didn't need them yet. I asked him if he was sure. He said he was sure. Minutes later, a basketball ricocheted off the rim and hit him square in the face. His glasses immediately snapped in two. When he realized what had happened, he shook his head, picked the broken pieces up off the court, tried in vain to mush them back together, looked up, realized that I was looking at him, then said, "Is this a movie?" Coaching middle-school basket-ball was a fun, funny thing.
14. Corneal Erosion Syndrome, which sounds super made up.
15. In 1996, Worthy's goggles were inducted into the Smithsonian. That's not a joke. Someone at the Smithsonian was legit like, "You know what we should have here?" Then someone else was like, "What?" And then that first person was like, "James Worthy's goggles." And then that other person was like, "Oh fuck."
16. The average height of an NBA player has been 6'7" literally every year since the 1981 season.
17. He played 13 seasons in the league, winning three championships with the Bulls in 1996, 1997, and 1998 (though, in the interest of accuracy, I'd like to point out that he missed the 1997 playoffs due to an injury). The most memorable moment of his career was when Jordan passed the ball to him at the end of the 55-point game against the Knicks in 1995 and Wennington dunked it to win the game.
18. I went to a Rockets game one time and during the pregame shootaround Yao Ming was literally dunking the ball without jumping. That was actually pretty impressive. Standing dunks have a valuation of 2.5 points.
19. Since we're here, let's also go ahead and adjust the valuation of Dikembe Mutombo's blocks. Prior to now, he received zero points for a block. That's a real tragedy. Let's give him some points for each one. We'll make it a fluid thing. He can get one point for every wag of the finger following a block.
20. ⊗

WHICH DUNKS ARE
IN THE DISRESPECTFUL DUNK
HALL OF FAME?

On March 28, 1999, Shaquille O'Neal, who is like if a mountain came alive and started doing commercials, dunked on Chris Dudley, then a center for the New York Knicks. It was true devastation and real anarchy, the dunk. Shaq caught the ball in the low post, dribbled it a few times as he backed Dudley down closer to the rim, put his shoulder into Dudley's chest to uproot him, pivoted toward the basket, jumped, and then hit Dudley in the forehead with a dump truck.

Poor Dudley, man—he looked like the boat in that scene in *The Perfect Storm* when it tries to ride up that giant wave and gets crushed. It was very much a disaster. He was just getting bounced all over in Shaq's wake as Shaq pounded on him. And what's worse is that, despite getting banged around, he never all the way lost his balance, which was bad because if he'd lost his balance he could've just fallen down and that would've been the end of it. Since he didn't fall down, though, he was able to contest the dunk, which only made things more horrible, because when Shaq dunked it, he pulled himself up on the rim a bit, and when he did so he opened his legs up and so there was Dudley, right in the middle of that warfare, with Shaq's dick all of a sudden on his chest, and, I mean, if we're ranking places you'd be displeased to find Shaq's dick on your body, the chest is probably the third or fourth worst. The mayhem didn't end there, though.

Shaq finished the dunk and as he came down, Dudley was trying to hold on to him to prevent himself from falling, but Shaq being Shaq, he just shoved Dudley to the ground. And what's maybe the best part of the whole thing was that Dudley, who—how could you even blame him by that point?—he was so furious from everything that had just happened, he jumped up, grabbed the ball, then threw it at Shaq's back as hard as he could as Shaq was jogging back down the court. The refs blew the whistle to call a couple technical fouls (Dudley got one for throwing the ball, Shaq got one for shoving Dudley) so the game stopped for a moment, but the camera made sure to stay on Dudley's face as he was staring at Shaq and you could very plainly see him shout "FUCK YOU!" at Shaq. The whole situation was just really, truly excellent, because if someone dunks on someone else so hard that the dunkee responds by throwing the ball at the dunker and then cussing at him, then that's a pretty great and exactly perfect example of a disrespectful dunk, which is what this chapter (and the one that follows it) is about.

Shaq's dunk on Dudley definitely belongs in the Disrespectful Dunk Hall of Fame. Let's go over some other disrespectful dunks from the DDHOF, and let's give each of them Disrespect Scores so as to keep everything nice and tidy, and let's go in ascending order of disrespect.

▶

Before we get to The Disrespectful Dunk Hall of Fame, a few questions:

Are all dunks disrespectful?

No. In fact, most dunks aren't disrespectful. That's what makes the disrespectful ones so much fun. You know how when you pour a bowl of Lucky Charms and it's mostly those little brown pieces with a few marshmallows sprinkled in? That's this.

How do you know when a dunk is disrespectful?

That's like asking me "How do you know when you're in love?" or "How do you know when to masturbate?" You just sort of know because you feel it. It's those big dunks; those nasty dunks; those violent dunks. Dunks where, when they happen, you just instinctively go, "OH FUCCCCCCCCCCCK!" or you go, "YOOOOOOOOOOOOO!" or you go, "HAHAHAHAHA OH MY GOD." It's dunks like that. Dunks that go over someone, or, maybe more accurately, *through* someone.

Think on it like this: Most dunks just happen and that's it. There's the dunk and then it's over. (As an example, picture, say, 2004 Jamaal Magloire dunking it all alone on a fast break.)[1] A disrespectful dunk, though—a disrespectful dunk has an echo, and I mean that literally and, more importantly, I also mean it figuratively. They live on.

---

1. I have no idea why Jamaal Magloire, a 6'11" iceberg, is running a fast break in this pretend scenario.

You mentioned a thing earlier about Disrespect Scores. That means there must be some kind of scoring system for all of this, right? Something that'll help quantify everything?

Yes. It's easy. You just have to look at six different categories.[2] You have to look at:

- **CATEGORY 1: HOW DIFFICULT AND/OR IMPRESSIVE WAS THE ACTUAL DUNK?** This one is scored on a scale of 0 to 20, with easier dunks scoring lower, while more impossible dunks score higher. Using the abovementioned death-by-dickening of Chris Dudley by Shaq as an example, Shaq would earn 18/20 here. Athletically, it wasn't an especially difficult dunk to pull off like, for example, when Vince Carter hit Chris Mullin with the midair double-pump dunk in 1999, but the ferocity of it shoots its score way up.
- **CATEGORY 2: WHAT DID THE DUNKER DO IMMEDIATELY AFTER THE DUNK?** (Also scored on a scale of 0 to 20.) The more interesting or turbulent a post-dunk reaction is by the dunker, the higher the score. In Shaq's case, again, he shoved Chris Dudley to the ground, which is about as gnarly as it gets. 18/20.
- **CATEGORY 3: HOW HARD DID THE DEFENDER TRY TO STOP THE DUNK FROM HAPPENING?** (Also scored on a scale of 0 to 20.) For a dunk to become a truly elite disrespectful dunk, either the defender has to make a genuine and intense effort to stop the dunk (which Dudley absolutely did, God bless him), or he has to try and take a charge and then get annihilated, like what happened to Steve Nash when he tried to take a charge on Ricky Davis in 2002 (which we'll go over in a bit), or what happened to Steve Nash when he tried to take a charge on Kobe Bryant in 2006, or what happened to Steve Nash when he tried to take a charge on Josh Smith in 2009. Dudley's effort earns a 19/20 here.
- **CATEGORY 4: IS THERE A BACKSTORY BETWEEN THE DUNKER AND THE DUNKEE?** (Scored on a scale of 0 to 15.) There are two ways to score high here. First, if there's a very intense and vitriolic backstory between the two people involved in the dunk, then that's one way to shoot the score up. The second way is if the dunk is so devastating that it forever ties the two players together, creating a sort of instant backstory in the present, if that makes any sense. What I mean is, okay, the Shaq and Chris Dudley dunk—before it happened, there wasn't some long and drawn-out history between the two.[3] But, following that dunk, from now until forever, anytime someone brings up Chris Dudley,[4] someone else is going to bring up what Shaq did to him. That's why Shaq gets a good score here despite there having been no serious animosity between the two beforehand. 13/15.
- **CATEGORY 5: DID THE BALL GO STRAIGHT THROUGH THE NET OR DID IT RATTLE AROUND A LITTLE?** (Scored on a scale of 0 to 5.) Style is important. 5/5.
- **CATEGORY 6: HOW DID EVERYONE WHO WAS NOT DIRECTLY INVOLVED WITH THE DUNK REACT?** (Scored on a scale of 0 to 20.) You have to consider what the other players on the court did, what the guys on the bench of the dunker's team did, what the guys on the bench of the dunkee's team did, what the crowd did, what the people calling the game did, what the refs did, and on and on. The bigger and more dramatic the response from everyone else, the higher the score. In the Shaq/Dudley case, Ben Davis and Herb Williams both decided that they didn't want to be on the Knicks anymore as soon as they saw the dunk. Next season, they were both playing somewhere else. Shaq dunked two players off the Knicks roster, is what I'm saying. 17/20.

So we grab the score from each category, add them up, and that's how we see that the Shaq dunk on Dudley was 90 percent disrespectful to Dudley. Any dunk that earns a Disrespect Score of 85 or higher gets inducted into the Disrespectful Dunk Hall of Fame, which means this dunk is in the DDHOF.

▶

To be clear, I'm not going to go over *all* of the dunks in the Disrespectful Dunk Hall of Fame, but I do have one for every level of percent disrespectful from 85 to 100 percent, and it definitely ends with the only dunk that's ever been 100 percent disrespectful. First, though, some DDHOF dunks that aren't talked about at length but should be mentioned:

Dr. J on Bill Walton when he tossed the ball at his head afterward (1977), Dominique Wilkins's double-pump shotgun dunk on all of the Bucks (1984), Dominique Wilkins's fury dunk on Robert Parish (1988), Tom Chambers's flying knee dunk on Mark Jackson (1989), Kevin Johnson's dunk on Hot Rod Williams (1992), Shawn Kemp's Game 3 high-speed alley-oop from Gary Payton (1992), Michael Jordan over Alonzo Mourning (1993), Shaq's "You Thought This Was a Game?!" dunk on David Robinson in the All-Star Game (1996), Allen Iverson's putback dunk when he rode Marcus Camby like a horse (1998), Grant Hill's revenge dunk on Alonzo Mourning (1998), Vince Carter's Top Shelf dunk on Dikembe Mutombo (1999), the dunk where Gilbert Arenas bounced an alley-oop to Jason Richardson (2002), Kobe Bryant's "Buckle Up" up-and-under dunk (2003), Kobe Bryant's "Welcome to the NBA" dunk on Dwight Howard when he was a rookie (2004), Robert Horry's extend-o arm dunk over Richard Hamilton in Game 5 of the Finals (2005), Vince Carter's *Desolation of Smaug* dunk on Alonzo Mourning (2005), LeBron's End All Life dunk on the Celtics (2008), Dwyane Wade's "That's How You Fucking Do It!" and-one dunk on Anderson Varejão (2009), Blake Griffin's "Welcome to America" dunk on Timofey Mozgov (2010), Derrick Rose's *Armageddon* dunk on Goran Dragic (2010), Gerald Green's Around the World windmill alley-oop (2012), Paul George's beheading of Chris Andersen (2013), LeBron's LOL dunk when he literally jumped over tiny John Lucas (2012), LeBron's Broken Nose dunk over Serge Ibaka (2014), and Manu's FOH hammer-dunk on Chris Bosh in the Finals (2014).

---

85 PERCENT DISRESPECTFUL:
Michael Jordan on Dikembe Mutombo
(May 13, 1997)

This is maybe one of my personal favorite dunks, and I say that less because it was just such a big and extraordinary dunk (it wasn't) and more because of the pieces tucked away inside of it. To wit:

(1) Prior to the dunk happening, this great video came out of Jordan and Mutombo playfully arguing in a locker room about how Jordan had never dunked on Mutombo. Patrick Ewing was in there, too. He jumped in on the conversation: "He ain't ever dunked you?" he asked. Dikembe: "No!" Ewing: *"Never?"*

(2) Mutombo is one of the most endlessly likable NBA players of my lifetime. I remember seeing him participate in this 60 Days of Summer event that the Basketball Hall of Fame held. He was there being interviewed and a fan named Jeffrey began to ask him about the Jordan dunk. As soon as Jeffrey said Jordan's name, Mutombo smiled and rolled his head back and ultra-grumbled in his very distinct Dikembe Mutombo voice, "Ooooooh, there we go," and then turned the opposite direction and said, "Keep going, Jeffrey. I'm listening. I'm not looking at you." It was perfect and I smile every time I think about it.

(3) After Jordan dunked on Mutombo, he gave Mutombo the finger wag that Mutombo would do after he blocked shots, and that's just such a deliciously petty move.

(4) Despite it not being a mega colossal dunk like, say, Jordan over Patrick Ewing or Jordan over Kelly Tripucka or Jordan over Alonzo Mourning, it was still pretty impressive considering that Mutombo finished first in blocks in the league from the 1994 season to the 1998 season.[5]

---

2. This methodology was a thing I came up with for a recurring column about Disrespectful Dunks I wrote for *The Ringer* during the 2017 NBA season.

3. One possible backstory: In 1994, Chris Dudley started an organization called the Chris Dudley Foundation, which aimed to help children with diabetes. Perhaps Shaq is secretly pro-diabetes? Maybe he dunked it on Dudley and shouted something like, "Bang! That's a sugary thunder-dunk for them little diabetic ass kids of yours." It seems unlikely, but I wanted to toss the possibility out there.

4. Chris Dudley is one of only six players in NBA history with a minimum of 1,500 free throw attempts with a worse free throw percentage (45.8) than Shaq (52.7).

5. As I write this, Mutombo is still the only player in NBA history to lead the league in blocks for five straight seasons.

86 PERCENT DISRESPECTFUL:
Kevin Johnson on Hakeem Olajuwon
(May 15, 1994)

Nine things to point out here: (1) It was the playoffs. (2) Hakeem was the MVP that season. (3) Hakeem was second in the league in blocks that season (and, FYI, would go on to eventually become the all-time greatest shot blocker in the history of the NBA). (4) Hakeem was listed at 7 feet tall and Kevin Johnson was barely over 6 feet tall, and little guys dunking on big guys is the best kind of dunk. (5) Hakeem was called for a foul as KJ dunked it, which always magnifies everything. (6) They were playing in Phoenix, and so the arena went all the way berserk. (7) The Phoenix bench, otherwise subdued given that the Suns were down 11 points prior to the dunk, erupted in chaos; arms and legs were everywhere. And what's even better is that the play happened on Phoenix's side of the floor, so all of their reactions were captured in the shot as the play was happening. (8) KJ was so fired up that he literally celebrated all the way past half court as he jumped and flexed and yelled to himself, at Hakeem, at everyone. (9) As KJ was on his victory march, one of the guys calling the play declared, "Look at the determination and intensity in this man's . . . *soul*." If a player dunks it with so much gusto that another man decides he can see that player's soul, then that player is getting into the Disrespectful Dunk Hall of Fame.

87 PERCENT DISRESPECTFUL:
DeAndre Jordan on Brandon Knight
(March 10, 2013)

This one was the opposite of the KJ-on-Hakeem dunk, in that that one was a little-guy-on-a-big-guy dunk, which are (generally) the most enjoyable kinds of dunks, while this one was a big-guy-on-a-little-guy dunk, which are (generally) the most destructive.

Chris Paul dribbled the ball out near the three-point line. DeAndre rolled toward the rim. Chris Paul saw him (because he sees everything), so he tossed the ball up way too high for an alley-oop. DeAndre, who is the closest I have ever seen a human come to being a space shuttle, went after it, and as he jumped so too did Brandon Knight, a brave and foolish warrior with more courage than ability. DeAndre caught it and cocked it back and the force from his gigantic body knocked Knight's body off balance, and so DeAndre Incredible Hulk-ed the ball through the rim as Knight fell some 8 feet straight down onto his back. There was a real and literal "thud" from Knight hitting the floor. It sounded like what I imagine it'd sound like if you dropped a slab of meat off the Empire State Building. It was gross, and the Staples Center goddamn loved it. The whole thing. As soon as it was over, everyone went, "Well, that's definitely going to be the best dunk of the year," and it absolutely was.

88 PERCENT DISRESPECTFUL:
Baron Davis on Andrei Kirilenko
(May 11, 2007)

Baron Davis, attacking the rim with the same ferocity of a Viking storming a beach, jumped, put his axe through Andrei Kirilenko's chest, and then in the raucous ruckus afterward, he picked up his whole jersey to show his torso to Kirilenko. Showing your nipples to the guy you just dunked on is a very elite alpha male move.

89 PERCENT DISRESPECTFUL:
Shawn Kemp over Chris Gatling
(April 30, 1992)

This one is a famous dunk because the dunkee, Chris Gatling, after he got obliterated for an and-one dunk by Shawn Kemp, he literally dapped Shawn Kemp up. Kemp powered it home and then as he stood there celebrating after the ref's whistle, he reached his hand out and Gatling was like, "Yeah, you got me," and then grabbed it and celebrated with him. In a way, I guess this dunk was so disrespectful that it was respectful, which is at least a little bit confusing, probably.

Note: Gatling's post-dunk reaction is the secondmost effective way to handle getting dunked on. It's just hard to be like, "Hahahaha, you got dunked on real bad," when the guy who got dunked on real bad is like, "Hahahaha, I got dunked on real bad," you know what I'm saying? The first most effective way to handle it is what Joakim Noah did when LeBron dunked on him in 2015.

Cleveland and Chicago were playing and LeBron had the ball on the wing. He spun on his man and got into the lane and then dunked on Noah, who'd slid over to contest the dunk. LeBron and Noah hadn't liked each other for a long time by that point, so LeBron glared at Noah and shouted something not nice to him. The ref called a tech on LeBron, and if it had ended right there and then, LeBron would have won. But it didn't end there.

Noah immediately charged at LeBron and shouted, "You're still a bitch, though." The cameras tried to hurry away from Noah's face as he said it, but it was too late. He'd lobbed that atom bomb out into the universe and everyone had seen it happen. There was nothing LeBron could do in return. Because he knew then what I'm telling you now: Shouting "You're still a bitch, though" is the first most effective way to handle getting dunked on. It's the first most effective way to handle anything, really. It instantly delegitimizes whatever happened right before it. Imagine the best, most noble, most unimpeachable thing you can think of, like—okay, imagine the guy who invented prosthetic limbs for children who were born without parts of their arms and their legs. Now imagine him presenting his invention very proudly and profoundly to an auditorium of afflicted children, and as he does, one of the little kids in the back shouts, "You're still a bitch, though." Guess what, then? He's still a bitch, though.

---

90 PERCENT DISRESPECTFUL:
Amar'e Stoudemire on Michael Olowokandi
(December 20, 2002)

I watched this dunk happen on TV at my grandma's house. I was home from school visiting her and my mom and dad in San Antonio. I'd actually moved in with my grandma when I started sixth grade. By the time ninth grade showed up, my whole family was living there, too. It was me, my mom, my dad, my sisters, and my grandma. She lived with us (or, "we lived with her" is probably more accurate) until she passed in 2008. I remember taking this class later in college and part of it was a weekly discussion about whatever it is we were supposed to have been reading. One week, the reading was some story about a family—I don't remember the specifics, but I do remember that the conversation in class that day ended up being centered around when it was okay to send your grandparents or parents to live in an assisted living home. Everyone was sitting there talking about it and I was so fucking confused. The teacher, this very nice and smart and insightful woman, called on me. She said something like, "Shea, at what age do you think sending your grandparents or parents to live in a home is acceptable?" I said, "I have no idea." She asked, "Why?" I said, "Because Mexicans don't do that. We just move them in with us until they die." Mostly everyone laughed. I wasn't joking, though. I don't know. That's the first thing I think about when I think about this dunk. You can't control how your brain works.[6]

---

91 PERCENT DISRESPECTFUL:
Tracy McGrady on Shawn Bradley
(April 25, 2005)

So many excellent pieces to this one: (1) It was a playoff game. (2) It was a playoff game between the Rockets and the Mavericks, and the Rockets and Mavericks hate each other. (3) The Rockets were on the road and had already stolen Game 1 and were looking to steal Game 2. (4) To that point in his career, Tracy McGrady, for all his otherworldly talents, had never made it out of the first round of the playoffs.[7]

(5) The actual dunk itself was just this devastating, crippling felony. T-Mac had the ball in the corner, and he was being guarded by Dirk (which really meant that he wasn't being guarded by anyone), so he just dribbled right around him. When he did so, he saw that Bradley, a 7'6" tall tree branch, had slid over to try to protect the

rim, and if you watch the play in slow motion it looks like when McGrady saw it he actually got mad that Bradley had done it, because he just fucking accelerated straight at him. He jumped, and Bradley, knowing there was nothing left to do except accept his fate, turned his back and waited to get dunked to dust.

(6) McGrady was so high up that when he let go of the rim he literally slid down Shawn Bradley's back, which, I mean, if we're being technical here, I think that means he turned Bradley into a playground slide.

(7) Kevin Harlan, the primary announcer for the game, shouted, "OH! HE JUST SUCKED THE GRAVITY RIGHT OUT OF THE BUILDING!" (8) The crowd—and remember, the game was in Dallas—the crowd screamed in delight like it was one of their guys who'd just had that great dunk. (9) The play happened on the Rockets side of the floor, and so in the background of the play you could see one of the Rockets bench guys, Jon Barry, roll out onto the floor in shock. (10) *And* the refs called a foul on the dunk.

---

92 PERCENT DISRESPECTFUL:
Blake Griffin on Kendrick Perkins
(January 30, 2012)

When you're the defender in one of these dunk situations, there are five ways to handle it. You can do the thing where you just go ahead and step right on out the way on some "Live to fight another day" shit (the coward's way out, as it were). You can try and take a charge (the dumbest way to go about it). You can stand there and put your arms straight up and just hope something good happens (shoutout Roy Hibbert). You can jump and try desperately to actually block the dunk (the bravest

way to go about it). Or you can just foul the hell out of the dunker, hoping, if nothing else, to at least preserve your own integrity.[8]

Kendrick Perkins chose for the fouling option when Blake Griffin started his dunk, only except the bad thing for him was that Blake, who, by then had gotten the taste of dunk blood, was just too big, too strong, too forceful, too mean to be stopped. He jumped, Kendrick put both arms into Blake's chest, clobbering him, hoping to stop him (or at least stun him enough to cause him to miss), and Blake just went through him, dropping a nuclear bomb onto Kendrick's whole everything.

---

6. The dunk was heavy. Stephon Marbury passed the ball to Amar'e following a very soft pick and roll. Stoudemire, who dunked with exceptional speed, caught the ball in the lane, rose up, then Rose Up, then ROSE UP, and then fucking shoved Olowokandi into an ocean trench. And as good as the dunk was, the best part was Stephon Marbury, who made a face like what it would look like if someone's face was melting off of their skull.
7. In 2003, McGrady led his Magic to a 3–1 lead in their playoff series against the Pistons. In an interview after Game 4, Tracy expressed gratitude and thankfulness for being able to get his team to the second round of the playoffs so early in his career, which he assumed they'd do since they had what looked like an impossible-to-lose lead. They lost the next three games. Pistons won the series 4–3.
8. The most famous recent example of this was Draymond Green doing it to LeBron James at the end of Game 7 of the 2016 NBA Finals when LeBron tried to create his own personal *San Andreas* in Oakland.

WHICH DUNKS ARE
IN THE DISRESPECTFUL DUNK
HALL OF FAME?

...continued

93 PERCENT DISRESPECTFUL:
John Starks on the Bulls
(May 25, 1993)

Let me say three things here, none of which are specifically about the actual dunk: (1) I love the John Starks origin story. He played at three different junior colleges, went undrafted, played sparingly for the Warriors in 1989, played in the Continental Basketball Association and the World Basketball League,[1] then worked stocking groceries while trying to land on a team. He was at a Knicks camp (and about to be cut) when, during the final practice, he tried to dunk on Patrick Ewing. He ended up twisting his knee (Ewing blocked the dunk), so the Knicks couldn't cut him until he healed up.[2] But right around the time he was healing up, another Knicks player, Trent Tucker, got hurt, so the Knicks kept him on, and he just never went away after that. (2) This dunk for sure was instantly iconic and will remain that way, but its most lasting impact was that the defense that led to it would eventually change basketball hugely. "That was the first time . . . that I had ever seen in the NBA any team force the ball to the baseline in the side pick-and-roll," Jeff Van Gundy, then an assistant coach with the Knicks, told ESPN in 2012. (3) This was the biggest dunk ever *on the Bulls* during the Knicks–Bulls rivalry. It actually put the Knicks up 2–0 in their playoff series that year. They went on to lose the next four games. The biggest dunk ever *on the Knicks* during the Knicks–Bulls rivalry was the one Scottie put down over Patrick[3] in 1994 (it's discussed later). His team won that game, but then eventually lost the series, same as what happened here with the Starks dunk for the Knicks. The universe is weird.

94 PERCENT DISRESPECTFUL:
Darryl Dawkins on backboards
(November/December 1979)[4]

(If you want to swap him out here for the times that Shaq yanked down basketball stanchions, then that's fine.)

95 PERCENT DISRESPECTFUL:
LeBron James on Jason Terry
(March 18, 2013)

A perfect revenge dunk.

LeBron and his Heat faced Terry and his Mavs in the 2011 Finals. After going down 1–2 in the series, Terry, a master needler, started talking to the media about how LeBron, the best player of his generation and one of the five best players of all time, wasn't going to be able to guard him well for a full series. And then somehow, improbably, unbelievably, unfathomably, it became true. Terry outplayed LeBron in Games 4, 5, and 6 (including a three over LeBron in the final seconds of Game 5 that basically won the game for the Mavs), and the Mavs ended up stealing the title.

But so two years later—and, mind you, this is two years later of Jason Terry bringing that up every chance he got—Terry was on the Celtics and they were playing the Heat, who, by then, were not only the defending champions, but also on a 22-game winning streak. He was bringing the ball up the court and Dwyane Wade snuck in from behind and poked it away. Wade flipped it to Mario Chalmers, who then tossed it to Norris Cole, who then lobbed it up for LeBron, who was all of a sudden heading toward Terry like that comet in *Deep Impact*. Terry, oh man, he kept jumping around trying to knock the ball away from someone, anyone, but he just

---

1. I have no idea what leagues these are. Had I not read about them in the *New York Times*, I'd have believed they were fake.
2. Teams can't cut injured players.
3. There is absolutely an argument to be made here that Michael's dunk over Ewing was the biggest.
4. Darryl shattered two different backboards in two different NBA games less than a month apart. The first one happened during a road game against Kansas City. He said he broke the second one, which happened during a home game, because he wanted to do it in Philadelphia so his fans could see it.

couldn't. He jumped for it when Norris threw it to LeBron, but it was too high, and so LeBron caught it, D-U-N-K-E-D it, then, before coming down, reached inside Terry's body, yanked out his spine and skull on some Sub-Zero shit, and then D-U-N-K-E-D that, too. Terry's body fell backwards, slapping against the court. LeBron stared at him long enough to prove his point (and get a technical), then walked away without saying a word.

Afterward, he told the media scrum, "I'm glad it happened to him." <3

96 PERCENT DISRESPECTFUL:
Dominique Wilkins on Larry Bird (October 30, 1982)[5]

Really, the only thing you need to know here is that it was Larry Bird trying to stop Dominique Wilkins on a fast break, and asking someone to try and stop Dominique Wilkins on a fast break in the '80s was like dropping an army infantry tank out of an airplane from 20,000 feet up and then asking someone on the ground to catch it. The dunk literally ended with Bird, who'd gotten spun all 360 degrees around in the air after he'd collided with Wilkins,[6] sitting on the floor just staring straight ahead refusing to move.[7] He looked like he'd just survived a car crash, which, I suppose in a way he did.

97 PERCENT DISRESPECTFUL:
Ricky Davis on Steve Nash (November 13, 2002)

Shawn Bradley tried to throw a pass to Dirk Nowitzki.[8] Ricky stole it, then shot up the court in his most turbo mode. Steve Nash, may God have mercy on his soul, tried to stop Ricky from scoring by stepping in front of him to take a charge; he'd have done better stepping in front of a train, really. Ricky planted his left foot down just inside the paint, jumped, somehow ended up with his knee on Nash's shoulder, and then Stone Cold Steve Austin'd a dunk down from 45 feet up in the air. Even Ricky was surprised by what Ricky had just done, which

was very crazy because Ricky had a very high opinion of himself.[9] The ref called a foul on Nash,[10] Ricky just stood there under the rim screaming, "OH SHIT! OH SHIT," one of his teammates shoved him, then Ricky celebrated for a few more seconds afterward because Ricky always celebrated for a few more seconds afterward.[11] Imagine the scene from *Game of Thrones* where The Mountain squishes The Red Viper's eyeballs into his head. That was this.

98 PERCENT DISRESPECTFUL:
Dr. J on Michael Cooper (January 5, 1983)

This is that dunk they always show on all the important NBA highlight reels where Dr. J and Cooper are heading full speed toward the rim and Dr. J swings the ball around from what feels like his feet to his forehead and then slams it home as Cooper curls up in the air like how spiders do when they die. It's the only dunk in the Disrespectful Dunk Hall of Fame that is more distinguished than it is ferocious, which is probably everything you need to know about Dr. J and his entire aesthetic.[12]

99 PERCENT DISRESPECTFUL:
Shawn Kemp on Alton Lister (April 30, 1992)[13]

There's just so much great stuff here to unpack. First, it was Game 4 of their first-round series in the 1992 playoffs, and the young and surprising Sonics, led by the human sneer Gary Payton and the human hightop fade Shawn Kemp, were up 2–1 on the higher-seeded Warriors (it was a 3–6 matchup) and looking to close them out. Second, Game 3 of that series featured an already disrespectful Gary-Payton-to-Shawn-Kemp alley-oop, and so you have to include that in here. Third, and this is maybe the second-best part, Kemp and Lister got into a fight during Game 2, so it was very clear and obvious that they didn't like each other. Fourth, you have Kemp's actual dunk, which was incredible all on its own. And then fifth, the part that tied everything together, you have Kemp's post-dunk celebration, hands down the best post-dunk celebration of all time and the first best part of this whole thing.

To recap the actual play and histrionics: Sonics guard Ricky Pierce dribbled his way into a trap on the left side of the court. He turned and tossed the ball out to Kemp, who caught it at the top of the key. Kemp realized the lane was wide open, took a dribble in, gathered the ball and held it in his arm like a running back does the football when he's in the opening field, and then began his jump. And just as he began his jump, Lister slid over and tried to take a charge.

Now, I don't mind telling you: Shawn Kemp was a bad motherfucker.[14] He remains, in no uncertain terms, one of the all-time great in-game dunkers. I was reading things about him and also about his dunks while I was researching for this book and the best description I came across for his dunks was when Dan Devine, writing for Yahoo! Sports, referred to it as "a doomsday device," which is exactly what it was. It was just this very ferocious, very violent, very terrifying act, and on this particular day, Alton Lister caught the ultimate worst of it.

He slid in and tried to take that charge, which I guess was noble, but it was too late; Lister caught a knee in the sternum, somehow propelling Kemp even higher into the air, and so there Lister was, falling backwards onto the ground, sliding some several feet across the court as Kemp tried to tomahawk dunk the Warriors out of the NBA.[15] The whole arena—they were playing in Seattle—the whole arena just went haywire. It was total madness. And Kemp, in the moment that would go on to be the signature play of his career, after the dunk, he landed, squatted down a little to get closer to Lister's eye level, and when he caught Lister's eyes, he pointed at him with both index fingers in a very "Haha, you just died" way.[16] Imagine that. Imagine hitting someone with a truck, jumping out, then pointing at them and laughing. That's basically what Kemp did. It was poetry. It was excellent. It was *excellence*.

---

5. Only the second game of 'Nique's career.

6. "I think that dunk I was just mad because I'd just got burnt three or four times by Larry. And that was probably just a dunk out of anger." —Dominique Wilkins, on TNT's show *NBA Posterized!* in 2007.

7. This was an and-one dunk, too. That should be mentioned.

8. This is the whitest, tallest sentence in the entire book.

9. Ricky was actually in Cleveland when LeBron first showed up. He lasted just a couple of months before he was traded. He told newspapers afterward: "I thought LeBron James was just going to be another addition to help me score."

10. During a retrospective on TNT where they were talking about the best dunks of all time, Steve Nash, talking about the Ricky dunk, said, "Well, I dare him to try that again. Now that I know where he's—I didn't know he was gonna dunk it or I'd have blocked it." Steve Nash is neat.

11. In several of the cases, the dunks mentioned in this section ended up being the plays most often associated with each player. For example, if I say, "Think of a Scottie Pippen play," you're almost certainly going to think of his dunk on Ewing first. That's not the case for Ricky, though. The moment most often associated with him is the time he shot the ball at his own basket at the end of the game just so he could get the rebound because he was one rebound short of a triple double. His explanation years later during an interview with *Grantland:* "It was probably a selfish thing. But I really wanted that triple double."

12. A neat aside about this dunk: As the date indicates, it happened in 1983. Dr. J and the Sixers had lost to the Lakers in the NBA Finals twice in the prior three years (1980, 1982). So make no mistake: For as breathtaking of a play as it was, there was ill intent behind it from the good doctor.

13. This dunk became known as The Lister Blister. I wish more dunks were named.

14. He was also, as it were, a mothermaker, if that's even a thing. He fathered at least seven children.

15. The Warriors actually only made the playoffs one time in the 14 years that followed the dunk.

16. What's lost in all of this is that after the play, Kemp jogged down court and gave a teammate a double low-five, probably the most secretly disrespectful kind of celebratory five to give. If we arrange all the celebratory fives from Least Disrespectful to Most Disrespectful, it goes: single high-five, double high-five, single low-five, double low-five.

> **100 PERCENT DISRESPECTFUL:**
> Scottie Pippen on Patrick Ewing
> (May 20, 1994)

The most disrespectful dunk of all time. Let's go through each of the six categories mentioned in the first part of this double chapter to make sure we don't miss anything.

- **CATEGORY 1: HOW DIFFICULT AND/OR IMPRESSIVE WAS THE ACTUAL DUNK?** Insanely difficult and impressive. You're talking about a full-speed, fast-breaking, taking-off-from-just-inside-the-lane, one-on-one-versus-Patrick-Ewing dunk. And let's add to it that, not only was it the playoffs, but it was the playoffs and the Bulls were down 3–2 in that series, meaning if they lost it was over, meaning that it happened under incredibly high stakes. 20/20.

- **CATEGORY 2: WHAT DID THE DUNKER DO IMMEDIATELY AFTER THE DUNK?** Oh God. Ewing, who'd tried so hard to block the dunk that he'd compromised his balance entirely, fell backwards to the floor. He grasped at Scottie to keep himself up, but Scottie just shoved his arms away, making it look like he'd shoved Ewing to the floor. What's more, Scottie's momentum carried him forward several steps after the dunk, and so he was literally standing over Ewing, his dick just two feet from Ewing's face, which, same as we saw with the Shaq–Dudley dunk, is just always extra points for the guy who's the dicker and bad business for the guy who's the dickee. Pippen wasn't even done there, though. He walked over Ewing, then strolled past Spike Lee, who'd gotten courtside seats to the game and was standing up screaming and yelling, and told him, "Sit your ass down." Then he smiled and did a fist pump and walked away from the carnage like what the Joker did in *The Dark Knight* after he blew up that hospital. 20/20.

- **CATEGORY 3: HOW HARD DID THE DEFENDER TRY TO STOP THE DUNK FROM HAPPENING?** So hard. As hard as anybody could ever possibly try to block a dunk without actually blocking a dunk. Give Ewing his due here: He had no fear about him during that play. 20/20.

- **CATEGORY 4: IS THERE A BACKSTORY BETWEEN THE DUNKER AND THE DUNKEE?** The Knicks lost to the Bulls in the playoffs in 1989. The Knicks lost to the Bulls in the playoffs in 1991. The Knicks lost to the Bulls in the playoffs in 1992. The Knicks lost to the Bulls in the playoffs in 1993.[17] Yes. There's a backstory. 15/15.

- **CATEGORY 5: DID THE BALL GO STRAIGHT THROUGH THE NET OR DID IT RATTLE AROUND A LITTLE?** Perfect. 5/5.

- **CATEGORY 6: HOW DID EVERYONE WHO WAS NOT DIRECTLY INVOLVED WITH THE DUNK REACT?** In the best way possible. The announcers went bonkers. ("OH MY!" "OH BABY!" "HOLY COW!") The crowd went bonkers. Pete Myers, a shooting guard for the Bulls, leaned over Ewing and barked something at him. Several Knicks players ran over and started shoving people. Several Bulls players ran over and shoved people back. The refs ran in and tried to get control of everything. It was chaos. It was beautiful, gory, disrespectful chaos. Scottie Pippen dunked almost 20,000 people into a feeding frenzy. It was all just so perfectly disrespectful. 20/20.

---

17. Additionally, this was the last Bulls game ever played at Chicago Stadium.

A memory hero is, in most (but not all) cases, someone who you remember as being way better than he or she actually was. Most times, the talent inflation happens because the memories were formed when you were a child or young person, and so since children and young people don't know things and are very bad at placing things in context,[1] that's how you end up having a moment when you're an adult where you say something like, "Whoa, wait, actually maybe *Bio-Dome* wasn't the best movie of 1996." Or, "Whoa, wait, actually maybe Wreckx-N-Effect wasn't better than Wu-Tang." Or, since we're talking about basketball, "Whoa, wait, actually maybe Vinny Del Negro wasn't a generational basketball talent," which is a thing I said to myself some years ago.

Vinny was one of my first memory heroes.[2] He played guard for the Spurs from the 1993 season to the 1998 season, and that's for sure part of the reason I really liked him. But an even bigger part of the reason I liked him so much was that someone lied and told me he was Mexican, and so of course I loved him, and of course I was also so incredibly proud to brag to everyone how a Mexican led the league in points,[3] rebounds,[4] steals,[5] assists,[6] and blocked shots[7] in 1995.

When Vinny started coaching the Bulls in 2008 is when I actually went back and looked through his stats and accomplishments and saw that he wasn't what I had him built up to be in my head. It should've maybe been a big moment for me, or a profound moment for me, or a sad moment for me. But here's the thing of it: It didn't matter. It didn't matter then and it doesn't matter now. The real truth on Vinny is that he was a role player who bounced around the league and also in and out of the league. The real truth on Vinny is that he didn't even hold a double-digit career scoring average when he was squeezed into retirement in 2002. The real truth on Vinny is that he made zero All-Star teams and zero All-NBA teams. But, again, none of that matters. He's my memory hero. And, given that he doesn't do anything absolutely irredeemable, I don't think that can change. I will love him forever, and well past then. Sometimes basketball is just metaphysical like that.

▶

A neat thing about memory heroes is how much people enjoy talking about them and thinking about them. As such, it made sense to me here to pull in some of my basketball friends and let them talk a bit about their memory heroes. That's what the rest of this chapter will be.

▶

BILL SIMMONS, ON NICK WEATHERSPOON: My dad bought a single season ticket for the '74 Celtics and carried four-year-old me into many of the games. Apparently, we won the title. My memory kicks in the following spring, when we blew the Conference Finals because someone named Nick Weatherspoon absolutely eviscerated us. The Spoon was a 1970s irrational confidence guy who came off Washington's bench and drained baseline jumpers instead of threes. Imagine blowing a Finals trip because of Dion Waiters or Nick Young. For the next 40-plus years, that's how my father and I bitterly remembered Weatherspoon: that random Bullet who ruined our three-peat because flames started shooting out of his ass. Every time a Boston opponent ever caught fire, my dad would grumble, "It's like Nick Weatherspoon!"

---

1. One time, one of my sons told me that he thought a gallon of milk cost $40 and that a new car also cost $40.
2. The other most notable one is Chris Mullin. Mullin, I came to find out later, was actually super fucking good (best stat: during Mullin's five-year peak, only Michael Jordan, Dominique Wilkins, and Karl Malone bested his 25.8 points per game). I mostly liked him, though, because he had a flat top, and for some reason I have always been fascinated by white men with flat tops. When I was plotting out all of the art that I wanted in this book, the only thing I knew for certain was that I definitely wanted a picture of Mullin, as a barber, holding court with other famous white men with flat tops. It's on the next page.
3. Incorrect. It was Shaquille O'Neal.
4. Incorrect. It was Dikembe Mutombo.
5. Incorrect. It was Scottie Pippen.
6. Incorrect. It was John Stockton.
7. Incorrect. It was Dikembe Mutombo.

Recently, I combed through Weatherspoon's stats and learned that he only averaged 13 a game in that series. What? Impossible! I couldn't find any YouTube footage or Google evidence, which makes me think (a) my dad and I exaggerated the Spoon's impact, (b) we imagined the whole thing, or (c) we're living in a simulation and the master computer forgot to add Spoon's 1975 heat check. Only one Internet tidbit gives me hope. Someone posted the Spoon's 2008 obituary on the APBR.org message board; one commenter wrote, "His baseline jumpers destroyed the Celtics in the 1975 playoffs." So maybe it happened. Maybe.

▶

CANDACE BUCKNER, ON DAN MAJERLE: I cried the day my favorite player announced he had HIV. For years following his retirement, I abandoned the NBA and wanted to light fires to the bandwagon carrying those front-runners called Chicago Bulls fans. But during the '93 season I discovered the greatest thing since Magic: Thunder Dan Majerle.

The only thing doper than his perfect tan and lead-character-in-an-'80s-soap-opera good looks was his shot. I don't think Majerle missed a three all season, who cares what the stats on Basketball-Reference say. I just remember watching the '93 playoffs on NBC and actually feeling the roar of the Phoenix crowd every time Majerle held his perfect form. Just money. My go-to player on NBA Jam, and the real reason why the Suns won 62 games that year.

This sounds goofy, I know, but Majerle was, like, my reverse Jackie Robinson: the first white boy I respected as a hooper. I wanted the Suns to crush the Bulls so badly that year that I would've sacrificed my own black card. Alas, MJ apparently wanted to preserve my heritage.

I quit the Suns after that season but had returned to my first love: the NBA. All because of Majerle's magic.

▶

JONATHAN ABRAMS, ON SEDALE THREATT: The Lakers experienced some dreary seasons in the '90s during that dark span between Magic Johnson's retirement and Kobe Bryant's emergence. The Lakers

and winning went together during my childhood, and the shocking and abrupt retirement of Johnson, a figure so revered that I used to practice smiling like him in the mirror, tossed the organization into turmoil. Sedale Threatt, a point guard originally obtained to back up Johnson, provided some light during the sucky years.

First of all, he had a great name for a guard who could pick your pocket at any moment, and the legendary Chick Hearn rightfully dubbed him "The Thief." Threatt led the Lakers in scoring one year and had his moments on the big stage, dropping 42 points in a game against the Knicks and 35 in a playoff game against the Suns. With his legend ensured, Threatt was gone from the Lakers by the time Kobe arrived and soon out of the league altogether.

Fast-forward a couple of decades and I found myself playing against his son, Sedale Threatt Jr., at a pickup game on USC's campus. I swear he had the athleticism and explosiveness to play in the NBA just like his dad, but Junior wound up playing quarterback at Lehigh, where he drew the attention of plenty of NFL scouts. I should have told him to thank his dad for getting me through those down years, but he was too busy getting buckets on me.

▶

ZACH LOWE, ON ANTOINE WALKER: I don't remember the game, or even the year, and I don't even want to. But I remember this: Antoine Walker snagged a defensive rebound, took it up the court himself, toasted someone around midcourt with a behind-the-back dribble, kept going, and eventually dished a behind-the-back pass to someone for a dunk.

I immediately called one of my college buddies I always argued about basketball with: "Did you see that? That, right there, is why I won't shut the hell up about Antoine Walker even though he's barely shooting 40 percent." It was why Walker, around 2000 or 2001, was my favorite player—by a healthy margin over Paul Pierce. In my crappy little apartment, the one I rented right out of college, I had a few pieces of sports memorabilia. One of them was a little plaque, about 4 inches by 4 inches, with an Antoine Walker basketball card mounted to it.

I was obsessed with Antoine Walker. I was convinced he could redefine the entire idea of a power forward. And he could have! Antoine Walker should have been Draymond Green, only with more offensive game, 15 years before Draymond Green became a thing.

That Walker clearly never would be was part of the appeal. Walker was deeply flawed, and deeply flawed athletes are always more interesting than the guys who do everything right. I regarded Walker as a wayward son. I lamented his, umm, lax approach to conditioning. I chastised him through the TV: "Concentrate less on jacking threes, and more on guarding all five positions! Pass more! Get to the basket! Why can't you realize I know what is good for you!"

Antoine Walker was my unrequited basketball love. He was possibility unrealized. Pierce realized his full potential eventually. That's cool. It made me happy for him, even proud. Those good Walker plays—those plays only he and maybe one or two other bigs could make during his prime—stick out because they represented proof of attainability. Walker's ideal version of himself was there, so obviously there, and yet you knew he would never reach it even if he could see it. He wasn't disciplined enough. He didn't get it.

He was a regular dude in that way. But I will spend my life wondering what Antoine Walker could have been. I still have that plaque.

▶

DORIS BURKE, ON MAURICE CHEEKS:[8] It's 1983 and I am all in for the game of basketball. My home was right next to a park and I'd be on that blacktop playing the game I loved, and that would shape my life every day from the time I was seven years old. The NBA team that was the epitome of cool that year: the Philadelphia 76ers. Julius Erving, Dr. J, was always on call to dissect an opponent or leave us breathless with the spectacular. Moses was brought in to bring them to the promised land and boy did he, with the emphatic Fo'-Fo'-Fo' declaration. The defensive stopper of the group was Bobby Jones. The too-often-overlooked and at times forgotten scoring machine was number 22, Andrew Toney. That guy could flat fill it up. But for me, my eyes

always drifted to the ultimate example of a floor general: Mo Cheeks.

This team ripped through the playoffs, going 12–1, one heavy of Moses's famous prediction. Every kid had a player they'd try to emulate. Could you fly like the Doctor or dominate with relentlessness like Moses? For me, Mo Cheeks was my guy, the be-all and end-all. I loved his handle, the unselfish, team-first approach, and yes, the defensive toughness. If the 76ers needed to get Moses the ball in his sweet spot, Mo would deliver the entry pass. If the break got started and the ball needed to find Dr. J in space to operate, Mo triggered it. An opposing player goes behind the back, gets into the lane, and you worry the game could turn? Think again. Mo gets a strip steal and turns the other direction.

His demeanor was calm, cool, dignified, and unflappable. It is no wonder, many years later, as a little girl was struggling with the national anthem before an NBA game, someone had to come to the rescue and help her finish the words to the song. That someone, well, of course, it was Mo.

▶

MIKE LYNCH, ON LIONEL SIMMONS: There's little debate about who the best basketball player in the world was in the late '80s and early '90s. It was, without question, Lionel Simmons. I was fortunate enough to grow up watching him rewrite the NCAA record books as a La Salle University combo forward. The L-Train was a big enough deal in Philly that you might see Charles Barkley in the crowd if he had a free night. That's affirmation. Simmons, the 1990 National Player of the Year, went to the Kings in the lottery and was runner-up to Derrick Coleman for 1991 Rookie of the Year. He was even NBA Player of the Week during a stretch in which he hung 38 points and 13 rebounds on Barkley's 76ers. But injuries (including the NBA's first recorded case of Nintendonitis, which was literally wrist tendinitis caused by excessive Game Boy use) took their toll. Now people consider some guy named Jordan the best of that era.

▶

SEAN FENNESSEY, ON GERALD WILKINS: Gerald Wilkins was better than Michael Jordan. You know how I know? Because when I was five years old, Wilkins averaged 19-4-4 while shooting nearly 50 percent from the field and 35 percent from three. In modern basketball terms, that is what we call A Good NBA Wing. But back then it was what we called *Oh Snap, Gerald Wilkins Just Dunked on MJ.* That was all it took to understand the power of Wilkins's silk, the ease of his game, the power of his windmill, the grace of his J. And though Jordan averaged more points, more rebounds, more assists, played better defense, dunked more memorably, and just generally seemed cooler, Wilkins had a try-hard charm that may have inspired my own more than I'd prefer to admit. And so for that reason Gerald Wilkins is the greatest player of his generation.

▶

RAMONA SHELBURNE, ON NICK VAN EXEL: I grew up in LA during the Showtime Lakers era, so I was super spoiled as a kid with Magic and Worthy and Kareem. I also had way too hard of a time letting go of that era, which caused me to believe that Nick Van Exel was way better than he probably was. Nick the Quick! He'd do these behind-the-back passes with his left hand that if you closed your left eye and squinted, seemed like something Magic would do. Then when he'd hit a big shot, he'd shadow box down the court. There was just something about the way Chick Hearn and Stu Lantz pumped him up that made me think he was capable of keeping Showtime going. He was never actually able to, but it was the hope that mattered.

▶

JASON CONCEPCION, ON PATRICK EWING: The thing about the '90s was there was never any debate about who was the best. Jordan was the best. He dunked on everyone, was on every poster, he had the best commercials, and everyone wanted to wear his shoe. So, even though my favorite player was Patrick Ewing, I never had any illusions that he was better than Jordan at anything besides copious perspiration and sadness. THAT SAID, as a kid, I was 100 percent sure that Patrick Ewing was the greatest center in the league. Better than Hakeem (he wasn't). Better than David Robinson (it was pretty much a push). Better than Shaq (based on the now-defunct theory that all the Diesel could do was dunk). Better than Rik Smits (fair, but the Dutchman was underrated). Better than Alonzo Mourning (THIS IS TRUE). Okay, so I was mostly right. Except for Shaq. And Hakeem. Whatever. I still believe in Patrick Ewing.

▶

KRISTEN LEDLOW, ON GRANT HILL:[9] Dad was in a sports bar in Tampa on March 28, 1992. With 2.1 seconds to go in OT, the defending national champions at Duke trailed Kentucky 103–102. I was four years old.

With the winner headed to the Final Four and the loser headed home, Grant Hill threw a pass the length of the court to Christian Laettner, who drained a jumper as time expired to win 104–103. Dad, half of the duo who raised me to love basketball, was cheering for Duke. Ask him, and he'll tell you it's because Coach Krzyzewski bred talent and Duke boasted class. Ask me, and I'll tell you it's because he's a born rebel and was surrounded by Kentucky fans. Either way, The Pass became an iconic moment in NCAA history.

When I was 12, Dad told me the story of The Pass as Grant Hill came to play for the Orlando Magic. He and Mom also bought me Grant's jersey. Thirteen years later, NBA TV decided to produce an *Inside Stuff* sequel with Grant Hill as host. I asked for an audition, just to tell Grant this story. I've never made a life-changing, full-court pass, but I'm glad he did. It changed mine.

---

8. To be sure, there are actually three players in this chapter who were picked as memory heroes who were truly incredible basketball players. Maurice Cheeks is one of them. Patrick Ewing is the second. And Grant Hill, the player Kristen Ledlow wrote about, is the third.
9. Told ya.

▶

SEERAT SOHI, ON LEANDRO BARBOSA: Leandro Barbosa, in his prime, topped out as an 18-point scorer on Mike D'Antoni's Seven Seconds or Less Suns, a team that helped inflate individual stats before it became fashionable. Not that those numbers are anything to sneeze at, but my fun-addled mind took the man with the off-kilter gaunt to be Manu Ginobili-lite. He operated at a different frequency from most players, and at the time, it was easy to confuse a different frequency for a higher frequency.

Barbosa with possession was mesmerizing, the way he galloped toward the rim with the fast-twitch muscles of Road Runner and the smooth finesse of a ballet dancer, and he consistently shot layups with the wrong hand—an appealing example for a right-hander who was sick of hearing coaches harp about fundamentals. There are moments, now past his 14th season, that Barbosa can summon the old tempo, but he was, in ways both figurative and literal, like a comet flying over the basketball universe, in the end representative of an ethos that defined those Suns teams: Given the right situation, anyone can be great.

▶

CHRIS RYAN, ON MARK MACON: Mark Macon was my first local basketball hero. Dr. J and Charles Barkley loomed like gods, but Macon—a 6-foot-5 two guard with a Dodge Ram engine, and Gamble and Huff jumper—was my generation, and he was part of a Temple University basketball boom that captured the competitive Philly sports moment.

Macon arrived at Temple University in 1987 after winning Mr. Basketball in Michigan in his senior year. His first year in North Philly, he led the Owls to a number-one ranking and a 32–1 record heading into what would be a heartbreaking loss to Duke in the tournament that I've never forgiven Coach K for. There was no basketball blog industrial machine to promote prospects back then, so a freshman phenom was like a ghost story. Where did he come from? He's coming to *Temple*? Macon came to Philly to play for John Chaney

and damn if he didn't look like the next MJ. He went eighth to Denver in 1991, but even then the genie was out of the bottle. He appeared like a dream, and was forgotten like one, playing out an itinerant career in the NBA, CBA, Italy, Venezuela, and Turkey. I know better now, but you couldn't tell me shit back then.

▶

REMBERT BROWNE, ON CHUCK PERSON: A great thing about growing up in the '90s was the sheer number of VHS box sets dedicated to players and games that happened only 3 to 5 years earlier. Quite often, you were watching classic games featuring players that were still in the league. One of the most memorable was this tape I had about Larry Bird. And the standout was a game in which he got absolutely torched by The Rifleman, Chuck Person of the Indiana Pacers.

There's something absolutely gorgeous about a basketball player who thinks he's the best player in NBA history when he's on the court with multiple future Hall of Famers. In Game 2 of the first round of the1991 playoffs, Person was that person, scoring 39 points in the upset, including 7 threes, many in the grill of the soon-to-be-concussed Larry Bird.

I think about Chuck Person when I need to be great, in the midst of greats. He's heroic, down to that rhombus landing strip of a coiffure he called a haircut. God Bless Chuck Person, the original Dion Waiters, my first Barack Obama.

WHICH NBA PLAYER'S GROUP
ARE YOU JOINING IF
THE PURGE BEGINS TONIGHT?

The Purge is a movie that came out in 2013. The foundation of its premise is as follows: In response to a crippling economic collapse, America creates "the purge," a once-a-year event where, from 7 P.M. to 7 A.M., all crimes are legal, including murder. (The killing helps to eradicate the nation's criminals and unemployed, we're told, as poor people and homeless people become the main cohorts of hunted humans.) They say things in The Purge like, "We can afford protection, so we'll be fine," so I suspect the movie wanted to be taken seriously on a level higher than the action horror genre it marketed itself as— something about classism or the privilege of cathar-sis as virtue or the amorality of wealth, or whatever, I'm sure. Mostly, though, it was just a thing that you watched and when you were done you said something like, "That was probably a better idea for a movie than it was an actual movie."[1]

But so what this thing is, the NBA Player Purge question—it's not some sort of clever play on how the NBA is, in a manner of speaking, like The Purge. It's not an extended analogy or euphemism or metaphor or anything like that because those things inevitably get clumsy and clunky after long enough. No, this ain't that. This is the real, actual, literal thing.[2] If America today adopted the purge and it was happening tonight and you had to join up with a squad led by an NBA player, current or retired, alive or dead, who's the player you're following?

I re-watched all three of The Purge movies before writing this. There were, by my measurement, approx-imately four kinds of people in them, so we'll separate a bunch of recognizable NBA players into one of those four categories. And for those categories, let's put in place that (a) any player you pick, you'll receive him

when he was at his strongest, and (b) only players from 1980 and forward are eligible.[3]

Additionally, there are three stats we'll use to try and frame out each of the groups as a way to keep things at least semi-organized.

· **ESTIMATED PERSONAL SURVIVAL TIME:** It's exactly what it sounds like it is: the estimated amount of time a person would survive during the purge. The stronger and more capable and more rugged and more dependable a person is, the longer you'll make it through the night following him. The weaker and less capable and less rugged and less dependable a person is . . . well . . . *does that thing where you drag your index finger across your throat*

· **ESTIMATED SQUAD MEMBER SURVIVAL RATE:** This refers to how many members of the group a player is leading would survive through the entire night under his watch. As a matter of consistency, let's pretend like each group consists of (a) one NBA player and (b) six regular people following him.

· **LIKELIHOOD HE'LL MURDER YOU:** With this one we're talking about what chance there is that the leader you've chosen ends up killing you for whatever reason he deems necessary.

Remember, the groupings aren't rooted in any sort of basketball skill level or anything like that. That's why someone like, say, the superstar debutante Steph Curry ends up way lower than someone like, say, 1994 Anthony Mason. I trust Steph Curry to destroy every-one on a basketball court. Off the court, I trust him to destroy a cashmere turtleneck or a suede long coat and that's about it. Give me Anthony Mason to get me through the night if our lives are on the line.

This whole thing is already ridiculous.

---

1. That being said, I liked it. And I liked the sequel, The Purge: Anarchy, which allowed itself to lean into its weirdness, even more. (The Purge: Election Year was fine.)
2. Inasmuch as it can be "real" and "actual" and "literal" given that it's a hypothetical question with a fictional movie as its underpinning.
3. Bill Russell obviously would've gotten you safely through the night. Jerry West, on the other hand, would've gotten you through the night safely one out of every eight tries.

GROUP 4: THE ANARCHISTS

SYMBOLIC FIGURE: Vernon Maxwell // 13
years in the league // Countless in-
game fights and confrontations // During
a game against the Trail Blazers in
1995, he walked into the stands and
punched a fan in the face because the
fan was making fun of him for playing
poorly that evening.

These guys don't get any of the stats I mentioned because this group is made up of players who are proactively engaging in Purge Night. They ain't trying to save anyone. Matter of fact, it's the exact opposite: These guys are the hunters. They don't care too much about anything beyond watching you and all your friends bleed and cry.

There are a ton of players who'd be good in this role. My number-one guy is Matt Barnes, who has a whole fight highlight reel on YouTube, which is a thing a UFC fighter should have, not an NBA player. The most insane Matt Barnes story is him driving 95 miles to fight Derek Fisher, a former teammate of his (by then the coach of the Knicks), because Fisher and Barnes's estranged wife were in a relationship.[4] Do you even know how fucking crazy you have to be to do some shit like that? I mean, I understand getting real worked up over something, but you have to figure by, like, mile 15 or something of the drive, a normal person would've calmed down or chilled out. Not Barnes, though. He held tough. He got to mile 85 and was like, "Just 10 miles more to go before I get to fuck this guy up." That's the level of determination that keeps a guy who averages eight points per game in the league for more than a dozen years.

He'd have a really great and productive night of purging, I'm sure of it.

More guys in this group: Anyone from the Bad Boys Era Pistons (not John Salley, though); nearly everyone from the Riley Era Knicks;[5] Latrell Sprewell (duh); anyone who shot over 50 percent from three point range for an entire season;[6] Arvydas Sabonis (he for some reason always looked like he was really into pile drivers); Kevin McHale; anyone from the 72–10 Bulls; anyone from the 2001 Lakers; and Bruce Bowen (he was running around legit kicking people during his career, so he's here, too). (Quick sidebar: Bruce Bowen's most egregious kicks, ranked: 4. Bruce Bowen kicks Amar'e Stoudemire in the Achilles during a game against the Suns in 2007; 3. Bruce Bowen kicks Ray Allen in the back during a game against the Sonics in 2006; 2. Bruce Bowen kicks Chris Paul in the chest after Paul falls down during a game against the Hornets in 2008; 1. Bruce Bowen kicks Wally Szczerbiak in the face during a game against the Timberwolves in 2002. IN THE ACTUAL FUCKING FACE, haha.)

More guys in this group: Metta World Peace (imagine how embarrassing it'd be to show up in heaven and have to tell people you were killed by someone with the last name World Peace); Kevin Garnett; Reggie Evans (anyone who's grabbed Chris Kaman by the dick is good to go here); Chris Kaman (anyone who's been grabbed by the dick by Reggie Evans is good to go here); Kendrick Perkins (I'm fairly confident Kendrick Perkins thought *The Purge* was a documentary); Art Long (he allegedly punched a horse in the face in 1995 four times during a traffic stop[7]); DeMarcus Cousins (he is killing SO MANY white people); George Gervin; Charles Shackleford;[8] Vernon Maxwell (I'm mentioning him again because I want to tell you about the time in 1994 when he

---

4. This is only a portion of the story. It's the main parts, though.
5. Patrick Ewing and John Starks and Greg Anthony aren't in this group.
6. The only six players in the history of the league to have done it are Kyle Korver, Steve Kerr, Tim Legler, Jon Sundvold, Jason Kapono, and Detlef Schrempf. Steve Kerr's the only player to have ever done it multiple times. He did it three times. Steve Kerr is a killer. My favorite Steve Kerr story I half-remember is him talking about when he got to the point in his career where he was spending most of his time on the bench, he'd do a shooting drill where he'd just sit down for, like, 30 minutes, then run out there and shoot one shot and then sit back down for another 30 minutes before doing it again.
7. His defense team said he was petting the horse, not punching it, which seems like a thing that is definitely not true.

waved an unregistered gun around during an argument in a Luby's parking lot in Houston, which seems like the exact kind of thing somebody who'd be really good at purging would do); anybody from the Jail Blazers Era of the Trail Blazers; Brad Miller; Danny Ainge (quietly a real killer); and Jerry Stackhouse.[9]

GROUP 3: THE "MAKE SURE YOUR FINAL WISHES ARE IN ORDER" GROUP

SYMBOLIC FIGURE: Steph Curry // 8 years in the league[10] // Endorsement deal with Express.

I love Steph. I truly do. He plays basketball in a way that feels less like he's a basketball player and more like he's a classically trained pianist. It's beautiful and it's transcendent. During a crucial part of a gigantic game, I trust him completely and entirely. But during a Purge Night, man, I don't know. Maybe it's because of his soft eyes or his pouty lips. Maybe it's because he flutters around the court like a butterfly. Maybe it's because he did a water-filter commercial (killers don't care about mineral filtration). I just find it real hard to say that Purge Night ends any other way than with the insides of his body on the outside of his body, you know what I'm saying. Bad news for anyone in his group.
• **ESTIMATED PERSONAL SURVIVAL TIME:** Less than two hours.
• **ESTIMATED SQUAD MEMBER SURVIVAL RATE:** Zero of the six people in his group are surviving the night.
• **LIKELIHOOD HE'LL MURDER YOU:** It's low. You're looking at a 5 to 10 percent chance, but it won't be an on-purpose kill. If it happens, it'll be completely by accident, like maybe you two are in a dark hallway and you call his name and he gets startled and accidentally shoots you in the chest.
    Some other guys in this group: Vince Carter (half-man, half-purged); Gilbert Arenas (smh[11]); Patrick Ewing (in all likelihood, Ewing belongs in Group 2, but I saw him at a Best Buy in 2005 a few days before Christmas and I waved hello to him and he ignored me so I'm

putting him here because that hurt my feelings[12]); the guys from *Space Jam* who had their talents stolen by the aliens;[13] Smush Parker (poor Smush[14]); the 1994 version of the Sonics; anyone who had a cocaine problem in the 1980s;[15] Ricky Davis (Is there a way to get a triple-double while you're getting purged?); everyone who was on the 2002 Sacramento Kings except for Mike Bibby[16] and Bobby Jackson;[17] Tracy McGrady (he probably wouldn't even make it out of the first round of the purge); Rik Smits (I could be argued the other way on this pick); Bryon Russell and Craig Ehlo (it seems like a good rule is: Anyone who was on the wrong end of an iconic play automatically gets a Group 3 designation); Wally Szczerbiak (You're seriously going to trust your life to someone named "Wally"?); Luke Ridnour (He's like if you were able to siphon all of the grit away from Kirk Hinrich); Penny Hardaway (a more handsome Tracy McGrady); Manute Bol (a less handsome Hasheem Thabeet); Amar'e Stoudemire; Mark Madsen (surprise landing here for the Mad Dog); Emeka Okafor; Kerry Kittles; Kris Humphries (He couldn't handle a Kardashian, how's he going to handle the purge?); Larry Hughes; Bob Sura; Andris Biedrins; Clyde Drexler;[18] Nick Anderson; Charles Smith; the 2007 version of the Dallas Mavericks; and Adam Morrison.

GROUP 2: THE "IT'S A TOSS-UP" GROUP

SYMBOLIC FIGURE: James Harden // 8 years in the league[19]// Can be absolutely devastating at times, but can also be a bit of a toad at other times.

The thing about Group 2 is that there are two versions of guys who fall into this category. They are:
1. The guys who would earnestly work their very hardest to keep everyone in their groups alive and they'd mostly be successful but sometimes they wouldn't be, and a good example here would be someone like Chauncey Billups or maybe Antonio McDyess.[20] Then there are . . .

2. The guys who, if they applied all of their effort and energy to keeping everyone in their groups alive then they absolutely could, but they'll never do that so they'll end up losing a portion of the people they're supposed to be protecting, and for this group a good and obvious example is someone like James Harden. Anyone he keeps alive during Purge Night is always going to only ever be the supplemental result of him trying to keep himself alive.

· **ESTIMATED PERSONAL SURVIVAL TIME:** Six to eight hours, possibly the entire night if Harden gets lucky.

· **ESTIMATED SQUAD MEMBER SURVIVAL RATE:** Half of the six people in his group are surviving the night and the other half are dying, due to either inability or neglect on the leader's part.

· **LIKELIHOOD HE MURDERS YOU:** There's a 60 percent chance that James Harden (or anyone in his subcategory) murders you in an attempt to save himself. There's a zero percent chance any of the guys from the other subcategory here murder you.

Some other Guys in Group 2, designated by whether they're a Good Group 2 Guy or a Bad Group 2 Guy: Karl Malone (bad); Rafer Alston (good); Antoine Walker (good, but bad with money); Jason Kidd (good, but bad with hair dye); Dwight Howard (bad); Chris Childs (good—I am forever in debt to Chris Childs for punching Kobe Bryant, so even if I knew I was going to die joining up with him, I'd still do it out of respect); Stephon Marbury (bad, but good with eyebrows); Shawn Kemp (bad, and worse with condoms); Matt Geiger (good); Isaiah "J.R." Rider (good); Chris Duhon (good); Doug Christie (good—Doug Christie one time punched Rick Fox so, same as Chris Childs, I would follow him right the fuck off a cliff if he asked me to); Fred Hoiberg (good); Cuttino Mobley (good); Rajon Rondo (good, but maybe bad, I'm not sure because sometimes he seems like the type of guy who would give his life to save a teammate's life and other times he seems like the type of guy who would sell one of his teammates to human traffickers if the opportunity arose); Tyson Chandler (good); Jamaal Tinsley (good[21]); Bonzi Wells

---

8. He had a spotty career in and out of the league, but there's a great story in Jayson Williams's book *Loose Balls* about how he got into an altercation with Armen Gilliam during a practice. Shack ended up cussing at Gilliam, who was very religious, and so it offended him a bunch. Gilliam challenged Shack to a fight later. Shack showed up with a fucking machete.

9. Jerry got in a fight with Kirk Snyder following a game in 2005 (he waited for him in the tunnel and then pummeled Snyder when he saw him), and it rattled Snyder so soundly that Snyder thanked him for beating him up when they came across each other the following season.

10. As of the 2017 season.

11. In 2009, Arenas and teammate Javaris Crittenton both brought guns into the Washington Wizards locker room following a gambling dispute on the team plane. It was a gigantic story that ended up unraveling the team. Caron Butler talks about it in his book *Tuff Juice*. He says he's fairly confident Arenas was joking. Crittenton, on the other hand, was serious. (He ended up being sentenced to 23 years in prison after pleading guilty to manslaughter in 2011.) Go with Crittenton, not Arenas.

12. This story is how I know that I belong in Group 3.

13. I'm just really trying to figure out a way to get Patrick Ewing in this category.

14. The only Smush Parker story worth telling is the one about Kobe Bryant, whom Smush played with for the 2006 and 2007 seasons, telling him that he didn't have enough accolades to talk to Bryant during practice. I wonder what the exact number of accolades one needs to talk to Kobe Bryant, or even what kinds of accolades are required.

15. There's a tiny thing in Bill Simmons's *The Book of Basketball* where he cites an article that ran in the *LA Times* in August of 1980 where the then-GM of the Atlanta Hawks, Stan Kasten, guessed that 75 percent of the players in the league were casual drug users.

16. So fucking clutch.

17. Here's a fun stat: Peja Stojakovic shot 41.6 percent from three in 2002. Do you know what he shot in Game 7 of the 2002 Western Conference Finals? He shot 0 percent. He went 0 for 6, including a wide-open air ball three that would've put the Kings up 2 with 12 seconds to go. Doug Christie also shot a wide-open three at the end of overtime that would've given the Kings a one-point lead. It didn't even hit the rim. I'm still hurt about this. The Kings ain't even my team and this loss still bothers me.

18. Clyde's inclusion here is conditional. If the purge takes place during any of the years Michael Jordan wasn't retired, then he belongs in Group 3. If it takes place when Jordan was retired, then you can move him up to Group 2.

19. As of the 2017 season.

20. I can't remember a role player who took not winning a championship as hard as McDyess did. There was a story about how after the Pistons had lost to the Spurs in a game during the 2005 Finals he didn't even get dressed back in his regular clothes, he just walked right the fuck to his car in his uniform and left.

(bad); Shareef Abdur-Rahim (good); Rip Hamilton (good); Dominique Wilkins (good); and Chris Dudley (good).

GROUP 1:
THE "REST EASY, MY FRIEND" GROUP

```
SYMBOLIC FIGURE: Ben Wallace // 16 years
in the league // Had a body like it'd
been carved out of the side of a moun-
tain, except the mountain wasn't a
normal mountain, it was a mountain made
of Ford F-250s // Was somehow the most
important player on a team that won a
championship despite not being able to
shoot from more than 2 feet away from
the rim.²²
```

You're surviving the night.
- **ESTIMATED PERSONAL SURVIVAL TIME:** At least 11 hours, though likely the entire purge.
- **ESTIMATED SQUAD MEMBER SURVIVAL RATE:** All six of the people in his group are surviving.
- **LIKELIHOOD HE MURDERS YOU:** There's a 3 percent chance he ends up being the one who murders you, though if he does it'll be because it was the one and only way to make sure that everyone else he was in charge of lived. In that sense, it'd be one of those honor killings, really.

Some other Guys in Group 1: Xavier McDaniel (he got into a fight with Charles Oakley and did not lose any of his arms or any of his legs, which is basically the same as them dropping the Hulk tens of thousands of feet to his death in *The Avengers* and him just shaking it off); Allen Iverson (all the tiny players in the league— Muggsy, Nate Robinson, Spud Webb, J.J. Barea, Isaiah Thomas, Earl Boykins,²³ etc.—are Group 1 guys); Gary Payton (he tried to bust Vernon Maxwell's head open with a 10-pound weight during a locker-room fight WHILE THEY WERE ON THE SAME TEAM); John Stockton

(like if a rattlesnake was a human); Delonte West (was one time arrested while driving a three-wheel motorcycle on a freeway in possession of two handguns, one shotgun, a knife, and 100 shotgun rounds, so yeah, I think he'd keep you safe); Alonzo Mourning; Udonis Haslem (I trust Udonis Haslem so fucking much and I'm not all the way certain why); Kenyon Martin; Steve Nash (it could be argued he's a Group 2 guy); Larry Bird; Tim Duncan (duh); Ray Allen; Pistol Pete and Andrei "AK-47" Kirilenko (any players who have gun-based nicknames are surviving); Dikembe Mutombo (anyone whose nickname is a landform is surviving); and Baron Davis.

Let's do some more, because I want you to have options: David Robinson (you're talking a 7-foot-tall hunk of muscle that's been trained by the military); Sam Cassell; Bobby Jackson; Chris Mullin; Young Charles Barkley; Stephen Jackson (the two things I will always remember Stephen Jackson for are (1) the regularity with which he delivered needlessly no-look passes to teammates and (2) charging into the stands to help Ron Artest fight someone who'd thrown a cup at him during a break in play); Larry Johnson (good with disguises); Thabo Sefolosha (not going to lie: I trust him a whole, whole bunch because I think he's very handsome); Steve Blake (another guy I trust and I'm not certain why); Jason Collins; Mario Elie; Theo Ratliff and LaPhonso Ellis (for some reason, these two guys exist in my head as the same person); Jermaine O'Neal; Kevin Duckworth; Dale Davis and Antonio Davis (they come as a 2-for-1 special); Scott Skiles (secretly one of the 15 toughest guys in the history of the NBA); Corliss Williamson; and Paul Pierce.

Paul Pierce was stabbed 11 times and also had a bottle smashed over his head during an altercation in September of 2000 and still came back and started all 82 games that following season. He fucking lived through the purge in real life then averaged 25 points per game in the days afterward. He's my guy. That's whose group I'm joining.

---

21. Tinsley was on that Pacers team involved in the Malice at the Palace brawl. There was a short clip of him swinging one of those dustpans that ushers use around at people. He was on some Jackie Chan Anything Can Be A Weapon shit.
22. Shoutout the 2004 Pistons.
23. Earl Boykins was 5'5". He weighed 140 pounds and benched 315. Figure that shit out.

WHAT'S THE MOST IMPORTANT NBA CHAMPIONSHIP?

PART 1

In 2015, a book I wrote called *The Rap Year Book: The Most Important Rap Song from Every Year Since 1979, Discussed, Debated, and Deconstructed* was published. The subtitle, while clunky, does a good job of summarizing the premise: Each of the chapters is about whatever rap song it was that happened to be the most important of a given year. For example, the first chapter is about the most important song from 1979,[1] the second chapter is about the most important song from 1980,[2] the third chapter is about the most important song from 1981,[3] and it just goes on like that all the way through to 2014.[4]

I mention it here because when I started telling people that the next book I was writing was going to be this basketball book, a person I know and kind of like but not all-the-way like made a joke close to "Is it going to be about the most important NBA championship of each year?" Now, of course that's semi-funny because there's only one NBA championship per year, but what if we toggled the settings a bit? What if, rather than make it a Per Year thing, we just make it a By Importance thing? That, I think, becomes an interesting discussion. So here's the new version: What's the most important NBA championship? Meaning: Which NBA championship had the greatest, biggest, most substantial impact on the NBA?

To answer that, what we need to do is set up the borders of the conversation. To measure the weight of the importance of a particular NBA championship, we have to look at four things:

1. WHAT, IF ANY, EFFECT DID THE CHAMPIONSHIP HAVE ON THE LEAGUE? This is an easy category to identify, but also an essential one. The clearest way to look at it: The 1984 Finals featured the first pro championship matchup between Magic Johnson and Larry Bird (more on this one later). It was obviously bigger and more important for the league than, say, when the Washington Bullets, a 44-win team, beat the SuperSonics, a 47-win team, to win the championship in 1978.[5]

2. WHAT, IF ANY, EFFECT DID THE CHAMPIONSHIP HAVE ON A PARTICULAR PLAYER'S LEGACY? An easy example: Bill Walton is a member of the basketball Hall of Fame and was also picked by the NBA as one of the league's 50 best players in history in 1996. Those things happened largely because of his performance in the 1977 Finals, where he averaged 18.5 points, 19 rebounds, 5.2 assists, 3.7 blocks, and was named the Finals MVP. The two years before that, he was mostly injured, and in just about all the years after that, he was injured, too.[6] It's very likely that without that one Finals, we don't remember him near as fondly as we do today.

3. WAS THERE A PARTICULARLY ICONIC GAME DURING THE FINALS? A good rule for this one is "Does one of the games in the Finals for whatever year it is you're talking about have a name?" If yes, then it was iconic, and thus made that Finals more important than a Finals that didn't have a game with a name. (Think: The Flu Game, The Isiah Thomas Sprained Ankle Game, The Junior, Junior Skyhook Game, The Willis Reed Game, etc.)

4. WAS THERE A PARTICULARLY ICONIC MOMENT DURING THE FINALS? Same as above: "Did a moment in one of the games in the Finals for whatever year it is you're talking about get a name?" If yes, then it was iconic, and thus made that Finals more important than a Finals that didn't have a

---

1. "Rapper's Delight" by the Sugarhill Gang.
2. "The Breaks" by Kurtis Blow.
3. "Jazzy Sensation" by Afrika Bambaataa and the Jazzy Five.
4. "Lifestyle" by Rich Gang, featuring Young Thug and Rich Homie Quan.
5. I understand the thinking behind owner Abe Pollin changing the name of the Washington Bullets to the Washington Wizards in 1997, but I don't agree with it. (I'm willing to admit that at least a portion of my ire toward the name change was that I really enjoyed drawing the Bullets's logo when I was a kid. I always thought the way they used the two Ls in it to make arms shooting a basketball was dope.)
6. He missed three full seasons because of injuries, and only one time during his 10-season career did he play in more than 67 games in a season (1986). My favorite Walton injury stat: He injured his foot in 1978, missed the final 22 games of the season, and somehow still managed to win the League MVP.

moment like that. (Think: Iverson's Step Over, Dr. J's Behind-the-Backboard Layup, MJ's Shrug, LeBron's Chasedown Block, etc.)

We just take all of the championships, run them through a grading rubric based on those four questions above, and there you go: That's how you figure out what the most important NBA championship was.

One thing to keep in mind, and this is maybe inflammatory or controversial (probably not, though), but I'm automatically going to eliminate any of the championships from before 1980 from contention. Originally, I'd intended to sort through all the championships from the NBA-ABA merger (1976) to now, but that seems like just empty space since none of the championships from 1977 to 1979[7] finished anywhere near the top of this What's the Most Important NBA Championship? conversation. Also, 1980, which is when Larry Bird and Magic Johnson entered the NBA, was essentially the beginning of the NBA as we know it today. So that'll be the starting point: We're only considering championships from 1980 to today.

▶

TIER V : ARRANGE THESE FINALS INTO JUST ABOUT ANY ORDER YOU'D LIKE.

It won't change much.

There are 37 championships that need to be arranged by importance. This last tier is the one where, I mean, okay, if we're being all the way honest, the order here isn't really all that important. These championships definitely belong in this section, but basically you can arrange them into just about any order you'd like and it's not going to affect too, too many things. It always works like that with any sort of list that's longer than, say, 20

spaces. You get to number 34 and it's just like, "Really, how much different is this one than 33 or 35?"—you know what I'm saying? If I ask you for your four favorite memories as a kid, you're probably going to have a very firm list of meaningful moments for me. If I ask you for your 37 favorite memories as a kid, by the time you get to 33 you're going to be like, "Um . . . I watched an episode of *Family Matters* that was pretty good when I was 12," or whatever. That's just the way it goes.

That said, this is the actual correct order these championships belong in:

37. The 2004 Championship (Pistons beat Lakers, 4–1): This was the year that the Lakers supersized themselves (Shaq, Kobe, Gary Payton, Karl Malone), only to have their legs cut off in the Finals by a team that had no real, discernible superstar.[8] Chauncey Billups was the first guard since Isiah Thomas to win Finals MVP. The main notable things that happened after this championship were things that were likely going to happen regardless of the outcome—it was the last series Shaq and Kobe ever played together; it was the end of Phil Jackson's first stint as a Lakers coach; the league introduced new rules during the off-season meant to eliminate hand-checking on defense, which eventually opened up the game—so I can't really credit it for causing the changes.

36. The 1999 Championship (Spurs beat Knicks, 4–1): Rough season. Two big, bad things happened: (1) The lockout gobbled up more than a third of the games, and so no one was really expecting to even have any season at all that year, which equaled up to some not that great basketball.[9] (2) Jordan retired after the 1998 championship, and no Jordan meant the league lacked the top-tier megastar it had had during all its best seasons. Two good things happened, though, one of which was

---

7. The Trail Blazers won in 1977, the Bullets won in 1978, and the SuperSonics won in 1979.
8. This sounds like it's an insult but I mean it in the best way possible. This Pistons group was a great, fun team. And, on just a personal level, I will always be thankful to them for beating the Lakers in the Finals because that was the year Derek Fisher hit his 0.4 shot against the Spurs, and so of course I wanted to watch them wither away.
9. The league offensive rating was the lowest it'd been since the 1978 season.

substantial and the other of which was cool: (1) Tim Duncan, the fifth greatest basketball player of all time, won the first of his five titles. I imagine it's a bunch like what that guy in *The Beach* was talking about when he was telling Leonardo DiCaprio the difference between a young shark and a mama great white shark who's killed before. Duncan became a mama great white shark after 1999, is what I'm saying. (2) The Knicks became the first-ever eighth seed to make it to the Finals.[10]

35. The 2005 Championship (Spurs beat Pistons, 4–3): A couple of neat asides happened—first Finals Game 7 since 1994; first time since 1987 the previous two champions met in the Finals; first time since 1960 the two previous champions played in a Finals Game 7—but those are all mostly just fun party favors. The main important thing that happened was this championship tied Duncan with Shaq for three titles and three Finals MVPs apiece.[11]

34. The 2012 Championship (Heat beat Thunder, 4–1): This was LeBron's first title, yes,[12] but really the most important thing that happened here is that the Thunder, who had a nucleus then of a 23-year-old Russell Westbrook, a 23-year-old Kevin Durant, a 22-year old James Harden, and a 22-year-old Serge Ibaka, lost out on winning a championship. They never made another trip back to the Finals, and by the summer of 2016, all but Russell Westbrook were playing for different teams.

33. The 2007 Championship (Spurs beat Cavaliers, 4–0): Tim Duncan's fourth title. Tony Parker becomes the first-ever international player who didn't play in the NCAA to win Finals MVP, which you could probably argue is pretty meaningful if you squint a little bit. This was also the first Finals appearance for LeBron James, though the Spurs dispatched him and his Cavs fairly easily. (This was of no fault of LeBron's. The Spurs basically guarded him with all five guys at once all game, every game. Besides, LeBron had already etched his name into the side of the Playoff Legends mountain in the previous series, when he put up 29 of the Cavs' final 30 points in a Game 5 double-overtime win on

the road against Detroit.[13]) The maybe most notable thing that happened was after the Spurs swept the Cavs, when cameras caught Tim Duncan telling LeBron James, "This is gonna be your league in a little while, but, uh, I appreciate you giving us this year," proving that Tim Duncan was a real human and not a statue that'd been brought to life by some sort of spell like in a movie, as many had assumed up to that point.

32. The 1994 Championship (Rockets beat Knicks, 4–3): This was a good one. We got (1) Hakeem vs. Ewing, marquee centers in the league who had played against each other in the 1984 NCAA championship and then went back-to-back as number-one picks in the NBA Draft after that; (2) the John Starks Game 7 disaster (2–18 from the field, including going 0–11 from three-point range, his final three somehow falling literally several feet short of the rim); and (3) every single one of the seven games was decided by single digits.[14] It was also (4) the first title for Hakeem, an all-timer; and (5) the first time a team from the Western Conference who wasn't the Lakers won the title since the 1979 Sonics. Of course, the everlasting knock on it would be that it came during the nearly two-year window of Jordan's first retirement,[15] which is or isn't valid, depending on your opinion of the Houston Rockets.

TIER IV : THE IN-BETWEENERS

Championships that fall into this category are the ones that are fun to remember and are certainly more impactful than those in Tier V, but don't quite have the reverb that the ones in Tier III have. Still, from here going forward, unlike Tier V, there's no wiggle room for the placement of a particular championship. It belongs where it sits.

---

31. The 1987 Championship (Lakers beat Celtics, 4–2): It's the Lakers and the Celtics for the third time in four years, which is just fantastic because rivalries are fantastic, so that's one big thing. Another big thing is that Magic Johnson becomes the first player ever to win three Finals MVP trophies. A third big thing is that it's the last year Larry Bird appears in an NBA Finals, and so we have to pay respect to that history. And then a last big thing is that it gives Magic a 4–3 lead over Bird in championships, which means a lot in the Magic vs. Bird argument.[16]

30. The 1995 Championship (Rockets beat Magic, 4–0): An NBA Finals I have come to appreciate and respect and even revere, in part because of the excellence of Hakeem Olajuwon,[17] but mostly because this particular Rockets team was like every lovable NBA team from the 1990s, except they were able to win a championship and that's great because it feels a lot like it validates those teams. Think on it like this: The Rockets only won 47 games in the 1995 season. They were the sixth seed in the playoffs. They beat Karl Malone and the third-seeded Jazz in the first round, Charles Barkley and the second-seeded Suns in the second round, David Robinson and the first-seeded Spurs in the third round, then Shaquille O'Neal and the Eastern Conference champion Magic in the Finals. And they did all of that despite their second-best player being a slightly-past-his-prime Clyde Drexler. Imagine a Charlotte Hornets team from the early-to-mid '90s doing that. Imagine an Indiana Pacers team from the mid-to-late '90s doing that. Imagine the '01 Sixers doing that. That was

this Rockets team. So there was that. Plus, you've got: (1) the Rockets repeating off their 1994 championship, helping to quiet some of the But If Jordan Was Here . . . talk; (2) the first Finals appearance for Shaq; and (3) a cargo ship's worth of What Ifs (see Chapter 20).

29. The 1989 Championship (Pistons beat Lakers, 4–0): (I'm going to ignore that Byron Scott, an essential starter for the Lakers, missed the entire series because he pulled a hamstring during a practice before Game 1. And I'm also going to ignore that Magic Johnson, the most essential Laker, missed the end of Game 2, all but the first five or so minutes of Game 3, and then all of Game 4, also with a hamstring injury.) This was the first of two titles in a row for the Pistons, which means that, as a championship, it was the solidification of the Bad Boys model of basketball practices.[18] That's important, and even more so than it just being a thing that was attached to the Pistons, it also vibrated outward. What I mean is: The Lakers's coach that year was Pat Riley. He wouldn't coach another team to the Finals until 1994. His team that year? The New York Knicks, who took what the Bad Boys Pistons did and then cranked the dial all the way up.[19]

28. The 2010 Championship (Lakers beat Celtics, 4–3): A couple of neat things here: (1) This was a revenge championship for the Lakers, as they'd lost to the Celtics in 2008, and revenge championships are always

---

10. They are still, as of this writing, the only eighth seed to do so.
11. Robert Horry, then playing for the Spurs, had one of the greatest Finals performances of all that series. He scored 21 points over the final 18 minutes of Game 5, including the game-winning 3 in the final seconds. I've always referred to it as The Robert Horry Game, but I don't think it's actually an official thing like, say, The Flu Game. I don't know. I just know that I owe Robert Horry so much for those 18 minutes. (I actually saw Horry at a club in Houston one night while I was covering some record label anniversary or something. I was so excited to see him in person that all I could think to do was shout, "Yooooo! Robert! Game 5! Game 5!" at him.)
12. Also his first Finals MVP.
13. LeBron finished with 48-9-7, including 25 straight points to finish the game. He was 22 years old.
14. First time it'd happened that way since 1955.
15. This one, like the 2012 title, also carries with it a great What If: What happens to Patrick Ewing's legacy if the Knicks win the title that year?
16. Magic was a better player, Bird was more magical, which is for sure some kind of ironic.
17. His stat line for the series was a gross 32.8 points, 11.5 rebounds, and 5.5 assists.
18. Step 1: Clobber everything. Step 2: Clobber everything again. Step 3: Clobber everything one last time.
19. I think the most surprising thing about that mid-'90s Knicks team was that we somehow got through that era without Charles Oakley or Anthony Mason clanking someone over the head with a crowbar during a game.

fun. (2) This was Kobe's last title, and the one that put him permanently ahead of Shaq in the championship count (5–4) and temporarily ahead of Duncan, with whom he dueled for the Best Player of That Generation title. (3) This was Kobe's second Finals MVP in a row, and that meant that he'd become the first to do that since Shaq did it during their original title run together at the beginning of the decade, and also the first guard to do it since Jordan did it during his second three-peat. (4) From a broader, non-Kobe view, this was the championship that brought the Lakers to within one title of the Celtics (Celtics have 17, Lakers have 16). (5) And it also has packed into it a fun What If to toss around: The Celtics were up 3–2 in the series when Kendrick Perkins, a defensive anchor for the Cs, tore his PCL and MCL at the beginning of Game 6. He missed the rest of that game (Celtics lost by 22) and all of Game 7 (Celtics lost by 4). Do the Celtics win that series if Perk doesn't go down?[20] And if they do, how does that affect Kobe's legacy?

27. The 1997 Championship (Bulls beat Jazz, 4–2): Our first Jordan entry. It feels at least a little bit weird to put this one behind the 1996 championship (when the Bulls beat the Sonics). After all, this was the Finals that had The Flu Game, The Mailman Doesn't Deliver on Sundays Game,[21] and the lesser discussed GatorLode Game.[22] And it was also the one that gave Jordan not only his

fifth title, but also his fifth Finals MVP, which was a record until he broke it the following year. But the 1996 championship, while against a mostly less-interesting opponent and also while having no iconic Big Name games or moments, simply carried more historical impact. (I'll go over it when we get there.)

26. The 1985 Championship (Lakers beat Celtics, 4–2): Another example, like above, of a Finals that had a Big Name game in it; the Celtics drummed the Lakers by 34 in Game 1, which was played on Memorial Day, so it became known then as The Memorial Day Massacre.[23] "The Memorial Day Massacre" is probably the best name of all the Big Name games. There's maybe an argument to be made that "The Greatest Game Ever Played" is a better name (that was the name given to Game 5 of the 1976 NBA Finals, a triple overtime bonanza that the Celtics won by two points over the Suns), but I'd argue otherwise because I am, at least spiritually anyway, always more interested in names that are terrifying.

At any rate, some other stuff that happened in this Finals: (1) It was a revenge championship; (2) it was the first time the Lakers had ever beaten the Celtics in a Finals;[24] (3) it gave Magic a 3–2 lead in championships over Bird; and (4) Kareem Abdul-Jabbar became the oldest player ever to win a Finals MVP.[25]

---

20. A smaller, more docile What If: In Game 2 of that series, Ray Allen hit eight three-pointers. That was an NBA Finals record then and is still an NBA Finals record now. (The best of the bunch was his sixth one, because rather than call for the ball when he was already open, he made gigantic eyes at Rajon Rondo before he made any kind of move to get open, letting Rondo know he'd be open in just a second, then sprinted out off a Paul Pierce screen. It was a beautiful basketball moment.) But so if the Celtics end up winning that series, does that game gain more prestige? As it stands now, nobody really talks about it. But if they'd won, it'd almost certainly be a bigger part of that conversation, right?
21. An all-time great Finals moment. Karl Malone, the league MVP that year, was at the foul line with a chance to give the Jazz the lead in Game 1 of the Finals with 9.2 seconds left. Before Malone shot, Scottie Pippen walked over to him and told him, "The mailman doesn't deliver on Sundays." (They were playing on a Sunday.) Malone missed both free throws. On the next possession, Michael Jordan hit a game-winning jumper at the buzzer.
22. This one happened in Game 4. A Chicago Bulls team assistant accidentally gave the team GatorLode, a high-carb drink, rather than Gatorade. My favorite line about this was from Roland Lazenby's book *Michael Jordan: The Life*. He quotes then-Bulls-trainer Chip Schaefer: "It was like eating baked potatoes."
23. The original Memorial Day Massacre happened in 1937. Members of the Chicago Police shot and killed 10 protestors as they protested U.S. Steel signing a union contract. I'm willing to bet that when you picked up a book with a picture of cartoon squid watching a basketball game drawn on the front cover, you weren't expecting to read a footnote like this in it.
24. They were 0–8 up to that point.
25. He was 38 years old, but he played like a spry, fresh 36-year-old.

. . . continued

> ### TIER III : HINTS OF HISTORY
>
> Championships that fall into this category are ones that carry with them at least a discernible amount of historical significance.

25. The 2008 Championship (Celtics beat Lakers, 4–2): Two great moments from this series:

First, in Game 1, after contesting a Kobe jumper, Paul Pierce crumpled to the floor in that way that players crumple when the insides of their knees turn to goop. He stayed on the floor for several moments, writhing in pain, crying. He was eventually picked up by his teammates and carried to a wheelchair, after which he was wheelchaired off the floor to the locker room. It very much looked terrible and felt terrible to watch. It felt a lot like his Finals, the first of his career, was over. Less than two game minutes later, though, he came hopping out of the tunnel, looking all the way like a superhero (the camera shot of him coming out was even shot upwards like the way they showed Superman in those old comics all the time). The arena erupted. He checked into the game, then just minutes later hit back-to-back monster threes. It was some real-life movie shit, and it was so exciting to watch. Paul Pierce deserved that moment, and those Finals. So did everyone watching who loved him, and loved basketball.

Second, after the Celtics won in Game 6, Kevin Garnett, who'd just won his first championship after chasing one for 13 seasons, was interviewed, and he just as-loud-as-he-could screamed, "ANYTHING IS POSSIBLLLLLLLLLLLLLLE!" Kevin Garnett deserved that moment, and those Finals. So did everyone watching who loved him, and loved basketball.

For historical stuff for this championship, you've got: (1) It was the first Lakers-Celtics Finals since 1987; (2) it gave the Celtics a record 17th title; (3) Kobe was denied his first post-Shaq title; and maybe the most important, (4) the Big Three model, which the Celtics leaned into when they brought in Ray Allen and Kevin Garnett to help Paul Pierce, became a road to a championship that several other teams tried to emulate, most successfully the Miami Heat, who had their Dwyane Wade, LeBron James, Chris Bosh triumvirate.[1] Speaking of . . .

24. The 2011 Championship (Mavericks beat Heat, 4–2): The iconic moment: Game 2. The Mavericks, down 1–0 in the series, were down 15 with 6:21 left to go and looked extra cooked, both for the game and for the series. Then they went on a 20–2 run to go up three with about half a minute left, only to leave Mario Chalmers about 100 yards wide open for a three of his own that tied it with 24 seconds left, only to have Dirk Nowitzki save them with what has to be the greatest Dribble in from the Three-Point Line, Spin Move, Layup that a 7-footer has ever done in the Finals. Being a San Antonio fan, I always disliked Dirk and the Mavs, and I was so super happy when they lost in the 2006 Finals, but it was impossible even for me to hate on what he did that game, and then what he did for the rest of that series.[2]

Anyway, some big outside stuff that happened this Finals: (1) Dirk gets his ring, escaping the Great but Could Never Go All the Way tag that fell on guys like Barkley, Ewing, Malone, etc. (2) LeBron goes 0–2 in the Finals, sure, but what's bigger is he loses a Finals series for the first time when his team was favored, and he did so in an especially bizarre way (his worst game: Game 4, where he scored just 8 points on 11 shots; he ended with half as many turnovers as points). That was his first year in Miami, and the general tone surround-

---

1. The least successful Big Three: 2012 Minnesota's combo of Kevin Love, Ricky Rubio, and J.J. Barea. And to be clear, they were never, ever, ever advertised as a Big Three, but it's just fun to think of them as such.
2. The very best part of it was at the end of Game 6 after the Mavericks had won, he disappeared off into the locker room before anyone could grab him or even realized that he was gone. He said later that winning that title was an overwhelmingly emotional experience for him and he just needed to be alone for a moment. I love that. (Also, this was a revenge series for Dirk, as his Mavs lost to the Heat in the 2006 Finals, but, minus just a couple of pieces, it was mostly new teams so I'm not sure how accurate it is to call it an all-the-way revenge series like, say, when the Pistons lost in 1988 to the Lakers and then beat them in 1989.)

ing him and the Heat was that he was a bad guy for leaving Cleveland and the Heat were the bad team for Voltroning up with him and Bosh, and so of course him losing that year allowed for people who didn't like LeBron to stare at his lackluster stat sheets and masturbate furiously.

23. The 2013 Championship (Heat beat Spurs, 4–3): Gross. I'm going to close my eyes and just speed through this one: (1) This series featured four former Finals MVPs (LeBron, Wade, Duncan, Parker).[3] (2) LeBron wins his second title, and Dwyane Wade wins his third. (3) LeBron becomes just the 10th player ever to win multiple Finals MVP awards. (4) Ray Allen hits a three or whatever. Done. Shut up.

22. The 2000 Championship (Lakers beat Pacers, 4–2): The first appearance in our countdown from the Shaq and Kobe era of the Lakers. This was (1) the first title for Shaq;[4] (2) the first title for Kobe; (3) the seventh coaching title for Phil Jackson, who proved he didn't need the greatest basketball player of all time to win a championship so long as you gave him two of the other greatest players ever;[5] (4) the only appearance in the Finals for Reggie Miller; (5) the Finals where we got Kobe's Sprained Ankle Game, the second best Sprained Ankle Game in Finals history; and (6) the moment when it became clear that, at least for the next few years, you were going to have to have a dominant big man if you wanted to seriously contend for a title.[6]

21. The 2006 Championship (Heat beat Mavericks, 4–2): There were a bunch of smaller things that happened in this Finals. Shaq temporarily moved ahead of his low-post rival Tim Duncan, four championships to three. Shaq temporarily moved ahead of his petty rival Kobe Bryant, four championships to three. Dwyane Wade

became the first shooting guard since Jordan to win Finals MVP and also the youngest guard since Magic to do it. Pat Riley won his fifth title as a coach (this was the series where Shaq said Riley dunked his head in a bucket of water and held it there for three minutes to show how badly you had to want it to win a championship, which is a weird way to try to get your team to better defend the pick and roll but I guess that's why Riley has five rings as a coach and I have zero).

The main important thing, though, besides Pat Riley revealing that he was a fish who'd learned to talk, was that Dwyane Wade showed how utterly unstoppable an attacking guard could be in a league that no longer allowed hand-checking. In 2016, I wrote an article for *The Ringer* about Wade's brilliance in that series. The part that's most applicable here: "With his Heat down 2–0 to the Mavericks in the 2006 Finals, Wade put up 42 points and 13 rebounds in Game 3, including a stretch over the final six and a half minutes in which he fucking exploded the universe, single-handedly bringing the Heat back from down 13 to win it. In a Game 4 win, he put up 36 points, six rebounds, and three assists. In Game 5, he put up 43 points, four rebounds, four assists, and three steals, hitting two free throws with the Heat down one with 1.9 seconds left to win the game. In Game 6, he put up a super GTFOH stat line (36 points, 10 rebounds, 5 assists, 4 steals, 3 blocks) to close the series out." He was 24 years old when he did that.

20. The 1982 Championship (Lakers beat Sixers, 4–2): Magic won his second title here,[7] temporarily putting him ahead of Larry Bird in titles 2–1 (and also up 2–0 in Finals MVPs), and also this was the first title for Pat Riley's hair, but probably the biggest impact here was that it was the third time the Sixers lost in the Finals since signing Dr. J (1977, 1980, 1982). (I also like that it set up a super revenge championship in 1983, what with

---

3. And also a future winner, too, as Kawhi Leonard would win the award the next season.
4. Shaq was unbelievable in this series. He averaged 38 points and nearly 17 rebounds per game.
5. LOL.
6. From 1999 to 2007, eight of the nine titles were won by teams that had either Tim Duncan or Shaq.
7. He ended the series with a 13-13-13 triple double, a number set that is oddly satisfying to look at.

the Lakers and Sixers meeting again after the Sixers had lost twice in the Finals to the Lakers in three years.)

TIER II : BIG SOUNDS

Championships that fall into this category are ones that can stretch their legs out and admire their long-lasting importance to either the history of the NBA or the future of it.

19. The 1996 Championship (Bulls beat Sonics, 4–2): Lots and lots happening here. The Bulls are able to close out what currently stands as the single greatest season by a team in NBA history, finishing the regular season with a record of 72–10, one less win than the 2016 Warriors, sure, but the Bulls leapfrog over them in history because they ended their season with a championship and the Warriors ended their season in heartbreak. Jordan gets his fourth ring and also sets a record with his fourth Finals MVP. The fourth ring officially puts Jordan ahead of Larry Bird in the championship tally. And maybe most substantially: It's the first post-first-retirement title for Jordan, which killed off any of the He'll Never Be Able to Do What He Did Before His Retirement talk that started up after he'd returned at the end of the 1995 season and couldn't summon the full force of his strength in the playoffs when Shaq and Penny and the Magic came rumbling through.

18. The 2002 Championship (Lakers beat Nets, 4–0): The four main things that happened here: (1) A friend I grew up with began calling Nets center Todd Mac-Culloch "The White Shaq," which was funny to me then and is still funny when I think about it today.[8] (2) This championship is the one that gives the Lakers their three-peat, which makes it harder to argue they're not a dynasty no matter how much you dislike them.[9] (3) Shaq joins Michael Jordan as the only players to win three straight NBA Finals MVPs, a stat that still stands today and, were I to guess, will stand for a great deal longer. (4) Phil Jackson gets a third three-peat, which

ties him with Red Auerbach for Most Championships Won by a Coach, and puts him into a category all by himself for Most Championships Won by a Coach Whose Shoulders Sit Up Higher Than His Ears.

17. The 1991 Championship (Bulls beat Lakers, 4–1): I love all the parts of this series. There's a great storyline in it. (The Jordan vs. Magic angle.) There's the creation of a demigod. (It was the first of Jordan's six titles.) There's the ending of an ugly narrative. (The whole Jordan Can't Win Titles storyline that had followed him into the off-season during each of his previous playoff series losses.) There's a nice little barb cooked into it. (Jordan averaged 11.4 assists per game for the series. It was the first time he'd ever averaged double-digit assists, making it a not-so-subtle Fuck You to those who'd labeled him a selfish, bucket-hungry player.) There's an iconic move in it. (This was the series where Jordan switched hands during a layup midair, prompting Marv Albert's "Oh! A spec . . . tacular move by Michael Jordan!" call.) There's a sad ending in it. (It was the last time Magic would play in the Finals, his career cut short by his HIV diagnosis, which he announced in a press conference five months later.) And there's a very strong What If in it. (If the Lakers had won that series, could a case have been made that Magic, who'd have then had six rings to Jordan's eventual five, was better than Jordan?)[10]

16. The 2009 Championship (Lakers beat Magic, 4–1): You get Kobe, after failing to win his first post-Shaq championship in 2008, finally getting there this year, and so of course that's important. The title also helps him tie Shaq in the championship count, which is big because Kobe knew that if he was going to pass Shaq in the All-Time Best Players ranking he was going to have to have more rings than him since Shaq had racked up the Finals MVP trophies during their three-peat together. The title here also gives the Lakers a total of 15 championships, good for second best behind the Celtics, and it also gives Phil Jackson 10 rings as a coach, one more than Red Auerbach for the most ever. Probably what's most important, though, is that Dwight Howard, centerpiece for the Magic team here, does not win a championship.

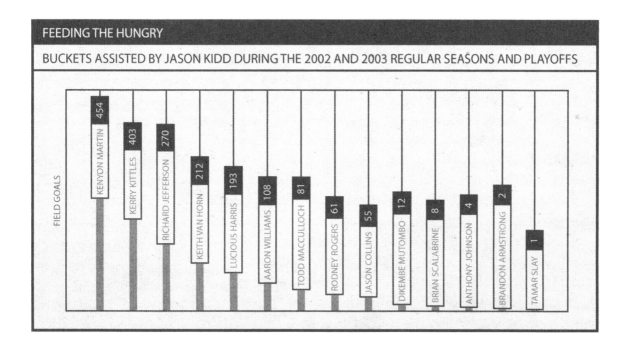

FEEDING THE HUNGRY

BUCKETS ASSISTED BY JASON KIDD DURING THE 2002 AND 2003 REGULAR SEASONS AND PLAYOFFS

FIELD GOALS

KENYON MARTIN — 454
KERRY KITTLES — 403
RICHARD JEFFERSON — 270
KEITH VAN HORN — 212
LUCIOUS HARRIS — 193
AARON WILLIAMS — 108
TODD MacCULLOCH — 81
RODNEY ROGERS — 61
JASON COLLINS — 55
DIKEMBE MUTOMBO — 12
BRIAN SCALABRINE — 8
ANTHONY JOHNSON — 4
BRANDON ARMSTRONG — 2
TAMAR SLAY — 1

15. The 2003 Championship (Spurs beat Nets, 4–2): A quick personal note: I worked as a waiter in college for a very brief bit in 2003. I was working the night of Game 2. I spent something like 45 minutes in the bathroom on my phone because a friend of mine took my call and then just set the phone down by the TV so I could listen to the fourth quarter. When it was over, I came out of the bathroom and everyone—all my tables, my boss, etc.—was super fucking pissed. I decided it'd be easier to just not work there anymore than fix everything, so I just left. I was not that great of a waiter, I suppose.

As far as the historical ramifications of this title, we're looking at: (1) My beloved Tim Duncan wins his second title and also his second Finals MVP. (2) It's the last season for David Robinson, a first-ballot Hall of Famer and also God's favorite and most perfect creation.[11] (3) It's the first title together for Duncan, Manu Ginobili, and Tony Parker, a group that would go on to be the winningest Big Three in the history of the league.[12] (4) And it's the fifth straight year after Jordan's retirement that the championship is won by a team with a monster big man roaming around in the paint.

8. Imagine you're Jason Kidd and you're getting ready to go to war against the 2002 Lakers and you look over there at their bench and see Shaq and then you look at your bench and see Todd MacCulloch.

9. A semi-nerdy stat: The last time the Lakers had three-peated before this was when they won the 1952 title, the 1953 title, and the 1954 title. Every time I get to looking at championship stats and whatnot from basketball that happened before, like, 1976, the first thought I always have is a very dismissive "I wonder how many playoff games this team could win if you dropped them into any year after 2000?" I just have a hard time seeing George Mikan and Slater Martin doing anything against Shaq and Kobe besides getting pounded into the earth.

10. I would argue no, mostly because Jordan was always the best player during each of his titles.

11. I'm assuming.

12. Their 575 regular season wins and 126 postseason wins are both records for a group of three teammates.

WHAT'S THE MOST IMPORTANT
NBA CHAMPIONSHIP?

PART 3

... continued

14. The 1990 Championship (Pistons beat Blazers, 4–1): This was a big one, really. (1) The Pistons were able to repeat off their 1989 title over a hobbled Lakers team, and so it helped to quiet all of the Y'all Would've Lost Last Year If Magic and Byron Hadn't Been Hurt criticisms, and that sort of validation is always important historically.[1] (2) It was the first Finals since 1979 that didn't feature either the Lakers or the Celtics, which was great because it meant the league was opening up some (the Lakers made it to the 1991 Finals, but following that one neither the Lakers nor the Celtics would make it to the Finals again for nearly a decade). (3) The Pistons's win here also was a war horn of sorts, signaling that a meaner, angrier version of basketball was what would be the next new trend in the NBA. (4) We get a retroactive Big Name game, what with Joe Dumars putting up a crushing 33 points and 5 assists in Game 3 and then finding out as soon as it was over that his dad had passed away.[2] (5) And also Mariah Carey sang "America the Beautiful" before Game 1, and that's maybe not super duper important to basketball, but it's super duper important to me.

13. The 2015 Championship (Warriors beat Cavaliers, 4–2): Seven things happened here. Let's go in order from most important to least important: (1) In the regular season, Steph Curry and Klay Thompson combined for 525 threes, obliterating the previous record by 41.[3] Then, in the Finals, the Warriors made a record 67 three-pointers. Anyway, but so the point is: This was the exact moment when it became impossible to argue that a jump-shooting team couldn't win a title, as the Warriors were, at that moment, the most jump-shootingest team of all time and won it. (2) It's the fifth Finals in a row for LeBron, which is a thing that nobody had done for half a century. It's wild to think about. Kobe never did it. Jordan never did it. Only LeBron.[4] That said . . . (3) LeBron loses in the Finals again, dropping his record down to 2–4.[5] (4) Steph Curry officially enters his name into the Who's the Greatest Shooter Who Has Ever Lived? debate. (5) It was the first Finals since 1998 that didn't feature Tim Duncan, Kobe Bryant, or Dwyane Wade. (6) The Warriors become the first team since the 1991 Bulls to win a Finals without any of their players having had any sort of Finals experience. (7) Steve Kerr becomes the first rookie head coach to win a title since Pat Riley did it in 1982.

12. The 1988 Championship (Lakers beat Pistons, 4–3): While working on this book (and specifically this section), I was going back and watching each NBA Finals. Of all of the main runs, I think the Pistons's run from 1988 to 1990 was secretly my favorite, and this Finals was the best of that bunch. You've got (1) Magic winning his fifth ring, which would end up being his last; (2) James Worthy picking up the Big Game James nickname after throwing up 36-16-10 in Game 7, a game that, oh by the way, was decided by only three points—still the record for Closest Finals Game 7 since the merger;[6] (3) the Lakers becoming the first team

---

1. With their 1990 win, the Pistons had become only the third franchise in NBA history to win back-to-back titles.
2. Isiah Thomas after the game: "You know he made one shot today, going down the lane, the shot clock was running down. And he threw it real high in the air and it went in. We kind of looked at each other and smiled. I said to myself, 'Your dad threw that one in.'"
3. The previous record was 484 by Curry (261) and Thompson (223) in 2014.
4. And James Jones, who was on each of those LeBron teams.
5. This one, same as the 2007 championship, was not his fault. He averaged 35.8 points per game, 13.3 rebounds per game, and 8.8 assists per game, which is just a very goofy and gaudy stat line. (He became the first player ever to lead both teams in points, rebounds, and assists.) And also he was without Kevin Love, who'd had his arm yanked out of its socket by Kelly Olynyk in an earlier series, and Kyrie Irving, who suffered a knee injury during overtime of the first game. That meant he was going up against a 67-win team in the most high-stakes situation of all and his best teammates were Matthew Dellavedova and Iman Shumpert, both of whom are basically scarecrows.
6. There were actually four Game 7s before the merger that were closer: the Syracuse Nationals beat the Fort Wayne Pistons 92–91 in 1955, the Celtics beat the St. Louis Hawks 125–123 in double overtime in 1957, the Celtics beat the Lakers 95–93 in 1966, and the Celtics beat the Lakers 108–106 in 1969.

since the '60s Celtics to repeat as champion; (4) Isiah Thomas's Sprained Ankle Game, when he badly turned his ankle in the third quarter of Game 6 and still managed to pour in 25 points that quarter, which remains a record; (5) the Phantom Foul on Bill Laimbeer that put Kareem at the line at the end of Game 6 with the Lakers down one, and of course he sank both free throws and gave the Lakers the one-point lead that they'd eventually win by. It was all just such great theater.

11. The 1983 Championship (Sixers beat Lakers, 4–0):
(1) This was the Fo'-Fo'-Fo' playoffs where reigning league MVP Moses Malone, who the Sixers had added to their roster after losing to the Lakers in six games in the Finals the year before, said that his team was going to sweep its way through the then three rounds of the playoffs to a title. (He nearly delivered, too. They lost one game in the Conference Finals to the Bucks.) (2) It was the first Finals sweep since the Warriors swept the Bullets in 1975. (3) It was the only title not won by either the Celtics or the Lakers from 1980 to 1988, which is kind of insane. (4) And there were four already NBA MVPs in the series (Kareem, Dr. J, Moses, and Bob McAdoo) and one eventual NBA MVP (Magic). It was super big boy shit here, for real.

10. The 2014 Championship (Spurs beat Heat, 4–1):
A personal note: This was the single most enjoyable championship that I have ever experienced in my life, and likely will ever experience in my life. I for real was so nervous during Game 1 of this series that rather than watch it, I sat in a car in the driveway with my wife and listened to it. I don't know why I thought that would help, but I did.[7] Okay, but so big picture stuff: (1) This was a revenge championship for the Spurs, which is great, and they did it the very next year after Ray Allen stole the 2013 championship from them with his unreal three in Game 6, which made it even better.[8] (2) Better than it just being a revenge series, it was a revenge killing: The Spurs outscored the Heat by 70 points, the most in Finals history. (3) Tim Duncan gets his farewell championship, his fifth, tying Kobe and also passing Shaq. (4) Tim Duncan wins a title in three different

decades, which is a very strange and kind of overwhelming stat to think about. (5) The Spurs shoot the highest field goal percentage in the Finals of any team ever. (6) This series marks the arrival of Kawhi Leonard, but more importantly it marks the end of the Big Three era in San Antonio regarding championships and Finals appearances, and Tim, Tony, and Manu end it as the winningest Big Three in playoff history.[9]

TIER I : HALLOWED GROUND

Unquestionable.

---

9. The 1986 Championship (Celtics beat Rockets, 4–2):
(1) This Celtics team (67–15 on the season, including 40–1 at home) is regularly argued to be one of the best NBA teams of all time, if not *THE* best NBA team of all-time. (2) Bird plays maybe the all-around best game[10] of any of the 31 he played in the Finals.[11] (3) We get an all-time great Infamy Game in the series when the 7'4" Ralph Sampson punches the much, much, much smaller backup Celtics guard Jerry Sichting (6'1") in Game 5.[12] (4) It's the Finals debut of Hakeem Olajuwon who, after having watched him play about 20 games while working on this book, I am officially in love with. (5) It's the first time since 1981 that the Lakers don't make it to the Finals. (6) It's a reverse revenge championship, in that the Rockets had lost to the Celtics in 1981, and then they lost again to them here.

8. The 2001 Championship (Lakers beat Sixers, 4–1):
You have almost all of the parts here that you need when you start to talk about the best, most influential, most substantial championships. You've got an absolutely and grossly dominant and impressive team (the Lakers were 11–0 in the playoffs entering Game 1 of the Finals, and then finished the playoffs at 15–1; they were like if a herd of rhinos were driving giant steamrollers). You've got a player making a big leap up in the All-Time Player rankings (Shaq wouldn't yet pass Hakeem Olajuwon on that list, but he would tie his champion-

ship count and also his Finals MVP count). You've got Kobe two seasons away from averaging more than 30 points per game for the first time in his career and also from beating Shaq in Win Shares for the first time, too. You've got Phil Jackson adding to his legend with an eighth title as a head coach. And you've got an Iconic Move that happened during a game (Allen Iverson's Step Over in his masterful Game 1 performance).

7. The 1980 Championship (Lakers beat Sixers, 4–2): (1) It's Magic's first title, and it happens in his first season in the league, and his first season in the league is the one that came after him winning an NCAA title. (2) We get the single greatest Magic in the Finals moment of his career: his 42-15-7 in Game 6, which is the game where everyone talks about how he played all five positions, including center (Kareem was out with a severely sprained ankle so Magic filled in, but mostly what he did was just do the jump ball). (3) It was the first NBA Finals that featured a three-point line, which is at least a little bit weird to think about[13] (and of course the inclusion of the three-point line changed basketball forever).[14] (4) And also this was the series where we got Dr. J skywalking for the One-Handed, Behind-the-Backboard Scoop Layup move, which, even looking at it today, feels less like you're watching a basketball move and more like you're watching a Leonardo da Vinci paint stroke.

6. The 1981 Championship (Celtics beat Rockets, 4–2): A couple of good smaller things, and also one big and very strong thing. The good smaller things: (1) It's Larry Bird's first title, tying him with Magic at one apiece. (2) Magic won his in 1980, then Bird won his in 1981, and so this one really helped to build the fervor of a potential high-stakes showdown between the two. (3) There's a great sort of sidebar, and that's that Cedric Maxwell ended up being the Finals MVP this year, meaning he'd become the only Finals MVP who'd not eventually make his way into the basketball Hall of Fame.[15] The big and very strong thing: This was the title that represented the beginning of a new era for the Celtics. The Celtics had 14 championships by this point, but the first 11 were Bill Russell teams, and the 12th and 13th had guys like John Havlicek and Don Nelson on them, and both of them had been part of the Russell run. This one, though, had exactly zero players on it who'd won a title with the Celtics the last time they'd won it (1976). It was Bird's franchise from here going forward.

5. The 1992 Championship (Bulls beat Blazers, 4–2): The most important thing here is the Bulls repeat as champs, which makes this championship wildly meaningful because it very clearly, very obviously, very loudly declared that Jordan was legit, which was a thing people weren't all the way willing to accept after the 1991

---

7. And it did. The Spurs won that game. I watched Game 2 with my eyes like a schmuck and they lost that game.

8. The secretly best part of the whole thing was after the Spurs beat the Thunder in the Western Conference Finals, Tim Duncan, who, to that point in his career had never really done any kind of thing that could have ever been construed as trash talk, told David Aldridge, the postgame interviewer, "We've got four more to win. We'll do it this time." It was like hearing Tupac bark, "First off, fuck your bitch and the clique you claim," at Biggie at the beginning of "Hit 'Em Up."

9. Together they won 126 games. Second place is Magic, Kareem, and Michael Cooper, who won 110 together.

10. I'm pretty sure his actual best Finals game was his Game 5 in the 1984 series against the Lakers. (More on that one soon.)

11. His stat line: 29-11-12. This is how Bob Ryan, columnist for the *Boston Globe*, started his recap after Game 6: "The Houston Rockets were like an unwary couple pulled over on the highway for going 3 miles over the speed limit by a burly Georgia cop with the mirrored sunglasses. It wasn't their day. The cop's name was Bird. The bailiff's name was Bird. The court stenographer's name was Bird. The judge's name was Bird. And the executioner's name was—guess what?—Bird."

12. We also get a great needling. Sichting told the *LA Times*: "My little boy hits harder than that, and he is 3 years old."

13. Outside of the three-point line, the main thing that makes watching old Finals games technically different than watching newer Finals games is that they didn't have a bar on the screen all the time that showed the score. You don't realize how essential that is until it's not there.

14. How many threes do you think the two teams made during that Finals? It's a remarkable answer. Here's the number: one. The two teams were 1/20 from the three-point line that series. Julius Erving made it during Game 3.

15. The other two guys who have a shot at pulling this off are Chauncey Billups, who won it in 2004, and Andre Iguodala, who accidentally won it in 2015.

title. Also, this was the series where Jordan delivered The Shrug, his most iconic Big Name moment of all.[16] (A smaller thing is he becomes the first player to ever win consecutive Finals MVPs, a record he'd break the very next year by winning his third.)

4. The 1993 Championship (Bulls beat Suns, 4–2):
You've got Jordan at his most dominant vs. Barkley at his most dominant.[17] You've got the triple-overtime in Game 3 that the Suns, down 0–2 in the series, absolutely have to have (and end up getting).[18] You've got Barkley putting up a goofy 32-12-10 stat line in Game 4, only to be outdone by Jordan's obscene 55-8-4, including the and-one on Barkley that sealed the game.[19] You've got Barkley telling Ahmad Rashad after the Suns manage to win Game 5 in Chicago to keep the series alive that "God want[s] us to win the world championship," then you've got John Paxson proving Michael Jordan was more powerful than God when he hits the go-ahead three in the final seconds of Game 6 to give the Bulls the title. You've got this title making the Bulls the first team since the Celtics in the '60s to win three championships in a row, and also Jordan becomes the first player ever to win three Finals MVPs in a row.[20] You've got Jordan averaging over 40 points per game for the entire Finals (it's the only time he'd done that, or would do that). And you've got Jordan's first retirement just a few months away.[21]

All that equals up to: You've got the fourth most important Finals in NBA history.

3. The 2016 Championship (Cavaliers beat Warriors, 4–3): Whoa. All the things this Finals did: (1) It tied LeBron with Duncan, Shaq, and Magic for second-most career Finals MVPs (three). (2) It was the first pro championship for Cleveland in over 50 years, making it, in the estimation of many, the fulfillment of a destiny grander than even LeBron's quarter-mile-wide shoulders. (3) It prevented the Warriors from completing what would have been considered the greatest single season in NBA history.[22] (4) It took the Steph Curry Is Having One of the All-Time Best Offensive Seasons Ever conversation, dumped it into a muddy river, and replaced it with the Wait, Should We Very Seriously Start Talking About How LeBron Could Possibly Finish His Career As the Greatest Basketball Player of All Time? talk. (5) It was the first time a team in the Finals had come back from being down 3–1 in the series. (6) It gave us the defining play of LeBron's career[23] and gave us one of the cruelest, most ironic death sentences of all.[24] (7) And it changed the fortune for not only the Cavs franchise, but also the Warriors and the Oklahoma City Thunder, as Kevin Durant, who left the Thunder to sign with the Warriors less than a month after the Warriors had lost, told *Rolling Stone* that had the Warriors won that series, he'd have not joined their team. LeBron had already

---

16. Somehow, his pose after hitting the jumper at the end of Game 6 of the 1998 Finals never became known as The Pose.
17. Cumulatively, both teams scored the exact same amount of points combined in the six games in the series, and every game was decided by 10 or fewer points.
18. Neat thing: The only other triple-overtime game in the Finals happened in 1976. That game also featured the Suns (they lost that one 126–128 to the Celtics), and it also featured Paul Westphal, who played for that 1976 Suns team and then coached the 1993 Suns team.
19. The highest-scoring game of any Finals of Jordan's career. Also, and this is just a guess and probably wrong, but there was a moment during the third overtime of Game 3 where Barkley stole a bad pass from Stacey King to Jordan and then hit a layup to put the Suns up five with less than two minutes left. Immediately after he'd done so, he ran down the court holding his arms in the air in triumph. In Game 4, after Jordan hit the and-one on Barkley to give the game to the Bulls, Jordan ran down the court holding his arms in the air in triumph. I don't imagine that Jordan did his move because Barkley did his move, but I also don't *not* think that.
20. He also tied Magic Johnson with three Finals MVPs here, too.
21. You've also got the great What If Barkley Had Won This Title? angle.
22. They won more games that season than any team in history (73 in the regular season, 88 if you include the playoffs).
23. The Chasedown Block on Andre Iguodala at the end of Game 7 to save the championship.
24. Steph Curry spent just about the entire season putting defenders into the torture chamber when they tried to guard him out at the three-point line. Then, at the end of Game 7, with the game tied and the championship waiting to be won or lost, the Cavaliers ran a screen play to put Steph Curry into a position where he had to guard Kyrie Irving, an offensive wunderkind, all alone at the three-point line. Irving danced on him a bit, then hit the three that effectively buried the Warriors. The universe can be a real cold place sometimes.

won two titles in Miami, but it was his one here, with Cleveland and for Cleveland, that made him a true, no joke, no hyperbole, basketball legend.

2. The 1998 Championship (Bulls beat Jazz, 4–2):

The coronation of the greatest basketball player of all time. Jordan wins his sixth title, which put him up past Magic's five and also tied him with Kareem (only former Celtics had more championships at the time). Jordan sets a still-standing record with his sixth Finals MVP. Jordan hits an updated version of The Shot, his iconic moment from the 1989 playoffs when he hit the series-winning jumper over Craig Ehlo, only this time he hits it over Bryon Russell and it's for a championship. Karl Malone loses again in the Finals (he'd never make it back as a member of the Jazz, and he'd flat-out never win a title, either). Jordan retired after the series was over, Phil Jackson never coached another Bulls game, and Pippen was traded before the next season arrived. It was as dramatic and certain an end to a dynasty as the NBA had ever seen.

1. The 1984 Championship (Celtics beat Lakers, 4–3):

Almost too much stuff to sort through, truly: (1) This was when the playoffs moved into the format they still fall under today, which is to say that all of the teams from here going forward would have to win four series to win the championship. (2) This was the Finals where Larry and Magic FINALLY played against each other for the NBA championship for the first time, a scene that'd been set in motion in 1979 when they played for the college championship and then both entered the league the summer after and began winning championships perpendicular to one another, and of course their rivalry

is the one that the modern NBA built itself up on so there's really no way to overstate how important of a moment this was. (3) The Celtics won, meaning Larry and Magic both now had two titles, and them both having the same number of titles helped to make everything feel even more electric and intense. (4) Larry was the league MVP that season (his first such award) and then won the Finals MVP, too, a thing that only three players had done up to this point.[25] (5) There were a couple of major basketball gaffes to point back to, and major basketball gaffes are always interesting.[26] (6) There was the press conference after the Celtics got blown out in Game 3 where Bird famously said the Celtics had played "like sissies," which led to the even more famous Kevin McHale Clothesline Foul on Kurt Rambis in Game 4 that turned the series from a basketball contest to full-scale warfare.[27] (7) There was Game 5[28] being played at the Boston Garden under an oppressive, relentless, unforgettable heat (it was 97 degrees in the building that day, but to hear the players talk about things it was closer to 970 degrees). (8) There was how this was two full years after the NBA Finals had been taken off tape delay, and so everyone was actually watching it as it was happening. And then also, somehow, improbably, perfectly, (9) there was a Game 7 in the Boston Garden. The Celtics ended up winning. The crowd ran out onto the court at the buzzer. If you watch the clip closely, you can see Bird crashing into people, shoving them, plowing through them as he full-speed-bumper-cars his way to the locker room, to salvation, to prosperity. It wasn't exactly a metaphor for what the NBA would do over the next four decades, but it's close enough.

Nothing could've been more perfect than this championship. Nothing ever was.

---

25. Willis Reed did it in 1970, Kareem did it in 1971, and Moses Malone did it in 1983.

26. Third-place gaffe from that Finals: Magic throwing the ball right to Robert Parish near the end of regulation in Game 4 (the Lakers lost in overtime). Second-place gaffe: Magic accidentally and inexplicably dribbling out the clock at the end of Game 2 (the Lakers lost in overtime). First-place gaffe: James Worthy's cross-court lob pass at the end of Game 2 that was stolen and then converted into a layup, allowing for the Celtics to force overtime and then win a game they should've lost. If they win that game they head home up 2–0, all but assuring themselves of the title.

27. The best summary of the effect of that moment came from Cedric Maxwell: "Before, the Lakers were just running across the street whenever they wanted. Now they stop at the corner, push the button, wait for the light, and look both ways."

28. The best Larry Bird Finals game. The series was tied 2–2 and he was playing against his super rival and also they were playing in a fucking oven and he put up 34 points on 15/20 shooting and also grabbed 17 rebounds.

What you are about to witness is real. The participants are not actors. They are actual litigants with a case pending in civil court. Both parties have agreed to drop their claims and have their cases settled here before the judge in our forum, the Basketball Court.

[The doors to the courtroom open. Dwyane Wade walks in and toward the plaintiff's table.]

NARRATOR: This is the plaintiff, Dwyane Tyrone Wade Jr. He says that for all of his success and influence on the way NBA basketball is played now and will be played moving forward, he is not mentioned nearly enough when it comes to discussing the league's all-time most influential players. It's unfair, he says. He's a top-10 name, easy, he says. He's suing for Allen Iverson's spot in the Important Players in NBA History, Ranked conversation.

[The doors to the courtroom open again. Allen Iverson walks in.]

This is the defendant, Allen Ezail Iverson. He's the sixth most important player in NBA history.[1] He says of course Wade feels that he's underappreciated. That's what happens when you owe two of your three championships to another person.[2] That's not Iverson's fault. He's accused of not being as important as he allegedly is. He is countersuing for Dwyane Wade's 2013 NBA championship.

COURT OFFICER: All parties, please raise your right hand. Do each of you, in the case now pending before this court, the Basketball Court, solemnly swear to tell the truth, the whole truth, and nothing but the truth, so help you God?

WADE AND IVERSON [TOGETHER]: Yes.

[A side door to the courtroom opens. The judge walks in.]

COURT OFFICER: All rise. The honorable judge Bill Russell, 11-time NBA champion, presiding.

[He hands a form to the judge.]

The litigants have been sworn in, your honor.

JUDGE [SETTLING INTO HIS SEAT]: Alright, Mr. Wade, you are suing for Allen Iverson's spot in the Important Players in NBA History, Ranked conversation because, according to you *[He looks at the form.]*, you think you're at least as important to NBA history as he was. Is that correct?

WADE: Yes, sir.

JUDGE [TO IVERSON]: And you are countersuing Mr. Wade for *[He looks at the form again.]* his 2013 NBA championship?

IVERSON: Yes, sir.

JUDGE: Why?

IVERSON: I just want it, your honor.

[Crowd laughs a tiny amount.]

JUDGE [TO WADE]: Let's get started. Talk to me, Mr. Wade. What's going on here?

WADE: It's simple. I think that Allen Iverson's placement in the Important Players in NBA History, Ranked conversation is suspect. I don't feel he deserves to be as high up as he is. I think I've been way more important to not only the micro view of the NBA, but also the macro view. We can star—

IVERSON [TO WADE, INTERRUPTING]: Micro, macro, macaroni, Makaveli. What are you even talking about? What have you ever done? Better question: What have you ever done *first*? Firsts are important. Firsts are iconic. Iconic moments are important. All of your best moments are like the half-off versions of more iconic moments from other players.

JUDGE [TO IVERSON]: Please direct your statements and issues to me, Mr. Iverson. What do you mean?

IVERSON [TO THE JUDGE]: Okay, I first noticed it in 2009, your honor. The Heat were playing the Cavs. This was back when LeBron was with the Cavs the first time so it was LeBron vs. Wade, so everyone was watching. And there was a play in the first quarter where LeBron went in for a dunk and it got blocked. Wade grabbed the loose ball, took off down the court, charged into the lane, then rose up and dunked it over Anderson

---

1. It goes Jordan, Russell, Wilt, Magic, Bird, Iverson. And to reiterate: We're talking about important, not best.
2. Oh, hey, LeBron.

Varejão, and he did it with such force that it knocked Varejão onto the ground. Now, Wade's momentum was clearly carrying him in one direction. But Wade very deliberately stopped, pivoted, then walked back in the opposite direction just so he could step *over* Varejão while Varejão was on the floor. It was contrived.[3] That's my imprint. Does he ever even think to do that if I don't do The Step Over against Tyronn Lue in the 2001 Finals?

WADE: You're not the only one who can step over people, Allen. I step over people all the time.

IVERSON: *[He makes a very Get the Fuck Outta Here face at Wade.]*

WADE: Your honor, when my first son was born— I'll never forget this—when my first son was born I remember the doctor handed him to me. I looked at him. That little baby looked at me. A lot of people say babies can't look at you when they're first born, but my son did. He was the most beautiful thing I'd ever seen. And you know what I did? I took him and I set him down right on that hospital floor and then I stepped over him. It was the first thing I did as a father.

JUDGE: Mr. Iverson, please expand on your comment. The implication was that there were more instances like that. Are there?

IVERSON: Sure. There was a time during a 2010 playoff game against the Celtics where he hit five 3s in a half and then stared at his hand and pretended it was on fire. That's like what Jordan did when he hit six 3s in a half against the Trail Blazers in the 1992 Finals and then gave The Shrug to the announcers, except less classic. There was a time where he tried to have his own version of The Flu Game, another Jordan rip-off. Jordan did his in the Finals against Stockton and Malone and the Jazz, Wade did his in a December game against Trey Burke and the Jazz. There was the time he shot a game

winner from just beyond the elbow and it hit the front of the rim, bounced straight up, then fell in the rim at the buzzer. Ralph Sampson had a shot that did the exact same thing, except his shot sent his team to the 1986 NBA Finals. Wade's sent his team to the team plane so they could go to their next regular season game. He's like the MetroPCS of players.

JUDGE [TO WADE]: Any response to these?

WADE: I can't control what the ball does when I shoot it, your honor. I shot it, it hit the rim, it went in. But I guess since we're talking about firsts, why don't the three of us share what it was like when each of us won the first of our multiple championships. Championships are important, right A.I.? We're talking about important things, right?

IVERSON: Man, come on.

JUDGE: We're not comparing numbers here, Mr. Wade. Stats alone do not equate importance or influence.

WADE [TO JUDGE]: Your honor, did you know that I'm one of only seven players in NBA history to have at least 2,000 points, 500 assists, and 150 steals in a single season?[4] Sounds important to me.

IVERSON [TO WADE]: Bro, I did that twice.[5]

JUDGE: I won't tell you again, Mr. Wade. We're discussing importance and influence. We're trying to figure out whether or not you've had a greater impact on basketball than Mr. Iverson. That's it. Argue toward that.

WADE: How about this angle, then: The style of play that Iverson brought into the league, the Shoot-First Point Guard, which was wildly inefficient, that whole style is dead now. The NBA doesn't run like that anymore. I don't think it's any coincidence that the period of time when Iverson was really at his greatest also generally coincides with the time period consid-

---

3. Dwyane Wade is kind of a nerd so he catches a lot of slack for being so clunky in his attempts to throw his coolness around, but it cannot be said that he doesn't understand the importance of good basketball theater. If there was a moment to be had in a big game when he was at his apex, he would have it. Another great one he pulled off against the Cavs was in 2007 when he stole the ball, dribbled it down the sideline, dribbled it to himself around a player who was trying to draw a charge (Sasha Pavlovic), then lobbed it up from beyond the three-point line for an alley-oop to Shaq, who was playing for the Heat, because he played for, like, 25 fucking teams during his last few years in the league.
4. 2009.
5. 2005 and 2008.

ered by many to be among the worst of any NBA era. It's a whole new league now, and it will very, very, very likely never go back to that style. That has to take away from Iverson's influence, doesn't it? How can you say a person is truly important if his fingerprints aren't on the game anymore?

Meanwhile, I convinced LeBron and Chris Bosh to come to Miami and play with me, and within that one thing you find the two big pieces of my argument for taking Iverson's spot.

First, all of everything that happened in the NBA from 2010 going forward, it was all part of the reverb of me getting LeBron to Miami. It was a response to that move. I mean, that's an insane storyline. How different does the NBA look today if LeBron never left Cleveland that first time for Miami? Does Kevin Durant still go to the Warriors? Do the Bulls make the Finals in 2011? Does Paul George still break his leg in that exhibition game?[6] Does Linsanity still happen? Is the 2013 NBA Draft still so terrible? Does Tom Thibodeau take Derrick Rose out in the fourth quarter of that easy-win playoff game before Derrick Rose's knee goes out? And it just keeps going and going like that. Cleveland for sure never gets Kyrie and probably doesn't get Kevin Love either, so LeBron probably never gets his title, which would've been an incredibly unjust way for the universe to treat him. There are so many spider legs there.

IVERSON [TO WADE]: What the fuck are you talking about spider legs?

WADE: So that's one way I was very important: The whole NBA landscape would look different if I don't get LeBron and Bosh to Miami. Second, and this is even bigger, but our championship Heat teams—we were really the true Super Team of that era. I don't even just mean the numbers stuff, either. I mean, okay, we were the first-ever team to win 17 games in a calendar month, and also the first team to go to at least four

straight Finals since the Celtics.[7] But what I mean is it is within reason to say that our Heat team solidified Super Teams, and more than that, we even set the framework in place for the Team-First version of basketball that all the teams in the league aspire to now.

IVERSON [TO WADE]: You should probably do some stretches before you try and reach like that.

WADE [IGNORING IVERSON]: So you have all of those things, all of those ways that basketball moves forward, and there's one person at the center of it . . .

IVERSON: Yeah, LeBron.

WADE: . . . Dwyane Tyrone Wade Jr., the new sixth most important player in the history of the NBA. And that's nothing to say of the fact that there was a very real stretch of time when I was arguably the best basketball player on the planet, which is its own argument.

JUDGE [TO IVERSON]: Would you like to respond?

IVERSON: Yes. Let me shoot some holes in all these untruths. First, he mentioned the Shoot-First thing, and while doing so he said that the NBA doesn't work like that. So then how do we explain Steph Curry and Russell Westbrook and Kyrie Irving and Damian Lillard and John Wall and all them?

WADE: You know whose name you didn't say? Chris Paul, maybe the best point guard in the league for a decade.

IVERSON [TO WADE]: Chris Paul literally called me the most influential player of all time, so what are you even talking about?[8]

[Turns to address the judge.]

It ain't that hard, your honor. You can point to the way I almost single-handedly forced the league to create a dress code for players. You can point to how I helped to show that smaller guys could be as big as the biggest guys. You can point to the way I took the tattoos and cornrows and shooting sleeves and other things like that and turned them into a thesis state-

---

6. I'd say no. I'd say the Pacers would've either won the 2014 NBA Finals or lost the 2014 NBA Finals. Either way, they'd have gotten there, and that probably would've been enough to make PG skip it so he could rest up a little during the summer.

7. 1984–1987.

8. "I grew up in North Carolina and I loved Michael Jordan to death, but I think Allen Iverson had a bigger influence on the game of basketball than anybody. You know, I don't even think it's close." Chris Paul, talking to a media scrum following Iverson's retirement announcement.

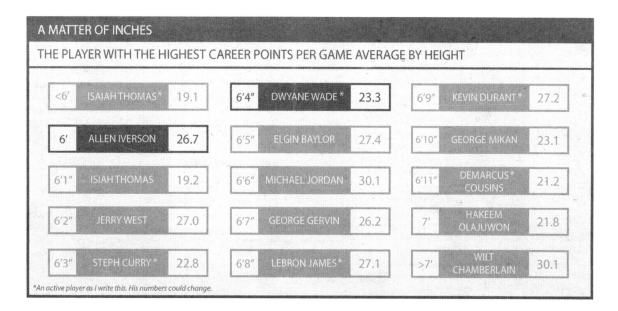

A MATTER OF INCHES

THE PLAYER WITH THE HIGHEST CAREER POINTS PER GAME AVERAGE BY HEIGHT

Height	Player	PPG	Height	Player	PPG	Height	Player	PPG
<6'	ISAIAH THOMAS*	19.1	6'4"	DWYANE WADE*	23.3	6'9"	KEVIN DURANT*	27.2
6'	ALLEN IVERSON	26.7	6'5"	ELGIN BAYLOR	27.4	6'10"	GEORGE MIKAN	23.1
6'1"	ISIAH THOMAS	19.2	6'6"	MICHAEL JORDAN	30.1	6'11"	DEMARCUS* COUSINS	21.2
6'2"	JERRY WEST	27.0	6'7"	GEORGE GERVIN	26.2	7'	HAKEEM OLAJUWON	21.8
6'3"	STEPH CURRY*	22.8	6'8"	LEBRON JAMES*	27.1	>7'	WILT CHAMBERLAIN	30.1

*An active player as I write this. His numbers could change.

ment for my own existence. But what I am, above all those things, or maybe with the confluence of all those things—what I am is the embodiment of the fusion of hip-hop culture and basketball culture.

Those two things had always been connected, always been intertwined, at least as far back as those two things being very popular are concerned. But when I showed up, it was like those two things got mushed together so perfectly and so thoroughly that they would never ever again be able to be pulled apart from one another. Dr. J did a version of that, M.J. did a version of that, and I did a version of that. That's where the line ends. Wade ain't in that line.

JUDGE: Is that it?

[Crowd laughs a tiny bit.]

IVERSON: There's also The Crossover.

[The courtroom falls into a hush.]

[There's a prolonged pause of silence.]

[Everyone trades glances.]

[Judge Bill Russell looks through his notes one last time.]

[He looks up at the litigants.]

JUDGE: Anything else?

IVERSON: I took fucking Eric Snow and Matt

Geiger to the Finals, your honor.

[The courtroom erupts in raucous applause and hollering.]

JUDGE [BANGING HIS GAVEL]: Order! Order in the court! I will have order in the court!

IVERSON: Sorry, your honor.

JUDGE: Upon hearing both sides, the rulings are as such: Mr. Wade, while you and your contributions to the style and evolution of the NBA and its storylines and its play are surely undervalued historically, you are not, in totality, more important and more deserving of Mr. Iverson's spot in the Important Players in NBA History, Ranked conversation than Mr. Iverson is, so I am finding in Mr. Iverson's favor there. Verdict for the defendant. He gets to remain the sixth most important player in the history of the NBA. You are welcome to have Dirk Nowitzki's spot in that conversation, if you'd like it, Mr. Wade.

Mr. Iverson, in your countersuit against Mr. Wade, wherein you are suing to gain ownership of Mr. Wade's 2013 NBA Championship, I also find in your favor. Verdict for the defendant, you are now a one-time NBA champion. Court is adjourned.

[Bangs gavel.]

A couple of summers ago, I was riding around Houston with two of my three sons in the car. My phone was connected to my radio and Eric B. & Rakim's *Paid in Full* was playing.

Paid in Full, which came out in 1987, is a great rap album to play when your children are with you because it's one of the greatest rap albums of all time, and history is important, so that's one reason. But it's also great to play because there aren't really many curse words in it. Were I to guess, it's the rap album my sons have heard more times than any other rap album, really. But so since I knew they'd heard it a bunch, I asked them if they knew who it was by. This is the conversation:

ME: Do you remember who this is?
BOY A: No.
ME: Eric B. and . . .
BOY A: . . . I don't know.
ME: It starts with an R.
BOY A: Oh! I know!
ME: Thank you!
BOY A: Eric B. and Rodney!

Rodney. Eric. B and *Rodney*. That's what he thought. *Paid in Full* is an especially influential album. It moved rap forward in an almost uncountable number of ways. And I feel like there's just no way possible that album would've happened if Rakim had gone by the name Rappin' Rodney or some shit like that. It had to be "Rakim." That album's history was such that it needed to be made by a person with a name as heavy and influential as that. It just wouldn't have come to fruition otherwise.

(I'm realizing as I type this out right now that this is a kind of clumsy manner in which to make my way into a book chapter where I just change the first or last name of an NBA player and then make up an alternate legacy for him, like if Michael Jordan had been born Morgan Jordan or if Bill Russell had been born Phil Russell, but the general premise is clumsy itself so it all makes sense.)

(I don't know.)

(Whatever.)

(Let's just start.)

MORGAN JORDAN: Morgan Jordan got a job as an accountant at a midlevel accounting firm when he was 23. He and his friends had a big laugh at the small party he had for his 10-year anniversary when the cake showed up and they realized the bakery had accidentally transposed the *g* and the *d* in his first and last names. "Hold on," one of his friends said. "Does that say, 'Congratulations, Mordan Jorgan!'?" It became a running joke until the day he retired, 19 years later. He really loved his job there. Retirement was hard for him.

LEBRON JONES: He still made it into the NBA because "LeBron" alone is a strong enough name to get him there. His time there, though, was considerably shorter and also considerably less spectacular. He was drafted in the second round. He played two seasons for the Pacers (3.2 ppg) before getting bounced down to their D-League affiliate, the Fort Wayne Mad Ants. He washed out from there before enjoying a fine career as a solid role player on a team in the Italian League.

WILT CHAMBERLORD: Wilt Chamberlord was an even more dominant basketball player than Wilt Chamberlain. Adding "-lord" to someone's last name is always an upgrade. Imagine Sylvester Stallonelord or Serena Williamslord.

PHIL RUSSELL: Phil Russell became an activist, though he was never able to stick to one mission for more than a couple weeks. "Save the Whales," he'd shout one week. "Save the Owls," he'd shout the next. "Save the Elephants," he'd shout after that. "Don't you ever do any activism that'll help humans?" his father asked snidely one day. Phil was really hurt by that statement. He quit activism shortly thereafter. "Look, son," his dad started one night after dinner, "I didn't mean for you to stop. I was having a bad day. I was frustrated about work. They're laying off people at the plant. It was a me thing more than a you thing." Phil never forgot that night. It meant a lot to him. He eventually organized a labor strike that saved a bunch of jobs at the plant.

JUAN STOCKTON: (I legit don't know how this one plays out.)

KEITH DURANT: Keith Durant stopped growing when he was 5'10". He became very active in his church's youth ministry. One time he wore his shirt untucked and some of the kids mentioned how cool it made him look. He always untucked his shirts after that.

ANTHONY DAVENPORT:[1] Anthony Davenport became a semi-known R&B singer. He really liked Anthony Hamilton a lot but he really didn't like when people would tell him that he reminded them of Anthony Hamilton, even though he definitely sounded a lot like Anthony Hamilton. His song "Sometimes Love Hurts, Sometimes It Doesn't" was played on the radio a few times.

KRIS PAUL: Kris Paul ended up getting a job as a teacher but he hates it.

CARMINE ANTHONY: Carmine Anthony drives a truck in Brooklyn for his cousin's company.

DEREK NOWITZKI: Derek Nowitzki spends at least 30 percent of his day each day wondering how his German parents settled on the name "Derek" for him. When he finally asks them about it, they tell him that they'd intended to name him "Drek Nowitizki" but the handwriting on the birth certificate made it look like "Derek" so they just went with that. "Is 'Drek' a German name?" he asked them. "Nope," they said. The whole situation was very confusing.

JOHN HARDEN: John Harden starred in a block of second-rate action movies, which he also wrote the scripts for. They went on to gain cult fame because of how goofy they were in the most serious way a thing can be goofy. (His character's name was John Harder.) His most famous film, *Death Hammer*, ended with a scene where a mafia boss had just been found not guilty of a bunch of crimes he very clearly was guilty of. As the mafia boss and his associates celebrated, the door to the courtroom was kicked open. It was John Harder. The mafia boss laughed. "You look at me and you see a criminal," he said. "But Lady Justice? She's blind." John Harder stood stoic for two seconds, then he took out two pistols and fired one shot from each at the mafia boss across the courtroom. The bullet from John Harder's left gun hit the mafia boss's right eye and the one from the right gun hit his left eye. "So are you," said John Harder.

RUSSELL EASTBROOK: Russell Eastbrook worked retail in a department store. He had over 2,000 followers on Instagram, a thing he managed to bring up in conversation way more than was necessary.[2]

JAKE GRIFFIN: Jake Griffin is completely nondescript. When he went missing two years ago, police asked his neighbors for details about Jake that could help them find him. Nobody knew anything about him. "I think he owned a cat, but I'm not sure," one lady said.

TOBY BRYANT: Toby Bryant managed The Container Store in Tigard, Oregon. He started working there after college. It wasn't the job he wanted, but he made the most of it. He had eyes on a corporate job with the company but never got the call-up. He was happy for the guy they chose over him for the job, though.

KYLE MCHALE: Kyle McHale and Kevin McHale ended up exactly the same because Kyle is exactly the same name as Kevin. If you know someone named Kyle then the next time you see him say, "What's up, Kevin?" and he won't even notice. Same for if you know a Kevin. Just say, "How was your day today, Kyle?" He'll tell you how his day was.

ALLEN IVERDAD: ("Iverdad" is so stupid.) (I apologize.)

---

1. This is Anthony Davis. All the rest of the names you should be able to figure out pretty easily.
2. FYI: The necessary number of times the number of followers you have on Instagram needs to be brought up in a conversation is zero.

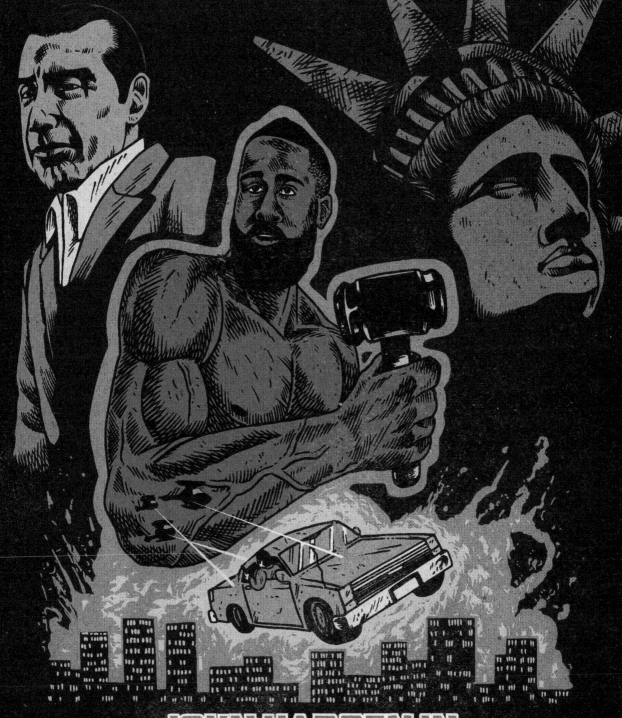

CARL MALONE: Carl Malone was super into woodworking. He was also super into putting Confederate flag bumper stickers on his truck. "They're not racist," he'd say whenever he was asked about it. "They celebrate history." All of his social media profiles were set to private.

CHARLES BERKLEY: Charles Berkley eventually became a college professor at the University of California, Berkeley. Anytime anyone asked him how work was going he would respond with, "Let's just say I wish I'd been born Charles Stanford." He always laughed when he said it. Nobody liked him that much.

BARRY BIRD: Barry Bird wore a sweater all the time. Even when it was hot outside he'd still wear a sweater. Whenever someone would ask him about it he'd say, "Sweaters are my thing. Everyone has a thing. Sweaters are mine." (Barrys are always super fucking weird. All of them. Barry Gibb, Barry Bonds, Barry Manilow, Barry Williams [the guy who played Greg on *The Brady Brunch*]. Barry White one time stole $30,000 in Cadillac tires, which is just about the weirdest thing to steal $30,000 of. Even fictional Barrys are weird. Barry Allen was the Flash, and superheroes are inherently weird. Steve Carell played a Barry in *Dinner for Schmucks*, and his character made dioramas out of stuffed mice. There's Barry Kripke from *The Big Bang Theory*, Barry from Pokémon, Barry from *High Fidelity*, Barry Zuckerkorn in *Arrested Development*.)

DANIAL LILLARD: Daniel Lillard worked at a Blockbuster all the way up until they started mass-closing stores in 2013. He spent a lot of time in the '90s trying to convince people that he was related to Matthew Lillard, then spent a lot of time in the '00s trying to convince people that he wasn't related to Matthew Lillard.

GEORGE PAUL: George Paul made it to the NBA same as Paul George, because guys who have a first name for a last name are generally pretty good at whatever it is they want to do, especially basketball (Michael Jordan, Kawhi Leonard, Tim Duncan, LeBron James, Julius Erving, Isaiah Thomas, Rick Barry, etc.).

TOM DUNCAN: Tom Duncan was a fighter pilot in the Navy. He had really nice hair even though he never bothered to try to have nice hair. Nobody ever said just his first name whenever they talked about him; they always used his full name. "Has anyone seen Tom Duncan?" "Goddamnit, you're gonna get us all killed, Tom Duncan." "We're ordering pizza, Tom Duncan. You want in?" Things like that.

JORGE "THE ICEMAN" GERVIN: He still became The Iceman, only instead of it being a basketball nickname, it's because he was the fourth biggest ice salesman in the Midwest. "Come on down to Jorge 'The Iceman' Gervin's Ice Depot," he proudly shouted in his commercials, which only ran regionally. "We've got more ice than we know what to do with," he'd say, as he took a big bite out of a piece of ice he was holding.

IRVIN "MAGIC" JOHNSON: The third biggest illusionist in the Midwest.

JULIUS "DR. J." EARVING: He became the second biggest furniture salesman in the Midwest. "Let the Doctor write you a prescription for cheap prices," he'd say in his commercials while wearing a long white coat. Then the camera would pan over to show Irvin "Magic" Johnson standing there. "Watch me make these high prices disappear," he'd say. Then the camera would pan over again and, oh fuck, it's Jorge "The Iceman" Gervin, too. "You're gonna need some ice to treat the burns from all these prices that are getting slashed," he'd say. All three started teaming up to form a supergroup to try and take down David "The Admiral" Robinsen, who'd two years earlier opened a superstore that specialized in ice, magic, and furniture and quickly became the most popular place to get any of the three.

Note: *You have to have read the previous chapter for this chapter's existence in a book about basketball to make any sense at all.*

In 2009, John Harden wrote, starred in, and directed *Death Hammer*, a low-grade action movie about John Harder, a hard-charging, steel-tough Detroit City cop with a mysterious past (no wife, no children, no siblings, no parents) and an affinity for physical force. Despite its 115-minute run time, almost no backstory was provided in *Death Hammer*. All we were told in it was (a) the mafia had moved in and taken over Detroit, and (b) Harder, in the middle of serving a three-week suspension for breaking a higher-ranking officer's arm while stopping him from beating on a suspect, was the only man capable of toppling their empire, which he did, piece by piece, always with violence and occasionally with a hammer.

It was an instant cult hit, and immediately catapulted the John Harder character up into the Who's the Greatest John in an Action Movie? conversation, alongside iconic figures like John Rambo (*Rambo*), John Matrix (*Commando*), John McClane (*Die Hard*), John Shaft (*Shaft*), and John Creasy (*Man on Fire*).[1]

In 2011, Warner Bros. greenlit a big-budget sequel. Seventeen months later, *Death Hammer 2: Hammergeddon* was released.

▶

The *Death Hammer 2: Hammergeddon* main cast:

John Harder: The film's protagonist. (See above for description.)

Xavier Gunz: John Harder's new partner. He's a rookie. He annoys Harder to no end, but by the end of the movie he's proven himself to be "a damn fine cop," which is how John Harder describes him to no one in particular as he sits and drinks alone in a bar one night.

Cassie Galloway: The nine-year-old daughter of the family that lives in the apartment across from John Harder. Every day when Harder comes home from work, he sees her outside playing on the stairs. "It's dangerous out here, Cassie," Harder always tells her. "You need to stay inside." "I'm not scared," she responds every time, smiling. "I know you'll protect me." It's their little routine. It's the only thing that makes Harder feel like maybe the world isn't rotting.

Demetrious Wolfe:[2] The main villain in the movie. He's the leader of The Blood Family, the ultravicious crime syndicate that moved in and took over in the years that followed John Harder ridding the city of the mafia. "The Blood Family kills for sport," explains Robert Webb, the Detroit chief of police, during an assignment briefing with the department. "They kill because they like the mess it makes. I worked a case a few years ago. This guy was in a club or some shit. Somebody bumped into him so he turned around and shoved the guy. Turned out, the guy was Demetrious Wolfe. Three days later the poor bastard's daughter opened a package she'd received in the mail. It was her father's arms. We've never seen evil like this before."

▶

John Harder was grizzled and ferocious in *Death Hammer*, and in *Death Hammer 2: Hammergeddon*, he's twice as grizzled and twice as ferocious, and I mean that figuratively, yes, but mainly I mean it literally, because hammers are rarely ever figurative. For example, in *DH*, Harder wore street-smart blue jeans. In *DH2:H*, he wears a pair of street-smart blue jeans over *another* pair of street-smart blue jeans. It's double fucking blue jeans.

A scene from *DH2:H*:

```
INT. JOHN HARDER'S CAR — NIGHT
John Harder and Xavier Gunz are on a
```

---

1. There are so many action-movie Johns. It's some sort of phenomenon. There's Johnny Ringo and John "Doc" Holliday (*Tombstone*), Johnny Lawrence (*The Karate Kid*), Johnny Utah (*Point Break*), John Triton (*The Marine*), John Carter (*John Carter*), John Smith (*Mr. & Mrs. Smith*), John "Hannibal" Smith (*The A-Team*), John Anderton (*Minority Report*), John Kimble (*Kindergarten Cop*), John Connor (pick a *Terminator*), etc.
2. My parents were visiting from San Antonio the week that I was writing this chapter. I was telling my dad about it one night and then the next morning he was like, "I have the perfect name for the villain of *Death Hammer 2*: Demetrious Wolfe." I was like, "Oh fuck. That is perfect." That's where the name comes from.

stakeout. They've been sitting in Harder's
car for more than three hours. Harder is
very focused. His eyes are burned onto a
building. He's hoping to see The Cannibal,
The Blood Family's most notorious hitman.
His plan is to tail The Cannibal back to
the Blood Family compound, which, to this
point, has remained hidden from the Detroit
police. Xavier, antsy, is fidgeting. While
searching for a snack he happens to notice
that Harder is wearing two pair of pants.

    XAVIER GUNZ
    Hold on. Are you wearing two pairs of
pants at the same time?

    JOHN HARDER
    (continues staring at the building)
    Yeah.

    XAVIER GUNZ
    Why?

    JOHN HARDER
    (still staring at the building)
    The criminals today are twice as tough
as they used to be.

    XAVIER GUNZ
    I . . . I don't think that's how it
works, man.

    JOHN HARDER
    (frustrated)
    Look, the guys we're going up against,
they're an army. We're fighting a fucking
army! And I'm just a man. One man. Like
every other man. Putting my pants on one
leg at a time. Two times in a row.

▶

Whereas *Death Hammer* focused mainly on the turbu-
lence of John Harder's life during his battle with the
mafia, *Death Hammer 2: Hammergeddon* contains flash-
back scenes that reveal his origin story, the most reve-
latory of which being that John Harder wasn't actually
born as "John Harder." He was born "Jonathan Hart," the
only child to a decent, hardworking family in Kentucky.

The story: When he was six years old, Jonathan
Hart's mother was killed in a drive-by shooting that was
never solved (it haunts him to this day). After the funeral,
he legally changed his name from Jonathan Hart to
John Hard, a literal representation of the philosophical
way he'd been changed by the trauma. Two years later,
John's father, struggling to raise John on his own, abandoned him in a grocery store parking lot. "I think you're
going to be better off on your own, John," his father told
him. "Dad, no. Please. I can't lose you, too," John said,
whimpering. "I'm sorry," his father said, eyes watery,
heart in pieces. "I just can't. You remind me too much
of her." Then he drove away. John watched his dad as
he disappeared into the night. He didn't cry, though. He
decided right then he would never cry again.

The next morning, he hitchhiked a ride to the DMV,
where he once again legally changed his name.

"Why the name change, Mr. Hard?" the county clerk
asked as he prepared to stamp eight-year-old John's
paperwork official. "It's just two little letters," the clerk
said with a smile. "And where are your parents, anyway?" John took the toothpick he was chewing out of
his mouth. "Just stamp the fucking paper," he said, then
he flicked the toothpick at the clerk.

John Harder was born.

▶

Another scene in *DH2:H*:

    INT. JOHN HARDER'S APT. - DAY
    Xavier Gunz is waiting in John Harder's
living room. He's looking around at the
place, which is surprisingly well decorated.

    XAVIER GUNZ
    (shouting to John, who is in the bedroom
getting ready)
    Ayo, John!

    JOHN HARDER
    (no response)

    XAVIER GUNZ
    (still shouting, still looking around)
    Ain't you supposed to be the hammer guy
or some shit like that?

    JOHN HARDER
    (no response)

XAVIER GUNZ
(still shouting, still looking around)
You're the hammer guy, right? So where are all your hammers? We been partners for four months and I ain't seen one single hammer.

(John Harder emerges from the bedroom.)

JOHN HARDER
Everything is a hammer if you swing it hard enough.

▶

Other titles the movie studio considered before settling on *Death Hammer 2: Hammergeddon*:
* *Death Hammer 2: The Awakening* (John Harder takes on apocalypse mummies)
* *Death Hammer 2: Chamber of Torture* (John Harder fights the bad guy from *Saw*)
* *Death Hammer 2: Gladiator X* (John Harder follows a crime lord back in time to the gladiator days of Rome)
* *Death Hammer 2: Pain Matrix* (John Harder just kicks the shit out of a bunch of dudes who look like Keanu Reeves)
* *Death Hammer 2: Ominous Calling* (While working part-time as a telemarketer, John Harder discovers a corrupt politician's plan to blow up City Hall)
* *Death Hammer 2: She's the One* (This was from the brief period where *DH2* was pitched as a romantic comedy)
* *Death Hammer 2: Furious Calculations* (John Harder fights guys who use math to kill people)
* *Death Hammer 2: Cosmic Void* (John Harder in space)

▶

A final scene from *DH2:H:*

EXT. THE BLOOD FAMILY COMPOUND - DAY
Two nameless henchmen are outside on sentry duty. They're both watching for John Harder, who's already torn through half of The Blood Family.

HENCHMAN #1
(lights up a cigarette, takes a drag)
I can't believe we drew this bullshit detail again.

HENCHMAN #2
(only half-concerned with HENCHMAN #1's words)
You shouldn't smoke.

HENCHMAN #1
(dismayed)
What?

HENCHMAN #2
You shouldn't smoke. It's bad for you.

HENCHMAN #1
Are you serious right now?

HENCHMAN #2
I'm just saying, with as much as we know about smoking now, you'd think you'd know better.

HENCHMAN #1
(exasperated)
I would have to smoke a pack a day every day for the next 10 years for someth—

(There's a sound behind them. Startled, they both turn around. John Harder is standing there. He's got a shotgun aimed at Henchman #1.)

JOHN HARDER
10 years? Let me save you the trouble.

(Harder pulls the trigger. *Bang!* The close-range shot explodes Henchman #1's chest. Harder turns the gun to Henchman #2.)

HENCHMAN #2
(terrified)
No, no, wait, wait, wait!

(*Bang!* Harder explodes Henchman #2's chest with a shot as well.)

JOHN HARDER
Secondhand smoke kills, too.

▶

The final 20 minutes of *Death Hammer 2: Hammergeddon* are "as tumultuous and heart-attack-inducing a stretch of film as has ever been produced," says Wesley Morris of the *New York Times*. "I couldn't take my eyes off the screen, but I also couldn't stop crying. Bravo to everyone involved. Bra-vo. I am so excited to watch John Harden win the Oscar for Best Actor this year, and even more excited to watch John Harder enter the annals of movie character lore."

I don't want to explain to you all of the things that happened during that final 20-minute stretch, so let me just tell you four parts:

1. Two big reveals end up happening. The first big reveal: Xavier Gunz is going to be a father. He and his wife take Harder out to dinner and they tell him and it's this very charming scene. Gunz tells Harder that he's taking a desk job because it's safer. Harder is upset, which is surprising because he didn't even realize he liked Gunz. He feels better, though, when Gunz tells him he wants Harder to be the godfather to his kid, an offer he happily accepts. The second big reveal is that it turns out that The Blood Family was responsible for the death of John Harder's mother all those years ago (!!!).

2. There are hammers in those last 20 minutes. So many fucking hammers. It's a gigantic hammer fight. Imagine all the hammers you can think of. Now double it. Now double it again. Now triple that. That's still not enough hammers.

3. The fight between John Harder and Demetrious Wolfe is, in a word, transcendent. It's devastating. It's masterfully nihilistic. It is so, so, so hard to watch because of how horrific and graphic it is, but it's also beautiful and poetic in this very satisfying way. It ends with John Harder barely alive and Demetrious Wolfe all the way dead, his head caved into his neck from hammer blows.

4. The last shot of the movie is John Harder, bloodied and gouged and broken but victorious, walking up the steps to his apartment. He can barely walk, it's so painful. He can barely breathe, it's so painful. But he's victorious. And he feels so good—better than he has in a long, long time. He takes a second; he sits on the steps. He takes a big, pained breath. He reaches in his pocket. He takes out his wallet. Another big, pained breath. He fishes something out of the wallet. The camera zooms in up and around him and over his back to show what he's looking at.

It's an old, tattered picture. The camera zooms in tighter. It's of him and his mom. The camera slowly pans up to his face. He's crying. It's the first time he's cried since she died. "We finally have peace now, Mom," he says. "Finally."

He gathers all of his remaining strength and uses it to pull himself up into a standing position. He walks the final few steps to his apartment, though really it's more like he staggers the final few steps to his apartment. There are two bags at his door, one large, one smaller. They both have ribbons and bows on them, and one of them has a card on it. Harder smirks. Gunz told him at that dinner he was getting him a thank-you present. Harder protested. "That kid never listens," Harder says, pretending to be disappointed, but happy to know that Gunz really does care about him.

Harder leans over, picks up the card. He reads it:

```
With love,
—D. Wolfe
```

His eyes widen. Everything stops moving. Demetrious mailed them to John before their fight. The card falls slowly from his hand to the ground. The camera moves down to the bags. Music builds in the background. "No," Harder says. "Please, no." He pulls on the ribbon of the first bag, and its contents spill out onto the floor. It's Xavier Gunz's dead body.

"Noooooooooooooooo!" he screams. It's a painful scream, and he breaks down into a teary mess, cradling Gunz. It's awful. It's ruinous. Then he stops. And he looks over at the smaller bag. He's can't move. Because he already knows.

He reaches for it. His hand is shaking. The entire universe is vibrating. He grabs the end of the ribbon. He pulls on it. The bag falls over as it opens.

It's Cassie Galloway's body.

She's dead.

John Harder is dead, too.

He's John Hardest now.

IF 1997 KARL MALONE
AND A BEAR SWAPPED PLACES FOR
A SEASON, WHO WOULD BE
MORE SUCCESSFUL?

Here's the play: Let's take a bear from a forest, and then let's take Karl Malone from the 1997 Utah Jazz, and then let's put the bear in Karl's place and Karl in the bear's place. That's the setup; a straight-up swap. And the thing we're trying to figure out here is: Who has a better outing that season after the swap, the bear playing power forward for the 1997 Utah Jazz or Karl Malone living as a bear in the forest?

Let's flesh out the specifics here first, of which there are really only two that need to be addressed.

First, we should sort out the type of bear that's going to trade places with Karl because that will affect things greatly. There are a bunch of different types of bears to choose from. We could use a polar bear. We could use a koala bear. There's a brown bear. There's a black bear. There's a Build-A-Bear (the second-most gentle of all bears). There are dozens of different Care Bears (Bedtime Bear is the first most gentle). There's the golfer Jack Nicklaus, who was nicknamed "The Golden Bear." There are the Chicago Bears. There's more and more and more and more. In this particular case, let's go with the black bear. That one seems to make the most sense since it's indigenous to Utah and also because it has a broad enough weight and height span that we could reasonably find one about the same size as Karl, who, at his peak, was 6'9" and somewhere near 256 pounds of carved oak.

Second, we should sort out the dynamics of the situation. Karl Malone has a long and recorded history of outdoorsmanship, so his side of the equation is fine. We can just take him and drop him into the forest and there you go. That's a very ordinary thing. The bear side is a little trickier, so let's just consider these things to be truths going forward so as to make talking about the situation as easy as possible:

- Once the bear gets placed on the team, nobody finds it weird or strange. It's seen by everyone as completely normal. The bear walks into the locker room and the situation is treated no differently than if John Stockton or Antoine Carr had walked into the locker room.
- The bear is anthropomorphic like a Ninja Turtle. He has many human qualities, including being able to talk and being able to understand the fundamental tenets of executing the pick and roll. He does some bear-like things occasionally (he regularly snacks on honey, things like that), but it's almost always seen as charming or eccentric.
- If the bear ever acts aggressively, it's only in a very human manner. For example, one time Karl Malone elbowed David Robinson in the back of the head and knocked him unconscious. Another time he elbowed Isiah Thomas and opened up a gash on him that required 40 stitches to close. The bear would do things like that. He would not, however, attempt to eat anyone or claw anyone across the throat.

With those things in place, all we have to do is measure the bear and Karl up against each other in a few categories. But first, a little background information about each.

▶

Karl Malone is one of the best, most powerful, most durable basketball players of all time. Here is a list of some of his more impressive stats:

- He played in 1,169 games during his NBA career, 193 of which were in the playoffs.
- He played 54,852 minutes of actual game time. That puts him second all-time in the history of the NBA.[1] (For perspective: That's enough time to watch *Pitch Perfect* 489 times.[2])
- He played 2,800+ minutes in a season 16 different times. Nobody else has ever done that (or likely will ever do it).

---

1. First place is Kareem Abdul-Jabbar, who played 57,446.
2. I feel like more things should be kept track of by using *Pitch Perfect* as the measurement device. Imagine you get arrested and the judge is like, "You have to serve two years in prison." That's awful and devastating. But imagine you get arrested and the judge is like, "You have to serve 9,385 *Pitch Perfect*s." That makes it way better.

- He missed a total of 10 games[3] in 18 seasons with the Jazz. That means he played in 99.3 percent of the games.
- He averaged 20 or more points per game 17 times over his career. That puts him tied for first all-time with Kareem Abdul-Jabbar.
- He played in 80+ games in 17 different seasons over his career. That puts him first all-time.
- He was an All-Star 14 times.
- He was the league MVP twice.
- He shot more free throws than anyone else and also gobbled up more defensive rebounds than everyone in NBA history except Kevin Garnett.
- He performed a Diamond Cutter on Dennis Rodman during a wrestling match at WCW's Bash at the Beach.

A bear is one of the best, most powerful, most durable animals of all time. Here is a list of some of a bear's more impressive stats:

- Very good swimmer.
- Very good climber.
- Can run up to 30 miles per hour.
- It's a fucking bear.

▶

The Utah Division of Wildlife Resources has an entire section on its site about bears, the most interesting part of which is about staying safe because "Utah's mountains and forests are home to thousands of black bears." My favorite parts:

"Go with a group, if possible."

This one made me sad to read because I realized that nobody I am friends with in real life would be of any help at all were we out in the forest camping together as a group and a bear ran up on us. That situation would very quickly turn from a Quality Time Bonding Experience to an Every Man For Himself kind of setup. Worse still, I don't even think it'd be, like, "Okay, there's a bear here now so let's just all run away and whoever the bear ends up catching is who the

bear ends up catching." There would be very deliberate sabotage in play, I'm sure. I mean, look, if it's between me and you to see who a bear eats, I'm pretty sure my first move there is to try and shove you by your face toward the bear in hopes that he grabs you first so I can get away. I promise I'll make sure to say something very nice about you and your heroism at your closed-casket funeral, though.

"Stay away from animal carcasses."

This seems like advice that would be applicable in all situations, not just bear-based ones.

"Keep kids in the center of the group."

Here's the thing: Kids are (probably) made of the softest meat, right? So my guess is they're the ones the bears are most excited about catching. So I say put the kids on the outside of the group, because the only thing worse than being attacked by a bear is being attacked by a bear who didn't even really want to attack you.

"Place bear unwelcome mats (wood planks with nails or screws protruding) in front of doors or windows."

This seems like an aggressively rude move.

"Get one or more dogs."

R.I.P. one or more dogs.

"Turn on garden hoses or sprinklers."

Just a guess, but I don't think spritzing an 800-pound bear with a hose is going to stop him.

"Always fight back. And never give up! People have successfully defended themselves with almost anything: rocks, sticks, backpacks, water bottles, and even their hands and feet."

Imagine you're the guy who defended yourself from a bear with a water bottle, and so you get to live on that story forever. Your toughness is unquestionable. You're a neighborhood hero. You get featured on the news. It's great. But then, like, two years later some new family moves in at the end of your street. And, turns out, the dad of that family was attacked by a bear once, too. So you go to talk to him about it. And you're like, "What kind of water bottle did you use to defend yourself?"

---

3. That's enough to watch *Pitch Perfect* a little more than four times uninterrupted.

And he's like, "Water bottle?" and then he laughs. Then he picks up his hands and they're covered in scars and he takes off his shoes and his feet are covered in scars, too. He's the guy who fucking boxed a bear and karate kicked a bear.

▶

There are five categories we need to look at to figure out who has the better season after the swap.

WHO IS MORE ADAPTABLE? Black bears are the most common bears in the United States. They're found all over the country. Per the Defenders of Wildlife website, "Black bears are extremely adaptable and show a great variation in habitat type." Karl Malone was only found in Utah (when he played for the Jazz from 1985 to 2002) and in LA (when he played for the Lakers in 2003). This category goes to the bear.

COULD KARL MALONE EVEN SURVIVE IN THE WILD? There's a show on TV that I watch occasionally called *Naked and Afraid* (and I'm legit in real time realizing right now as I type this that that sounds a lot like the title of a very specific kind of pornography). The premise of the show is the producers take a man and a woman and they drop them off in some remote area with no food and no shoes and no clothes and so on.[4] The people have to survive there for 21 days, and if they do that then they win. Usually, by day four both people are a wreck. They're hungry and thirsty and bitten up by bugs and are just generally miserable. Every few episodes, the contestants become so overcome with adversity that one of them will just quit and ask to be taken home. I do not fault them—I was stung by a wasp once in 2014 and called in sick to work three days in a row—but that doesn't make the truth any less true: Living in the wild is rough. It is not for the soft.

In most other cases, I'd argue against an NBA player surviving in the wilderness for seven months. Karl

Malone, though, is a unique case. He was, by his own explanation, raised to exist in the wild, and I don't mean that as a stylistic statement. I mean it literally. And the most straightforward example of that is him telling *Outdoor Life* in 2009, "When I was growing up in northern Louisiana, we didn't have much, but [my mother and grandfather] taught me how to survive on what I could catch or kill."[5] So there's that. Plus, you also have to factor in his incredible durability because that would prove exceptionally valuable here. So Karl scores a Yes here. Karl Malone could absolutely survive in the wild.

COULD A BLACK BEAR REPLICATE KARL MALONE'S PRODUCTION DURING THE 1997 SEASON? Karl played in all 82 games. He shot 55 percent from the field and 75 percent from the free throw line. He averaged 9.9 rebounds per game, 4.5 assists per game, and 27.4 points per game, which is fantastic. While I have no doubts that a bear could be a serviceable NBA player, what with his incredible size and overwhelming strength and also admirable intelligence and unique skillset, I suspect he would play a much more brutish brand of basketball. Don't take that to mean Karl Malone was a physically dainty player, because he absolutely was not. I just think a bear is going to play way more like an Anthony Mason than a Malone, who, in addition to his feats of physical strength, possessed no small amount of grace in his movements. So the bear scores a No here. He would not be able to replicate Malone's regular season production.

COULD A BEAR RUN THE PICK AND ROLL WITH JOHN STOCKTON BETTER THAN KARL MALONE COULD EAT SUCCULENT GREENS? This would be central. Karl Malone running the pick and roll with Stockton destroyed more defenses than I'm willing to even try to count. It'd be an absolutely essential thing for the bear to be able to do. And I think he'd be able to do it. This is the part of the traits section

---

4. Each person is actually allowed to bring a single item. Mostly they bring a knife or a fire starter or something like that. I always wonder if they're allowed to bring shoes as their one item. That would absolutely be my first pick.
5. My favorite quote about Karl Malone and hunting actually came from Charles Barkley. It's from a *SportsCentury* documentary ESPN did on Malone. Barkley said, "He'd always call me to go hunting. And I'd say, 'What are you going hunting for?' He's like, 'Mountain lion and black bear.' I'm like, 'What about squirrel and deer or something like that?'"

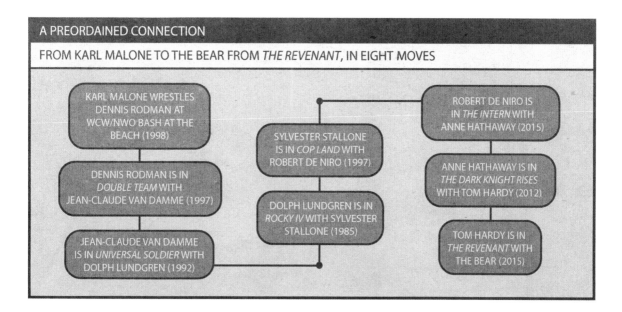

A PREORDAINED CONNECTION

FROM KARL MALONE TO THE BEAR FROM *THE REVENANT*, IN EIGHT MOVES

KARL MALONE WRESTLES DENNIS RODMAN AT WCW/NWO BASH AT THE BEACH (1998)

DENNIS RODMAN IS IN *DOUBLE TEAM* WITH JEAN-CLAUDE VAN DAMME (1997)

JEAN-CLAUDE VAN DAMME IS IN *UNIVERSAL SOLDIER* WITH DOLPH LUNDGREN (1992)

SYLVESTER STALLONE IS IN *COP LAND* WITH ROBERT DE NIRO (1997)

DOLPH LUNDGREN IS IN *ROCKY IV* WITH SYLVESTER STALLONE (1985)

ROBERT DE NIRO IS IN *THE INTERN* WITH ANNE HATHAWAY (2015)

ANNE HATHAWAY IS IN *THE DARK KNIGHT RISES* WITH TOM HARDY (2012)

TOM HARDY IS IN *THE REVENANT* WITH THE BEAR (2015)

about black bears at Bear.org that jumps out at me: "One of the more intelligent mammals. Navigation ability superior to humans. Excellent long-term memory. Can generalize to the simple concept level." His navigation ability would allow him to make his way through whenever teams tried to jam the pick and roll. His excellent long-term memory would help him remember how and where the most effective places to attack the defense were. And his ability to generalize to the simple concept would for sure let him master the pick and roll, what with there only being two steps to it (1. Pick. 2. Roll). So the bear would be fine in Malone's spot.

Measure that against Malone's willingness to subsist on a diet of plants and nuts and fruits and insects, which I assume would be low (he just seems like he's super into steaks and shit). Bears need all those specific types of food to help build up their body fat. Malone had a body fat percentage of 4.8 following his second MVP season (1999). That wouldn't be near enough for him to survive hibernation. This category goes to the bear.

WHO DOES THE SCHEDULE FAVOR? Karl Malone, a skilled hunter and survivalist, would likely maintain a very even wilderness performance, no matter the day or week or month. The bear, on the other hand, has a built-in two-part schedule that coincides almost perfectly with the NBA's regular season and postseason. According to Bear.org, bears typically hibernate from September or October until April. The NBA regular season runs from October to April. I think this means that the bear would be mostly uninspired during those months, which would start to lean this category toward Malone, as he was dominant during those months. The other side of that argument, though, is that the mating season for bears goes from May to June, which is when the later stages of the NBA playoffs are, including the NBA Finals. A bear who wants to mate would be an especially ferocious competitor. A super squinty way to look at this is that Karl was great in the regular season and less than great in the postseason (his Jazz reached the Finals twice and lost both times), while a bear would be less than great in the regular season and monstrous later in the playoffs. That's the one I want on my team.

The bear wins this category, which means he also wins the competition (three categories to two).

The bear would have a better season as 1997 Karl Malone than 1997 Karl Malone would have as a bear.

WHAT IF NICK ANDERSON

At the end of the 1995 NBA Finals, Jim Gray interviewed Nick Anderson, shooting guard for the Orlando Magic. The Magic had lost the series four games to no games to the Houston Rockets, who'd repeated as champions, and so Gray wanted to ask Anderson about that, but really he just wanted to ask him about the end of Game 1.

The championship series that year was mostly an unremarkable one, save for the first game, which remains an all-timer. The Magic, overwhelmingly talented[1] but still very young,[2] built up an early 20-point lead at home, only to give it all back later in the game. The fourth quarter was taut and perfect; no team had a lead larger than four points in the final six minutes. The Rockets's Kenny Smith hit a very contested three with just under two seconds to go, which sent the game into overtime, and then Hakeem Olajuwon won it in overtime by tipping in an errant Clyde Drexler layup with 0.3 second left. All most anyone remembers from that game, though, is what happened right before Kenny Smith's three.

The Magic had the ball and were up three with 55 seconds left in the game. After a bit of stalling, Penny Hardaway drove into the lane and missed a layup. Horace Grant grabbed the offensive rebound and dribbled it out so the Magic offense could reset itself (37 seconds left). The Magic ran down the clock a bit more, then Brian Shaw fired up a three-pointer. It missed. But Grant, banging around in the paint again, got just enough of his fingers on it to deflect the ball over to Penny (20 seconds left). Penny threw it out to Nick Anderson, and then Anderson and Brian Shaw and Penny played keep-away with the ball until the Rockets were able to foul Nick Anderson a few seconds later, sending him to the line (10.5 seconds left).

At that exact moment, the Magic had a game win probability of 98.5 percent.[3] Then all of the trees and birds and humans and animals in Orlando died.

Anderson short-armed his first free throw. It clanked off the front of the rim. The second free throw was even shorter, ricocheting back toward Anderson. After the ball was batted around some, Anderson managed to secure the rebound and was fouled again (7.9 seconds left). And at that exact moment, the Magic had an overall game win probability of 99.0 percent. "How can you expect to win an NBA Finals game if you . . . can't get a rebound after a really tough player like Nick Anderson misses two free throws?" Bill Walton, a large set of teeth acting as a commentator for the game, asked exasperatedly.

Nick Anderson settled in to shoot his third free throw. This time it was too long, and when the camera zoomed in on his face after the miss he was fake-smiling to himself and everyone knew right then that not only was there no chance he was going to make that next free throw, but that we were all watching a potentially legacy-altering, history-shaping meltdown, and that's exactly what happened. Anderson missed that fourth free throw, the Rockets (fucking finally) rebounded the ball, Kenny hit his three, Hakeem hit his game-winner, and the Magic never recovered. They lost the series, Shaq signed with LA 13 months later, Penny's knees turned into bubble gum, and everything went dark.[4]

But so that's why when Jim Gray was interviewing Nick Anderson after the Magic lost the series;[5] he wanted to ask him about those free throws. He said, "Would it have been a difference had you made one of those free throws back in Game 1?" And Nick, who, for my money, only ever handled the situation like a hero, stood right there and considered the notion and then said, "Yeah, maybe it would've. But, uh, yeah, I can't think about that. That's in the past. Can't change what happened."[6]

---

1. Shaq, Penny Hardaway, Nick Anderson, Dennis Scott, Horace Grant, Brian Shaw.
2. I mean this as far as the players go (Shaq and Penny, the team's two best players, were both 23), but also in relation to the franchise (it was only in its sixth season of existence).
3. This is according to Inpredictable.com's Win Probability Calculator.
4. Following the 1996 season, the Magic didn't make it out of the first round of the playoffs for 12 years, and five of those years they didn't make the playoffs at all.
5. A neat little note: Nick Anderson was actually the very first pick that the Orlando Magic ever made. They drafted him 11th in 1989.

Here's the thing of it, though: We *can* change what happened. At least, we can change it here anyway. So let's do that. What happens—*how are things different*—if Nick Anderson makes those free throws? How is the NBA different after that?

What happens in the Finals that year?
The Magic players talked a bunch later about how that Game 1 loss sapped them of their confidence. So let's assume the inverse is true, too: Let's say that Nick hit at least one of those first two free throws, and so they won that game, and so then they'd have really been feeling themselves. Then someone would've leaned in their ear and told them that home teams who win Game 1 of a best-of-seven series end up winning the series 85 percent of the time, and so then they'd have been feeling themselves even further. So then they're feeling unbeatable, which is what they become. They end up winning the Finals 4–2. (I can't say it'd have been a 4–0 sweep in their favor because even in a dream imaginary scenario with all of the knobs and levers turned to your favor, 1995 Hakeem Olajuwon is still going to beat you twice.) So the Magic win the 1995 championship. And if that happens, then the whole NBA as we know it today gets turned upside down.

Like what? How do you mean?
Well, there's an ESPN documentary that came out in 2016 called *This Magic Moment* that was all about how the Magic came within earshot of becoming a dynasty before watching it wash away.[7] As the credits roll at the end of it, Shaq and Penny are sitting in deck chairs by a pool talking about things. During their conversation, Shaq says that if Orlando had won a title, he'd have never left. So there's that: Shaq stays with the Magic.

And since we're rewriting pieces of history, let's go ahead right now and erase the parts where injuries stole Penny Hardaway's career. That means you've got a young and healthy Penny Hardaway, an unbroken Nick Anderson, an unflappable role player in Dennis Scott, a seasoned winner in Horace Grant, a wonderful basketball mind in Brian Shaw, and a not-yet-to-his-prime-but-already-dominant Shaq. And those guys all get to stay together for several years after having won a championship? Shit, man. It's murder for the rest of the '90s and early 2000s.

Yeah, but what about Jordan? He was all the way back from his retirement by then. And the Bulls swept the Magic out of the playoffs in 1996 in the version of the NBA that we know as true today. What happens there?
That's fair. But if the Magic didn't lose to the Rockets in 1995, I can't say for certain that the Bulls would've beaten the Magic in 1996. I'm just not quite sure how that series plays out, especially when you consider that the Magic knocked the Bulls out of the playoffs in 1995.[8] And, I mean, sure, that was the first year Jordan was back from his retirement and he only played in 17 games before the playoffs started so you can argue that he was not the fully formed Jordan that nobody could beat, but it still happened. We can't just ignore that. But, okay, let's go conservative: Let's say the Bulls did beat the Magic in 1996. They probably would've beaten the Magic in 1997, too (the Bulls were so good in 1996 that when they went 69–13 in 1997 it was somehow a regression). But let's at the very least give the 1998 championship to the Magic. That opens up a whole bunch of interesting doors, too.

---

6. By two seasons after the missed free throws, Anderson's free throw percentage plummeted from 70 percent to 40 percent.
7. How unlikely was the formation of that championship-caliber Magic team? The Magic not only had to win the number-one overall pick two years in a row to get there (they drafted Shaq with the 1992 pick; they had a 1/66 chance of winning the number-one pick in 1993), but they also had to be lucky/smart/dumb enough to trade Chris Webber, who was their number-one pick in 1993, for Penny Hardaway (and three first-round draft picks).
8. The defining play of that series also happened in Game 1 and also involved Nick Anderson, though his role in it was philosophically the exact opposite of his role in the Rockets Game 1 disaster: The Magic were down by one with 18 seconds left in Game 1. Anderson, guarding Michael Jordan, was able to poke the ball away from him, leading to a game-winning basket from Horace Grant.

Like what?

Well, let's jump back a bit first. So the Magic win the 1995 championship. Shaq falls in love with the way being a champion paints him, and so all of his side projects (the rapping, the acting, etc.) all get pushed aside as he tries to chase down more rings. That means that the leading role in *Kazaam* is open. And Hakeem, distraught from having lost the 1995 title and looking to boost his own signal, picks it up. So, boom, behind Shaq staying in Orlando, there's the next major thing that happens: We get Hakeem Olajuwon as Kazaam.

WHAT?

I know, right?

What else?

If the Magic get the 1998 championship then that means Jordan only gets five championships instead of six, and so all of a sudden his accepted status as the Greatest of All Time starts to get a little bit grayer.

What about Kobe? We're basically replacing Kobe and Shaq with Penny and Shaq. What happens to Kobe?

There are probably two ways that that situation plays out.

The first is that Vlade Divac, who the Lakers traded to Charlotte to get the rights to Kobe, decides he doesn't want to play in Charlotte. In January of 2016 he said he'd contemplated retiring when his agent told him that the Lakers had traded him to Charlotte. And so if that had happened, then: (1) Kobe plays for Charlotte,[9] which would've been a real disaster.[10] Kobe probably ends up with a career closer to, say, Tracy McGrady's or Vince Carter's. (2) We don't get the 2002 Sacramento Kings (Webber, Vlade, Bibby, Peja, Doug, Jackson), and let me tell you something: You can get fucked if you think I want to live in any branch of reality that doesn't include the 2002 Kings.

The second is that Vlade says, "Okay, fine, I'll play in Charlotte," then goes to Charlotte.[11] The Lakers get Kobe but they don't get Shaq, and so that means Kobe definitely isn't finishing with five rings. Here's the cool thing, though: Rather than teaming up with Pau, Kobe calls Kevin Garnett in the summer of 2007, tells him

he's sick of losing and also tired of seeing KG lose, and convinces KG to make the move to LA instead of Boston for the 2008 season, so we get at least three seasons of Kobe and KG together, which is like if you put a sun right next to another sun. That's good for two championships, maybe three. Of course, just as likely is that the Kobe/KG partnership turns toxic real quick and ends with zero titles for them and so then Kobe becomes Carmelo before Carmelo becomes Carmelo.

And all of that means the championships for 2000, 2001, and 2002 are definitely all up for grabs since the Shaq/Kobe Lakers aren't around to win them, and the 2008, 2009, and 2010 championships are possibly also up for grabs since the Celtics don't have Garnett to help them win in 2008 and Kobe doesn't have Pau to help him win in 2009 and 2010.

Who gets those?

The Magic beat the Trail Blazers 4–2 to win the 2000 championship, giving Shaq and Penny their third title together. (They cap off an amazing Game 7 fourth-quarter comeback when Penny throws an alley-oop to Shaq to put the game out of reach.) The Spurs beat the Sixers 4–3 to win the 2001 championship. (Allen Iverson steps over Avery Johnson.) The Kings beat the Nets 4–0 to win the 2002 championship. (Vlade Divac gives an all-world petty postgame interview where he talks about how none of anything would've been possible without the Lakers trading him to the Hornets for Kobe.) The Pistons beat the Pelicans 4–2 in 2008 (the lowest-rated Finals in history). The Magic (this time with Dwight Howard) beat the Nuggets 4–3 in 2009 (people start to talk about how Dwight vs. Carmelo is the next big rivalry because people are stupid). And the Cavs (!) beat the Lakers (!!) 4–3 (!!!) in 2010 (the highest-rated Finals in history).

What happened with Hakeem's acting career, though? It seems like you didn't talk enough about that. Were there any ripple effects from that?

With Hakeem at the lead, *Kazaam*, regarded now as *basura*, is an international smash success. Everyone loves it. *Kazaam 2: This Time Call Me Hazaam* is an even bigger hit. It sets into motion a two-year period where movie studios plug in basically any NBA player they can get into any movie that'll let them. We get *Titanic* starring Kate Winslet and Jason "White Chocolate" Williams (the scene where Jack and Rose go to a party in the bowels of the ship and dance gets replaced with a scene where Jack and Rose go to a 2-on-2 tournament in the bowels of the ship; Jack gives an Oscar-worthy speech to Rose where he delivers the iconic line "I'm throwing you a no-look pass with my heart, Rose. Will you catch it?"), *Good Will Hunting* starring Robin Williams and Latrell Sprewell (there's still the scene where Robin Williams's character chokes Matt Damon's character, except this time it's Williams choking Latrell and so everyone gets a big kick out of that), *Boogie Nights* starring Patrick Ewing (Pat Riley gets used for Burt Reynolds's part), *The Devil's Advocate* starring Al Pacino and Shawn Bradley (a total box-office bomb because Bradley decides halfway into the movie that Pacino actually really is the devil and so he refuses to film any of the remaining scenes with him so half of the movie is CGI'd), *Face/Off* starring Keith Van Horn and Kerry Kittles (shoutout the Jason Kidd–era Nets), *Armageddon* starring Reggie Miller, *American History X* starring Steve Kerr (Kerr gives a rousing performance as a reformed Nazi), and *Rush Hour* starring Shawn Kemp and Dennis Rodman (shamed by everyone because Rodman decides he's only doing the movie if the studio lets him do so in yellowface, which it does).

Holdonasecond. You're telling me that if Nick Anderson had made one of those four free throws, we'd have all ended up seeing Patrick Ewing's dick? That's what you're telling me?

That's exactly what I'm telling you.

Is that a good thing or a bad thing?

I suppose that depends entirely on whether or not you are pro–Patrick Ewing's dick or anti–Patrick Ewing's dick.

That's fair. So what's the tally? Where are we right now in this Nick-Anderson-Makes-A-Free-Throw version of the universe?

To this point: The Magic win the 1995 championship; Shaq stays in Orlando and he and Penny win three titles together; Hakeem Olajuwon does *Kazaam*, which vibrates out into Hollywood massively; Jordan wins five titles instead of six and his legacy isn't as guaranteed as it is now;[12] Kobe possibly wins two titles instead of five but probably actually wins zero; Duncan wins six titles instead of five; Chris Webber gets a ring (hooray!) but so does Dwight Howard (boooooooo!); Carmelo makes a Finals; we get LeBron vs. Kobe in an NBA Finals Game 7, which LeBron wins, which means he never goes to Miami; and everyone sees Patrick Ewing's dick. All if Nick Anderson makes one of those free throws.

---

9. Or the Nets. The Nets really wanted to draft him with the eighth pick that year. They were warned against it since he wanted to get to Los Angeles once he heard Jerry West wanted to trade Vlade for the pick to get him. The Lakers don't trade Vlade if Shaq never leaves Orlando, though.

10. Their roster that season: Rafael Addison, Muggsy Bogues, Scott Burrell, *Tom Chambers*, Dell Curry, Tony Delk, *Jamie Feick*, *Matt Geiger*, Anthony Goldwire, *Eric Leckner*, Anthony Mason, Ricky Pierce, Glen Rice, Malik Rose, Donald Royal, Tony Smith, and *George Zidek*. The five names italicized there are big white guys. Five big white guys is way too many big white guys to have on a team hoping to win a title in the mid-to-late '90s and beyond.

11. Vlade says it was Jerry West who talked him into going to Charlotte rather than retiring.

12. Thinking about Jordan with only five championships is somehow the weirdest part of this whole thing.

WHAT HAPPENED
IN THE MOMENT BEFORE
"THE MOMENT"?

At the end of Game 5 of the 2004 Western Conference Semifinals between the Lakers and the Spurs, Derek Fisher used every bit of the last 0.4 second left on the clock to hit a buzzer beater that gave the Lakers a one-point win and a 3–2 lead in the series. Do you know what happened on the play immediately before that? I do. I'll never forget it.

From 1999 to 2003, only either the Spurs or the Lakers won the NBA championship. And with the exception of 2000, each time they did so they had to go through the other team to get there.[1] It went like this:

- The Spurs sweep the Lakers in the Western Conference Semifinals on their way to winning the championship in 1999, the first in franchise history.[2]
- The Lakers sweep the Spurs in the Western Conference Finals on their way to winning the championship in 2001.
- The Lakers beat the Spurs 4–1 in the Western Conference Semifinals on their way to winning the 2002 championship.
- The Spurs beat the Lakers 4–2 in the Western Conference Semifinals on their way to winning the 2003 championship.

So what I'm saying is, by the time the Spurs and the Lakers met in the playoffs in 2004, they proper did not like each other, as tends to happen when one team plays another team 48 times in a six-season period. That's why I remember what happened before Fisher's 0.4 shot in 2004 so clearly.

There was a little less than six seconds to go and the Spurs, who'd had a 2–0 series lead and were now staring at a potential 2–3 hole with Game 6 to come in Los Angeles, were down by one and inbounding the ball. Whatever the inbounds play was got blown up by the Lakers, and so, too, did the backup play, because Tim Duncan ended up 20 feet from the basket with the ball

in his hands and Shaq's massive monster truck body hanging all over him. He took two dribbles to his left, then threw up a goofy, ill-advised, impossible, falling-down fadeaway over Shaq from the top of the key. And that bitch heat-seeking missile'd right through the net.

I was in college at the time and my mom and dad were in town visiting and so my dad and I were watching the game together and when that shot went in we both started jumping and screaming and *JUMPING* and *SCREAMING*. I was so overcome with emotion that I shoved him in the chest as hard as I could because that's just what my heart was telling me to do. It was great. It was so great. It was so, so great. And, I mean, the game and the stakes and the history and all of that stuff made it great, for sure, but the fact my dad and I were watching it together and experiencing that same set of emotions together is what I really remember. It was the exact kind of sentimental moment you hope to have when you're a sports fan. It was beautiful. It was so beautiful. It was so, so beautiful. And then it all got washed away.

Somehow, with just that 0.4 second left, Derek Fisher managed to catch an inbounds pass from Gary Payton, turn around, have himself a sip of tea, then toss up a prayer of a shot to heaven, and so of course God grabbed it and dropped it gently through the basket. It was devastating. The Lakers won the game and then closed out the series the next game.[3] That Tim Duncan shot was set to be one of, say, the top-five favorite basketball moments of my life, and it got disappeared just like that.

But so this three-part series of chapters is about that. It's about the moments that happened before The Moment, because I think those are just as nerd-interesting. As a matter of fence building, let's only rewind some of the big-time playoff moments (playoff

---

1. The Lakers won the championship in 2000 but they didn't play the Spurs in the playoffs. Tim Duncan tore the lateral meniscus in his left knee with just four games to go in the season. The Spurs made him sit out the playoffs. As such, they lost in the first round to the too-small Phoenix Suns, who the Lakers blitzed 4–1 in the next round.
2. Phil Jackson, who was hired to coach the Lakers in June of 1999, said the title deserved an asterisk next to it because it came during the lockout-shortened season. It legit hurt my feelings when he said that.
3. God bless the 2004 Detroit Pistons for beating the Lakers in the Finals.

moments are always more intense and impactful and memorable), and also let's start with Ralph Sampson's iconic buzzer-beater tip shot in the 1986 Western Conference Finals (going back through more than 30 years of plays seems like more than enough).

▶

THE MOMENT: 1986 Playoffs // Western Conference Finals // Rockets vs. Lakers // Game 5 // Series: 3–1, Rockets // Score: 112–112 // 1 second left // Rodney Mc-Cray, inbounding the ball from half court, threw it in to Ralph Sampson. Sampson caught the ball, then flipped it up over his shoulder before even landing. The ball bounced off the front of the rim, then the back of the rim, then all the rest of the parts of the rim, then fell through the hoop, winning the series for the Rockets.

THE MOMENT BEFORE "THE MOMENT": Byron Scott missed a wide-open 20-foot jumper. Five things here:

1. Sampson's shot sent the Rockets to the Finals for only the second time in franchise history. The first time they went was 1981. They lost in six games to the Celtics there, same as what happened in the 1986 Finals.
2. The Lakers were the defending champs. They'd beaten Boston the year before and had lost to Boston the year before that, so most everyone was very excited about a potential third meeting in a row between the Celtics and the Lakers. (The Lakers ended up winning the title in 1987 and 1988. Bird's Celtics never won another championship after 1986.)
3. That Rockets team (Olajuwon, Sampson, McCray, Lucas[4]) absolutely should've been good-to-great for the next decade. Injuries and drugs pulled them apart at the seams, though. Just 18 months after

Sampson's shot, he was traded to the Warriors. By the time Olajuwon got the Rockets back to the Finals in 1994, he was the only player on the team who remained from that 1986 squad.
4. Olajuwon had gotten tossed out of the game in the fourth quarter for fighting Mitch Kupchak. There's not a bunch of stuff I like thinking about more than Hakeem Olajuwon in a fistfight.[5]
5. In situations like these—where a player missed a shot before someone else on the other team hit a game-winning shot or a series-winning shot—I always wonder if it matters to the person who missed the shot whether or not the other team eventually went on to win the championship. Like, do you root for the team who beat you to win the championship because then you can say you at least lost to the best team that year? Or do you want them to not win the championship because you don't want someone to be able to point back to your miscue and say that it was your mess-up that sent them on their way to a title? I vote that I don't want a team to win a championship after they beat me.

▶

THE MOMENT: 1987 Playoffs // Eastern Conference Finals // Pistons vs. Celtics // Game 5 // Series: 2–2 // Score: 107–106, Pistons // 5 seconds left // Isiah Thomas attempted to inbound the ball on the Celtics side of the floor to Bill Laimbeer. Larry Bird jumped the passing lane, stole the ball, then passed it to a cutting Dennis Johnson. DJ made the layup, giving the Celtics a one-point lead with less than a second left on the clock. The Pistons failed to even get a shot off on their final possession, losing 108–107.

4. Technically, Lucas was kicked off the team for a failed drug test late in the regular season, but you get what I'm saying.
5. In 2012, Jonathan Abrams wrote an oral history for *Grantland* on the 1986 Rockets. In the part where people talk about the Olajuwon fight, the referee who broke up the fight, Jess Kersey, has this great line: "Somebody punched me in the head and I yelled up, 'I don't know which one of you just punched me in the head, but if I find out, you're going to be ejected.' With that, Bill Fitch [the Rockets coach] said to me, 'Jess, I know who punched you.' Of course in the heat of the moment, I look at Bill and say, 'Who was it?' He said, 'It was Kareem and Magic.'"

THE MOMENT BEFORE "THE MOMENT": The Celtics had the ball. Larry Bird inbounded it to Dennis Johnson.[6] Bird ran a flair screen and received the ball back from DJ. Rick Mahorn was guarding Bird. (Rick Mahorn was a fucking perfect name for Rick Mahorn.) They were both at the left wing three-point line. Bird gave a jab step to his right, then cut back left around Mahorn, angling his body toward the rim. He had Mahorn beat and also had Isiah Thomas beat (Thomas had cheated over to try and block the layup). It was a great play and should've resulted in a layup. It didn't, though. Because Dennis Rodman, an all-world defender who was guarding a separate player on the opposite end of the court, recognized what was happening and teleported through space like Nightcrawler, appearing at the rim to block Bird's shot back out to the three-point line. Jerry Sichting chased the ball down and tried to throw it off a Piston player before it went out of bounds. He wasn't able to, though. The ball went out of bounds off him. So the Pistons had the ball, up one, with five seconds left. All Isiah had to do was inbound it.[7]

▶

THE MOMENT: 1987 Playoffs[8] // NBA Finals // Lakers vs. Celtics // Game 4 // Series: 2–1, Lakers // Score: 105–106, Celtics // 7 seconds left // Magic Johnson hit a running baby hook over Kevin McHale and Robert Parish to give the Lakers the lead with two seconds left. The Lakers end up winning the game, taking a 3–1 lead in the series.

THE MOMENT BEFORE "THE MOMENT": Let's go back two plays:

1. On the play immediately preceding the baby hook, the Lakers actually had the ball. They were down two and Kareem had gotten fouled and so he was shooting free throws. He made the first and missed the second, but Kevin McHale ended up knocking the ball out of bounds while he was trying to grab the rebound.[9] If he grabs that rebound, there's no telling how the rest of that series plays out.[10] Maybe the Celtics win after they take Game 4?[11]
2. The Celtics possession prior to the baby hook was

beautiful. It started with Robert Parish setting a pick on Dennis Johnson's man (Magic Johnson), which forced Kareem to switch out onto DJ on the perimeter and Magic to switch down onto Parish in the post. DJ threw the ball down to Parish, and that's when everything turned to ash for the Lakers. Kareem ran back to help an undersized Magic, Parish passed the ball back out to DJ, both Michael Cooper and Magic panicked and ran out at DJ, DJ tossed it to a wide-open Danny Ainge, and then Ainge whipped it over to an even more wide-open Bird in the corner. It was a perfectly executed play. It was like the last 10 minutes of a season of *Breaking Bad* when all of the season's threads get braided together to form a noose around an unsuspecting someone's neck. It was real cool. And Magic Johnson baby hook'd it into the ether.

▶

THE MOMENT: 1989 Playoffs // Eastern Conference First Round // Cavs vs. Bulls // Game 5 // Series: 2–2 // Score: 99–100, Cavs // 3 seconds left // Michael Jordan hit "The Shot," a free throw line jumper at the buzzer over Craig Ehlo that gave the Bulls a one-point win and sent them to the second round of the playoffs.

THE MOMENT BEFORE "THE MOMENT": It was actually a very clutch play by Craig Ehlo, a reserve player for the Cavs who'd had himself a career night. During the 1989 season, Ehlo only averaged 7.4 points per game. That game, though, he put up 24 points, and the last two of them nearly won the series for the Cavs.

With six seconds left, Ehlo, standing near half court, inbounded the ball to Larry Nance. When Ehlo threw it, his man, Craig Hodges, turned all the way around to look at the ball. Ehlo realized he could get a step on Hodges and broke into a sprint (inasmuch as he could sprint, as he was playing on a sprained ankle). He ran right toward Nance. Nance passed him the ball back and Ehlo slithered his way to the rim, laying it in with just three seconds left, looking for all the world like he'd just won the game for the Cavs, like he'd just sliced the head off Jordan's shoulders.[12] And then: Doom.

▶   ▶

THE MOMENT: 1991 Playoffs // Eastern Conference First Round // Bulls vs. Knicks // Game 3 // Series: 2–0, Bulls // Score: 54–50, Knicks // With less than a minute to go in the first half, Michael Jordan got trapped along the baseline in a double team, pretended to retreat, pivoted back toward the baseline, then mega-dunked on Patrick Ewing, God rest his soul.

THE MOMENT BEFORE "THE MOMENT": Kiki VanDeWeghe, who played small forward for the Knicks, shot two free throws. They both went in. Quick aside: I really feel like Kiki VanDeWeghe has way too many capital letters in his name.[13] Two seems like the best amount. You can have three if you're either really outgoing or some sort of superstar. (The exception here is Josh McRoberts. He gets a pass because one time in the playoffs LeBron was driving in for a dunk and so rather than try to block him, McRoberts just fucking hit him with a forearm shiver right in the throat.) Four is just too many.[14] When he got to three capital letters one of his friends should've been like, "Kiki, you really don't need that W capitalized, man."

THE MOMENT: 1991 Playoffs // NBA Finals // Bulls vs. Lakers // Game 2 // Series: 1–0, Lakers // Score: 71–95, Bulls // With a little under eight minutes left in the game, Michael Jordan received a pass near the top of the key. He charged into the lane, jumped at the rim, then switched hands midair right-to-left for a driving layup. Marv Albert shouted, "Oh! A spec—tacular move by Michael Jordan!"

THE MOMENT BEFORE "THE MOMENT": Have you ever seen *Deep Impact*? It's a movie where a giant piece of a comet hits Earth and causes an ultra-tsunami that kills millions of people and causes billions and billions of dollars in damage. That's pretty much what Jordan was during this game. The hand-switch layup actually came at the end of a run where Jordan hit 13 straight shots. It was a real MOMENT. It was some Zeus Throwing Lightning Bolts shit. The play that happened right before it: A.C. Green missed a 17-foot jumper over Horace Grant. (Pretend like the sad noise from *The Price Is Right* when someone loses a game is playing right now.)

---

6. My favorite tiny moment from this play: Larry Bird smiled to himself as he walked toward the spot where he was going to inbound the ball from. Imagine that. Imagine being in a situation as pressure-packed as that one and the thing you do is smile to yourself. Larry Bird was so goddamn dope.

7. This was such a total turn of events that it's kind of overwhelming. Larry Bird had been magnificent in the game (36-12-9), but had missed a bunny that would've given the Celtics a three-point lead with under 30 seconds left. The Pistons came down, ran an iso for Thomas, and Thomas hit a massively clutch jumper to give the Pistons the one-point lead they ended up losing. So for Bird, he went (1) missed easy shot, (2) team loses lead, (3) gets shot blocked at the rim in astounding fashion. To go from that to one of the greatest playoff game endings in history is remarkable. Poor Isiah looked like he'd been shoved off a cliff.

8. The 1987 playoffs were fucking dope.

9. Chick Hearn was calling the radio broadcast of the game for the Lakers side. When the ball was awarded to the Lakers, to the ref, Chick, that beautiful bird, he said, "Last touched by a crying Kevin McHale." The game ended with Larry Bird just missing a shot at the buzzer to win the game. Chick, who thought the shot was good when Bird let it go, declared, "It was as straight as a mackerel going upstream." Chick was so wonderful.

10. Best guess: Things ultimately end up the same way they did. The only real change is that the Celtics hang on to win Game 4, tying the series 2–2. That being the case, I think the Lakers would've won Game 5 in LA and then Game 6 in Boston to close it out. The Celtics were just too beat up that series. McHale was hurt, Ainge was hurt, Bill Walton was hurt. They were just too old/beat up/fatigued.

11. They don't.

12. Jordan's stat line that game: 44-9-6. His stat line for Game 4: 50-3-4-3. He was not fucking around.

13. FYI: As a player, he only capitalized the first letter of his surname. In 2013, he adopted the original Belgian spelling to honor his grandfather.

14. Sorry, DeMar DeRozan.

. . . continued

THE MOMENT: 1992 Playoffs // NBA Finals // Trail Blazers vs. Bulls // Game 1 // Near the end of the first half, Michael Jordan hit his sixth three-pointer.[1] On his way back up the court, he turned toward the broadcasters' table, absorbed his own greatness, then shrugged at them in the most Get These Bitches Off the Court way that anyone has ever shrugged.

THE MOMENT BEFORE "THE MOMENT": On the play before Jordan's Three-and-Shrug, Clyde Drexler shot an air ball, and that's a very poetic thing because:

1. Prior to the series starting, there was some discussion about whether Clyde deserved to be in the Best Player in the League conversation with Michael.[2] Michael did not agree. Clyde Drexler was, at the time, one of the six or seven best basketball players on the planet. And Mike heard people saying their names in the same sentence and was like, "Well now I'm gonna destroy this man's whole life." That's incredible.

2. The year that Jordan was drafted (1984), the Trail Blazers had a chance to get him. They had the number-two pick that year. They chose Sam Bowie, a 7-footer with spaghetti for legs.[3] This is a thing most everyone knows. What a lot of people don't realize, though, is . . .

3. The year that Clyde was drafted (1983), the Bulls had a chance to get *him*. He was drafted 14th by Portland. Chicago had the 5th pick.[4] And there's another thing . . .

4. In Hakeem Olajuwon's book *Living the Dream*, he said that in 1984 the Trail Blazers offered Clyde Drexler and the second pick in the draft to Houston for their 7'4" center Ralph Sampson. The Rockets

declined. Had they taken the deal, they'd have had Clyde on their roster, then drafted Olajuwon first and Jordan second in the '84 draft. That's gross. But so you've got all of that backstory reflected in that one tiny moment where we watched the universe lift Michael Jordan up into the cosmos while karate kicking Clyde Drexler in the wiener.

▶

THE MOMENT: 1993 Playoffs // First Round // Celtics vs. Hornets // Game 4 // Series: 2–1, Hornets // Score: 103–102, Celtics // 3.3 seconds left // Alonzo Mourning hit a step back jumper over Xavier McDaniel at the buzzer to give the Hornets a one-point win and also send them to the second round of the playoffs for the first time in franchise history.

THE MOMENT BEFORE "THE MOMENT": We should rewind this back three full plays to get the full impact of the blow of this shot.

3. With about 55 seconds left and leading by one, the Hornets ran an iso for Larry Johnson at the top of the three-point line. He got a little careless with the ball and ended up getting it stolen by Sherman Douglas, who snuck off Muggsy Bogues to help. Douglas sprinted down the other way for a layup. It capped a 14–2 run by the Celtics that had given them a one-point lead.

2. The Celtics defended the Hornets well on their next possession, with Robert Parish swallowing up the rebound with about 32 seconds left. The game should've been theirs. But they SOMEHOW got called for a 10-second violation, which gave the ball back to the Hornets.

---

1. He set a Finals record for (a) threes in a half (it's not a record anymore—Ray Allen hit 7 threes in a half during the 2010 Finals) and (b) most points scored in a half (that one still stands).
2. He and Jordan appeared on the cover of an issue of *Sports Illustrated* in May and the subtitle of the article was "Michael Jordan and his No. 1 rival, Portland's Clyde Drexler, are primed for a playoff showdown."
3. The Rockets had the first pick. They chose Hakeem Olajuwon, although at the time his name was Akeem Olajuwon. He said he put the H on the front of it because it stood for all the "hoes" he was going to get as an NBA player. (That's not true.) (He actually said he was changing it from Akeem to Hakeem because he wanted it to be the proper Arabic spelling.)
4. They chose a power forward named Sidney Green. He played for the Bulls for three seasons.

1. The Hornets ran another iso for Larry Johnson after the 10-second violation call. He got a shot off that time, but he missed it. The Celtics bobbled the ball out of bounds.

So, to recap: The Celtics made this very wild run to get back in the game → then, short of punting it into the stands, they turned the ball over in the silliest way a professional basketball team can turn it over → then they couldn't gather a rebound after a miss → then Alonzo Mourning slit their throats. It was rough.[5] It doesn't rate as painful or regretful as some of the other ones because there's not one specific person we can pin it on and also the stakes were pretty low, but still. Rough.[6]

▶

THE MOMENT: 1993 Playoffs // Western Conference Semifinals // Suns vs. Spurs // Game 6 // Series: 3–2, Suns // Score: 100–100 // 11 seconds left // With about two seconds left, Charles Barkley hit a shot from the top of the key over David Robinson that won the game for the Suns. They moved on to the next round of the playoffs and I moved on to hating Charles Barkley.

THE MOMENT BEFORE "THE MOMENT": David Robinson, who'd shot 66 percent from the free throw line during the playoffs that year, hit two in a row to tie the game at 100. I was so fucking nervous for those free throws. It looked like he was, too. It looked like he'd just found out that he had legs. It was the first time (and only time) in his career I'd ever seen him look like anything less than perfect grace. But the fact remains: He made the free throws.

And then Charles Barkley happened. ☹

Probably the most sad thing about this is that that game was the last one the Spurs ever played in the HemisFair Arena. They moved into their new stadium after that.

▶

THE MOMENT: 1993 Playoffs // NBA Finals // Bulls vs. Suns // Game 6 // Series: 3–2, Bulls // Score: 98–96, Suns // 14.1 seconds left // Jordan brought the ball up court, tossed it to Pippen, who tossed it to Horace Grant, who kicked it out to John Paxson for a three. 99–98, Bulls. Game time.

THE MOMENT BEFORE "THE MOMENT": Dan Majerle airballed a very open 12-footer that would've given the Suns a four-point lead with 14 seconds left. These are the types of moments before the moment that hurt the most. (Quick thing: The Bulls only scored 12 points in that entire quarter and still managed to win.) (Jordan had nine of those points.) (Paxson had the other three.) (Jordan's scoring total for the series: 31, 42, 44, 55, 41, and 33. That's an average of 41 points per game, which is the highest in a Finals.)

▶

THE MOMENT: 1995 Playoffs // Eastern Conference Semifinals // Pacers vs. Knicks // Game 1 // Score: 102–105, Pacers // 16.4 seconds left // Immediately after having made a three to bring the score to 102–105, Reggie Miller stole the inbounds pass, retreated to the three-point line, shot it, and made it again, tying the game at 105–105. Six seconds later, Reggie hit two free throws to win the game for the Pacers.

THE MOMENT BEFORE "THE MOMENT": Let's call this one three separate rapid-fire moments. *What happened before Reggie's first three?* A pair of Greg Anthony free throws. *What happened before Reggie's second three?* Anthony Mason was like, "Fuck it," and threw the ball inbounds up for grabs. Reggie grabbed it. *What happened before Reggie's two free throws?*

---

5. Made maybe even more upsetting because Zo's shot went through the hoop with at least 0.7 second left but the clock operator just let it run until the buzzer sounded. They were doing wild shit in the '90s.
6. I'd like to say, though, that it was not rough for me. Rick Fox was on that Celtics team and so I just always loved seeing him lose, so that's one thing. But also, he was the one dribbling the ball up the court for the Celtics when they got hit with the 10-second violation. It was like Petty Christmas for me.

John Starks missed two free throws.[7] Ewing grabbed the rebound, missed a short shot, then Reggie grabbed that rebound and was fouled. The whole thing was a real collapse on one side and heroism on the other.

▶

THE MOMENT: 1995 playoffs // Western Conference Semifinals // Rockets vs. Suns // Game 7 // Score: 110–110 // 7.1 seconds left // Mario Elie received a cross-court pass from Robert Horry, shot a three-pointer, made it, then blew a kiss[8] to the Phoenix bench.

THE MOMENT BEFORE "THE MOMENT": Kevin Johnson was fouled on a drive. He shot two free throws. He made the first (which tied the game) and missed the second. Johnson actually shot 22 free throws that game.[9] He made all of them except that last one. I always wondered if that would have affected the way the game ended any. Does that game end differently if he makes that second free throw and gives the Suns a one-point lead? Does Elie still hit that three? Do they go for two instead?

▶

THE MOMENT: 1995 Playoffs // Western Conference Finals // Rockets vs. Spurs // Game 2 // Series: 1–0, Rockets // Third Quarter // Hakeem Olajuwon put David Robinson in a wood chipper. ⊗

THE MOMENT BEFORE "THE MOMENT": Shut up.

▶

THE MOMENT: 1997 playoffs // Western Conference Finals // Jazz vs. Rockets // Game 4 // Series: 2–1, Jazz // Score: 92–92 // The Rockets inbounded the ball with 6.7 seconds left to Matt Maloney.[10] He threw it to Clyde Drexler at the three-point line, and the Jazz immediately doubled him. Drexler threw it back to Maloney.[11] Maloney threw it to Eddie Johnson, who fired a rainbow three-pointer from his chin that splashed through the net just after the buzzer sounded.[12]

THE MOMENT BEFORE "THE MOMENT": John Stockton missed a free throw line jumper. Greg Foster missed a tip-in at the rim. Karl Malone grabbed the rebound and threw it out to Stockton, who reset the offense. Stockton drove, passed it to a cutting Hornacek, who then passed it out to Bryon Russell for a three. Russell missed it. So the Jazz went 0–3 over a 30-second stretch before Eddie Johnson's game winner. They can all share a little of the blame here.

▶

THE MOMENT: 1997 Playoffs // Western Conference Finals // Jazz vs. Rockets // Game 6 // Series: 3–2, Jazz // Score: 100–100 // 2.8 seconds left // Bryon Russell threw the ball in to John Stockton, who caught it near the edge of the Rockets logo at midcourt. He took one dribble in, then pulled up from about 27 feet. It was cash. Jazz won 103-100.

THE MOMENT BEFORE "THE MOMENT": Clyde Drexler missed a leaning one-hander that would've put the Rockets up by two. The pain in this one is more of an accumulation thing, though. The Rockets were up 10 with less than three minutes left and also up 7 with less than two minutes left. We can't blame this one all on Clyde. It's never felt like his fault.[13]

▶

THE MOMENT: 1997 Playoffs // NBA Finals // Jazz vs. Bulls // Game 1 // Score: 82–82 // 7.5 seconds left // The Bulls ran an iso for Jordan at the left wing. Bryon Russell was guarding him. Jordan gave a little stutter-step. Russell bit on it and jabbed at the ball. Jordan stepped through Russell's arm, then pulled up for an elbow jumper, then shit on all of Utah. Bulls won at the buzzer, 84–82.

THE MOMENT BEFORE "THE MOMENT": Following a John Stockton miss, Karl Malone chased down the rebound. While doing so, he was fouled by Dennis Rodman. The Bulls were in the penalty so he was awarded two free throws. Before he shot them, Pippen walked over to him and told him, "The Mailman doesn't deliver on Sunday." Malone missed them both. I laughed.[14]

▶

THE MOMENT: 1997 Playoffs // NBA Finals // Jazz vs. Bulls // Game 6 // Series: 3–2, Bulls // Score: 86–86 // 28 seconds left // Pippen had the ball out on the left wing. Jordan, who'd wanted it in the post, ran out to Pippen to go get it when they couldn't create the angle. Bryon Russell was guarding him and it was basically the same spot the two were in at the end of Game 1 when Jordan hit the jumper over him. This time, though, Stockton ran over to double Jordan. Jordan accepted the double team and passed the ball over to Steve Kerr. Kerr stuck his knife in the eyeballs of players on the Jazz, giving the Bulls a two-point lead with five seconds left.

THE MOMENT BEFORE "THE MOMENT": Shandon Anderson, who played guard for the Jazz, received a pass from John Stockton down to the baseline. Nervous that he was going to get blocked from behind by Pippen, he went up and under to the other side of the rim. His layup rattled out. It was super sad. It was also super tampered with. Scottie Pippen jumped to try to block Anderson but couldn't get to him because the rim was in the way and, likely out of reflex, Pippen grabbed the rim and pulled on it just enough to wobble the stanchion. It should've been called goaltending. It wasn't, though. The Jazz ended up losing by the two points Kerr scored on the next possession. Hard one to live with for the Jazz, I'm sure.

If you put together a list of things that have to happen at the end of a game for that game to become truly and unforgettably heartbreaking, it'd be (1) Did your team have a chance late in the game and blew it? (2) Did the refs miss a call that absolutely had to be made? (3) Did the other team end up capitalizing on that misfortune immediately after by making a go-ahead shot? (4) Did it cost your team a championship? (5) Was there a history of torment already in place between the person who made the final play and the person who was messed up/screwed over? This game hit the first four of those things. Just brutal.

THE MOMENT: 1998 Playoffs // Eastern Conference Finals // Bulls vs. Pacers // Game 4 // Series: 2–1, Bulls // Score: 94–93, Bulls // 2.9 seconds left // Reggie Miller came curling off a screen to receive the inbounds pass, shoved Michael Jordan into oblivion, caught the ball, turned around, let fly a three-pointer, then did an ultra-exciting I CANNOT FUCKING BELIEVE I JUST DID THAT jumping, twisty-twirly thing in excitement after the shot went in.[15]

THE MOMENT BEFORE "THE MOMENT": Scottie Pippen stole the ball (hooray!), was fouled (okay), missed the first free throw (oh no), then missed the second (SON OF A BITCH!). It's hard to look back at this and gauge exactly how upsetting it was because the Bulls ended up winning the series anyway and then

---

7. He super did not want to shoot those free throws. He had actually just made two a minute or so earlier. He should've been fine. He was just shook, though. I don't blame him. If I'd have been in that spot and the ref called a foul and I had to shoot those free throws, I'd have been like, "No, thank you," and then walked right the fuck out the stadium.

8. The "Kiss of Death," specifically. And he said in an interview in 2006 that he was blowing it at Joe Kleine. They'd been blowing kisses at each other during the series. I don't imagine Joe Kleine pretended to kiss Mario Elie in too many more games after that.

9. Additionally, he scored a career high 46 points that game.

10. Whoops.

11. Whoops again. (I just can't trust a guy whose name rhymes with bologna. It's the worst meat of all for your name to rhyme with.) (Better meat-rhyming names: Jake [steak], Chief Keef [beef], Phil [veal].)

12. Even as an impartial watcher, this was such a great and exciting moment. Johnson had surprised everyone by coming off the bench and putting up 31 on the Jazz in Game 3. So you add that with his buzzer beater in Game 4 and it just really felt like we were in the middle of an Eddie Johnson moment. Also: His post-shot celebration, where he just fucking high-stepped down the court until Barkley caught him and picked him up, was fantastic. Also, also: They were playing in The Summit, which held a little over 16,000 people for basketball games in 1997 but looked like there were something like 70,000–75,000 in there. All in all, it was just a great thing to watch happen.

13. There was only a five-point differential between the teams over the last three games. It was great.

14. Utah haunted San Antonio during the '90s. They made for great villains.

15. Another all-time great reaction.

the championship later. Pippen probably laughs about those misses. When you win six rings, you get to laugh at shit.

▶

THE MOMENT: 1998 Playoffs // NBA Finals // Jazz vs. Bulls // Game 6 // Series: 3–2, Bulls // Score: 86–85, Jazz // Jordan dribbled the ball up court to the left wing. He saw that Bryon Russell was guarding him and the Jazz weren't going to double him.[18] He took two hard dribbles toward the free throw line, crossed over on the second dribble to go back to the left, discarded Russell, pulled up, then cemented his case as the greatest basketball player of all time. Bulls won 87–86.

THE MOMENT BEFORE "THE MOMENT": Aw, man. Poor Karl Malone. Jordan stole the ball from him. First the missed free throws before Jordan's moment in 1997 and now this.

▶

THE MOMENT: 1999 Playoffs // Eastern Conference Finals // Pacers vs. Knicks // Game 3 // Series: 1–1 // Score: 91–88, Pacers // 11.9 seconds left // Charlie Ward tried to throw the ball inbounds to I'm not sure who. Jalen Rose (Pacers) tipped it up but Larry Johnson grabbed it. He was a couple feet outside the three-point line and Antonio Davis was guarding him. He sized Davis up, gave him a juke move, cut left, then shot a three. The ref blew the whistle. The shot went in. New York was loud.

THE MOMENT BEFORE "THE MOMENT": Doesn't matter. I don't honor it. That wasn't a foul. The Pacers won this game. They ended up going to the Finals. Congrats to the 1999 Pacers on making it to the Finals after all these years.

▶

THE MOMENT: 2000 Playoffs // Western Conference Finals // Blazers vs. Lakers // Game 7 // Score: 79–83, Lakers // 45 seconds left // Kobe, dribbling out a few feet past the three-point line, crossed over Scottie

Pippen, snaked his way into the lane, saw Portland's Brian Grant slide over in front of him to prevent him from getting to the rim, lobbed a chunk of meat into the air near the rim, then the Tyrannosaurus rex Shaquille O'Neal snatched it up and slammed it down.

THE MOMENT BEFORE "THE MOMENT": Scottie Pippen missed a three-pointer from the left wing. And that maybe doesn't sound like a big thing, and I suppose in and of itself it wasn't, but the "Kobe . . . TO SHAQ!" alley-oop was such an incredible moment because of the culmination of 10 different things:

1. The Lakers had a 3–1 lead in the series over the Blazers after Game 4.
2. Then the Blazers won the next two to tie it at 3–3.
3. Then the Blazers built up a 15-point lead with less than 11 minutes left in the fourth quarter.
4. Then the Lakers came all the way back to tie it.
5. Then the Lakers took the lead.
6. Then the alley-oop happened and I promise you I felt the floor rumble beneath my feet in Texas from how loud they were celebrating in LA.
7. It was, and remains, the biggest fourth quarter comeback during a Game 7 in league history.
8. This was the fourth year Kobe and Shaq were together but they'd yet to win a championship. Later, during their three-peat, it felt almost normal to see them rally back from big deficits. It was new here, though. I imagine they leaned on this particular comeback a lot when they got in those spots later.[19]
9. This was the first year Phil Jackson was the coach of the Lakers. It felt a lot like he'd finally gotten Kobe and Shaq to figure out their partnership during the season, and then it felt a lot like maybe it was all a ruse as the Blazers pulled away from them on their homecourt in a series where the Lakers had built up what was supposed to be an insurmountable 3–1 lead.
10. The Blazers had a stretch during the fourth quarter where they missed 13 straight shots. They finished the quarter 5 for 23 from the field and were outscored 31–13 overall. It was as much a collapse on their part as it was a comeback by the Lakers.

It was all just incredible. If the Lakers never make that comeback, who knows how different the NBA looks during the 2000s.

▶

THE MOMENT: 2001 Playoffs // NBA Finals // Sixers vs. Lakers // Game 1 // Score: 101–99, Sixers // 54 seconds left in overtime // Allen Iverson executes a perfect and unguardable step-back reverse crossover, pulls up, hits a 16-foot jumper, then executes his defender, Tyronn Lue, who'd fallen down, by stepping over him.

THE MOMENT BEFORE "THE MOMENT": Rick Fox overthrew a pass down to Shaq in the post. It sailed completely over his head and into the stands. Two things here: First, do you even understand how shook you have to be to overthrow a pass to Shaq? He's goddamn Shaq. He's 10 feet tall. The Lakers had been literally unbeatable that year in the playoffs. That the absolutely inferior Sixers had somehow managed to stay close to them for sure shook Fox.[20] Second, I wrote about the wonderfulness of the Iverson move for *Grantland* during the summer of 2014. Here's that excerpt:

Iverson rates as the Coolest NBA Player of All Time, and The Step Over was the single dopest moment of his career.

1.   It happened during Game 1 of the NBA Finals, so you have to calculate for that. Big stage, big consequences, lots of eyes.

2.   It was an away game, so you have to keep that in mind, too.

3.   The Sixers were playing the Lakers, a team that, if I'm remembering correctly, was something like 94–0 through the season and playoffs up to that point.

4.   It was overtime, with less than a minute left, and the Sixers were up by two before Iverson hit the shot that preceded The Step-Over.

5.   Iverson had already been brilliant the entire game, so you kind of had the feeling that he was maybe about to do something remarkable. (He actually ended up finishing with an unreal 48 points, 6 assists, and 5 steals, which is all the more crazy when you consider that nobody else on that Sixers team could shoot from farther than 4 feet away from the basket, so Iverson was always basically playing 1-on-5 whenever his team had the ball.)

6.   When The Step-Over happened, it happened DIRECTLY IN FRONT OF THE LAKERS'S BENCH. They were all standing up and seemed to be closing in on him, which definitely made it better.
     It was like he was standing in the middle of a crocodile pit. What a superhero.

7.   He set up The Step-Over by completing a ridiculous step-back-crossover-into-a-jumper move.

8.   The jumper, that beautifulBeautifulBEAUTIFUL thing, never even considered hitting the rim. It just swished straight through. The swish kind of matters, too.

9.   Iverson fully understood what he'd done as soon as it happened. He paused for a moment, then looked down at Tyronn Lue with a gravity-shifting amount of smugness and contempt, stuck a sword through his heart, then stepped over the body he'd just dead-ed.

10. And of course Marv Albert was calling the game, and gave the moment a triumphant ". . . and steps OVER Tyronn Lue" framing.
     The whole thing was flawless.
     All of that is still true, and will always be true.

---

18. WTF.
19. In retrospect, the alley-oop looks a lot like the big breakthrough moment for that version of the Lakers and their eventual dynasty.
20. This probably isn't true. It was probably just a bad pass. It's just I don't ever want to pass up an opportunity to poke fun at Rick Fox.

WHAT HAPPENED
IN THE MOMENT BEFORE
"THE MOMENT"?

PART 3 (2002-2016)

...continued

THE MOMENT: 2002 Playoffs // Western Conference Finals // Kings vs. Lakers // Game 4 // Series: 2–1, Kings // Score: 99–97, Kings // 11.8 seconds left // Kobe Bryant drove to the rim and missed a contested layup. Shaq rebounded it, then short-armed a put-back attempt. Vlade Divac, hoping to rid the Lakers of another chance at a close bucket, slapped the ball out of the fray. Unfortunately for him, it went straight to Robert Horry, who calmly collected it, then hit a buzzer-beating three to win the game.

THE MOMENT BEFORE "THE MOMENT": Vlade, who'd shot 8 of 10 on free throws in the game up until that point, had two free throws. He missed one of the two. Tough stretch for him, what with him having missed the free throw and then slapping the ball out to Horry. If he'd have either made both free throws or just not slapped the ball to Horry, the Kings probably would have won that game,[1] then probably would have won the series, too, after going up 3–1 with two of the remaining potential three games left at home. It's hard to say that there was ever any string of reality where the Lakers don't win the 2001 title (they were just so unstoppable that year), but you can for sure argue that they should've lost in 2000 to the Blazers and also in 2002 to the Kings. Shit's crazy, man.[2]

▶

THE MOMENT: 2004 Playoffs // Western Conference Semifinals // Lakers vs. Spurs // Game 5 // Series: 2–2 // Score: 72–71, Lakers // 5.4 seconds left // Tim Duncan received an inbounds pass at the right wing. The Lakers defense dissolved whatever it was that the play was supposed to be. Duncan, realizing things had turned

to poop, dribbled at the top of the key and threw up a prayer over Shaq. It went in with 0.4 second left on the clock.[3]

THE MOMENT BEFORE "THE MOMENT": Karl Malone set a pick for Kobe Bryant on Devin Brown at the left wing near the three-point line. Robert Horry, then playing with the Spurs, was guarding Malone and so rather than bother with him that far away from the rim, he sank back and waited for Kobe to drive. Kobe pulled up and shot a jumper from just inside the three-point line. It went in, giving the Lakers a one-point lead. I don't think Kobe Bryant ever, not one single time, missed a shot against the Spurs during the playoffs. I don't want to talk about this anymore.[4]

▶

THE MOMENT: 2005 Playoffs // NBA Finals // Spurs vs. Pistons // Game 5 // Series: 2–2 // Score: 93–95, Pistons // 9.4 seconds left // Robert Horry inbounded the ball to Manu Ginobili in the left corner. Rasheed Wallace, who was guarding Horry as he inbounded the ball, ran over to try and trap Ginobili. Ginobili threw it back to Horry, who was now wide open. Horry shot a three. It rattled in, giving the Spurs a one-point lead. The Pistons missed their final shot. Spurs win.

THE MOMENT BEFORE "THE MOMENT": Chauncey Billups missed a runner in the lane that would've given the Pistons a four-point lead with about 10 seconds to go. (The Pistons really should've won this game, and probably the series, too. The Spurs took a 2–0 lead and it looked for all the world like it was going to be a trouncing the rest of the way, then the Pistons, forever unshakable, won the next two games and looked to

---

1. I say the Lakers would've lost that game just because that's what logic tells me, but when I actually really and truly think about it, I have to assume that, given Phil Jackson's basketball life, the Lakers would've probably ended up hitting some sort of four-point play at the buzzer to win the game anyway.
2. I'm willfully choosing to ignore that the Kings had built up a 20-point lead by the end of the first quarter and then gave it all back later in the game.
3. ☺
4. In 30 career playoff games against the Spurs, Kobe made 336 of 711 shots. He made more shots in the playoffs against the Spurs than any other player in history. (Dirk Nowitzki is second at 265.)

have Game 5 sewn up. Then Robert Horry, who for the rest of his life will be beloved in San Antonio, went fucking nuts in the fourth quarter and overtime to steal the game for the Spurs. He scored all 21 of his points in the last 17 minutes, including the last five for San Antonio and also 15 of their final 20. I would also like to point out here that I watched the whole fourth quarter and overtime of that game standing up and also with the TV on mute, which no doubt helped the Spurs.)

(Note: To write these three chapters, I had to watch game tape from each game to find all the information I needed. Mostly, it was a fun and interesting exercise. The ones I had to watch where the Spurs lost, however, were less fun and less interesting. It's just hard to relive those moments, you know what I'm saying. Rewatching and reliving the Horry Game, though, has me in a real good mood and I don't want to burn that off. As such, I'm going to cheat for the last two bad Moment Before "the Moment"s that the Spurs were involved in and just do them real quick right now: In 2006, Dirk Nowitzki hit an and-one to tie Game 7 of the 2006 Western Conference Semifinals. The Spurs lost that game in overtime. On the play before Dirk's and-one, Manu hit a three to give the Spurs a three-point lead.[5] In 2013, Ray Allen hit a step-back three to tie Game 6 of the 2013 NBA Finals. On the play before that, LeBron missed a three. Bosh grabbed the rebound and threw it to Allen. I hate it. I hate everything.[6] I'll fucking fight you.[7])

▶

THE MOMENT: 2006 Playoffs // Western Conference First Round // Suns vs. Lakers // Game 4 // Series: 2–1, Lakers // Score: 98–97, Suns // 6.1 seconds left in overtime // Kobe collected a jump ball that'd been tipped out to him, dribbled up the court on the left side, zagged his way over to the right elbow, then raised up and hit a game-winner at the buzzer.

THE MOMENT BEFORE "THE MOMENT": This is one of those games people point to when they want to talk about how great Kobe was, and rightfully so, given that he hit a shot at the end of regulation to tie the game and send it into overtime, and then he hit a shot at the end of overtime to win the game for the Lakers (as well as hitting the shot before the game-winner to cut the Suns's lead to one), giving them a 3–1 lead in the series.[8] On the play before Kobe's game-winner, Steve Nash dribbled into a trap near the sideline between half court and the three-point line.[9] He tried to call a timeout, but the nearby ref called a jump ball between him and the much bigger Luke Walton instead. He lost the jump ball, then six seconds later he lost the game.

▶

THE MOMENT: 2008 Playoffs // Western Conference First Round // Suns vs. Spurs // Game 1 // Score: 104–101, Suns // 12.6 seconds left in overtime // Tim Duncan

5. Manu was also the one who fouled Nowitzki. It was one of those giveth-and-taketh situations.
6. It was 100 percent unreal that Miami managed to win that game. LeBron had two big turnovers in the final minute that should've put everything out of reach for the Heat (he also had 16 points in the fourth, to be fair). The Spurs went on an 8–0 run that gave them a five-point lead with less than 30 seconds left. Then LeBron hit a three, Kawhi missed a free throw, then Allen hit a three. And what's lost amidst all of that: Popovich took Duncan out for both of the final defensive possessions, and on both of those someone on the Heat missed a three and someone else on the Heat got an offensive rebound. I really feel in my heart that Duncan wouldn't have let that happen had he been in there. That's just me guessing, though.
7. I'm not sure if this is weird or not, but I kind of don't hate that the Spurs lost the 2013 Finals. I mean, please, do not get me wrong: When it happened, I was all the way devastated. I remember I went and took, like, what had to have been a two-hour shower after Game 6. And it was even harder to watch my beloved Tim Duncan upset after he missed a bunny in the final seconds of Game 7 that would've tied the game. But without 2013's heartbreak, we don't get the euphoria of 2014's win, which remains my all-time favorite basketball moment. There were just so many great redemption stories in that moment. So in a way, I think it needed to happen the way it happened. Does that make sense?
8. A 3-1 lead they would surrender, FYI.
9. It was almost the exact same spot where Nash turned the ball over at the end of regulation that led to Kobe's game-tying shot. All in all, it was a rough day for Steve.

received a pass from Manu Ginobili out at the right wing three-point line after setting a screen for Ginobili. Duncan, nobody within 28 feet of him, decided to shoot a three, which surprised everyone because he's fucking Tim Duncan. It went in. It was the first three he'd made all season. Tim Duncan is my boyfriend.

THE MOMENT BEFORE "THE MOMENT": This was an all-time great game, if we're talking about just watchability and enjoyability. Michael Finley hit a three near the end of regulation to tie the game (!), then Tim Duncan hit his three near the end of overtime to send it into a second overtime (!!), then Steve Nash hit a three near the end of the second overtime to tie it, setting up a potential third overtime (!!!), then Manu Ginobili hit a driving layup at the end of the second overtime to win it (!!!!). It was all great (though I'm sure it was less great if you're a Suns fan).[10] On the play before Tim's three, Amar'e Stoudemire was whistled for an offensive foul, giving the ball back to the Spurs. I'm super against the charge as an offensive foul, but I'm 100 percent in favor of the charge as an offensive foul any time it helps out the Spurs.

▶

THE MOMENT: 2009 Playoffs // Eastern Conference Finals // Magic vs. Cavs // Game 2 // Series: 1–0, Magic // Score: 95–93, Magic // 1 second left // LeBron James's attempt to create a backdoor lob got rubbed out so he cut back up the floor to the top of the three-point line. He got a pass from Mo Williams, then threw up a prayer three-pointer over Hedo Turkoglu. It rattled in, miraculously. Cavs win. Neat moment.[11]

THE MOMENT BEFORE "THE MOMENT": Hedo Turkoglu had the ball out past the three-point line winding the clock down. Once it got to five seconds, he attacked, dribbling past Sasha Pavlovic into the lane.[12] He pulled up just inside the free throw line, drilling a jumper over three Cavs, giving the Magic a one-point lead with one second left. I'd just like to take a moment to point out that in 2009, Dwight Howard was so good that he managed to drag a team where the second,

third, and fourth best players were Hedo Turkoglu, Rashard Lewis and Rafer Alston[13] to the Finals.

▶

THE MOMENT: 2010 Playoffs // NBA Finals // Celtics vs. Lakers // Game 7 // Score: 73–76, Lakers // Just over a minute left // Ron Artest received a pass from Kobe Bryant late in the shot clock. He gave just enough of a feint to slow down Paul Pierce, then shot a three over him, giving the Lakers a six-point lead. He blew a double kiss to the sky.

THE MOMENT BEFORE "THE MOMENT": Rasheed Wallace hit a three for Boston to cut the lead to three. Mostly I just wanted to bring up this shot because it lets me talk about how Artest ended up on the Lakers, which is one of my favorite things: In the minutes after Kobe and the Lakers lost the 2008 NBA Finals to the Celtics, Kobe was in the shower just being very mad and sad and heartbroken. Ron Artest walked in, told him he wanted to come to Los Angeles and play for the Lakers and help Kobe win a championship. Phil Jackson told that story during a radio interview and, wild as Artest may have been or might be, that's a really good origin story. All of that means it's pretty great he ended up being the one who hit the shot that really put the game out of reach for the Celtics in the 2010 Finals, even if it was pulverizing at the time.[14]

▶

THE MOMENT: 2014 Playoffs // Western Conference First Round // Rockets vs. Blazers // Game 6 // Series: 3–2, Blazers // Score: 98–96, Rockets // 0.9 second left // Damian Lillard came flying around a screen at the three-point line, clapping his hands at Nicolas Batum, who was inbounding the ball. Batum threw it to Lillard, who caught it, squared up, then shot a 27-footer. It splashed in. The Blazers win their first playoff series in 14 years.[15]

THE MOMENT BEFORE "THE MOMENT": Chandler Parsons grabbed a loose ball, then somehow flipped it up over his head into the basket.

▶

THE MOMENT: 2016 Playoffs // NBA Finals // Cavs vs. Warriors // Game 7 // Score: 89–89 // Just over a minute left // Kyrie Irving dribbled out a bit of the clock before the Cavs ran a pick and roll to get Klay Thompson off of him and Steph Curry onto him. After they did so, Irving put Steph into the torture chamber, dancing on him a bit with the ball before pulling up for a three. It went in, giving the Cavs a lead they would not give up. The Cavs win their first title in franchise history.

THE MOMENT BEFORE "THE MOMENT": Steph Curry missed a step-back three over Irving. And that was a big thing—Curry feasted all season on that shot—but we have to rewind things back two more plays to get the full effect of Irving's three. With just under two minutes left in a tied and ultra-tense Game 7, Andre Iguodala grabbed a rebound, then sprinted out into a fast break. They had a 2-on-1 with him and Steph against a back-pedaling J.R. Smith. It should've been an easy go-ahead bucket, and maybe against any other team it would've been. But against the Cavs, on that particular night, with the weight of the universe on the line, it was not. Iguodala passed it off to Steph, who immediately passed it back to Iguodala. Iguodala gathered it, ducked underneath Smith's outstretched arms, then laid it up. It was perfectly played and perfectly shot. And then LeBron James, who'd sprinted into position from about a mile away, erased it. He jumped, calculated the angles, calculated the age of the earth, calculated the exact age of the solar system, and then slapped the ball off the glass.

---

10. A better one for Suns fans was Stephon Marbury hitting a three-pointer at the buzzer of Game 1 of the Suns vs. Spurs first-round matchup in 2003. On the play before his three, Tim Duncan missed two free throws.

11. The Cavs were actually up 23 points in that game. It should've never been close. They ended up losing that series to the Magic, who then lost in the Finals to the Lakers.

12. Turkoglu vs. Pavlovic is the European version of Magic vs. Bird, probably.

13. Jameer Nelson was also on that team but he missed the whole run up to the Finals due to injury.

14. I was rooting for the Celtics that series.

15. One of my favorite things about this play is Mike Tirico losing his fucking mind calling the play. One of my other favorite things about the play is that while all the players were getting set up to run the play or defend the play, James Harden told Pat Beverley and Chandler Parsons to switch players. Pat, the best perimeter defender the Rockets had, was originally guarding Lillard. Harden fussed at them for a second, they switched, then Lillard sprinted off away from the slower Chandler easily.

WAS KOBE BRYANT A DORK?

(AND ALSO: HOW MANY YEARS
DURING HIS CAREER WAS KOBE BRYANT
THE BEST PLAYER IN THE LEAGUE?)

My first favorite Kobe Bryant memory is barely even a memory; it's more of an idea of a memory, or the edges of a memory, or the glow of a memory, which is how most of our important memories get registered, I think.

This was in 2007 or 2008, possibly 2009 or 2010, perhaps 2006 or maybe 2011. The Lakers had just played the Rockets, and they'd possibly played the Mavs the night before. NBA teams will, on occasion, do a Texas trip and play the Spurs, Rockets, Mavs in succession in whatever order, so I'm assuming here that the Lakers were on that trip. I'm also assuming they'd already played the Mavs by the night of their Rockets game, but that's only because Dallas is north of Houston if you look at a Texas map, which, admittedly, probably isn't a key factor that NBA schedule makers consider when they make schedules, so I'm not sure. It doesn't matter anyway. Because the memory has nothing to do with whether or not the Lakers had played (or were playing) the Mavs. It has to do with the Spurs, who the Lakers were scheduled to play after the Rockets.

But so the Lakers played the Rockets one night in one of those years possibly as a part of their Texas trip, and they lost to them or they beat them, who cares. The outcome of the game isn't relevant. What is relevant was that after the game everybody made a great big fuss about how well Shane Battier, who played small forward for the Rockets, had defended Kobe. It was the entire story from the game. All of the people who talked about basketball professionally seemed to be talking about it. There was this one clip that everyone was passing around and commenting on where Kobe was attempting a fadeaway jumper over Shane and Shane was all the way attached to him, as though he was part of him, as though he was an extension of his essence. It was, to be certain, excellent defense. In fact, it was picture-perfect defense. But as the chatter grew louder and louder about how picture perfect it was, all my brain could manage to think was, "Well, shit."

Because what I knew was that Kobe Bryant was going to see everyone talking about how well Battier had defended him, and he was going to come out the next game—the game against my beloved Spurs—and *go fucking nuts*. I knew it. I knew it was going to happen. I knew it like how you know when someone's about to die in a horror movie.

Now, I can't recall if the Lakers won that post-Shane game against the Spurs or if they lost it. And really, I can't even recall if Kobe played well or not against them. In my head, I remember him putting up something like 140 points and 25 assists, though I suspect that's an inaccurate recollection. But, again, it doesn't matter because, again, that isn't the point. The point is this: I was afraid. I was 100 percent afraid of what Kobe was going to do as a response to people talking about how well he had been defended. I didn't know exactly *what* was going to happen, I just knew it was going to be bloody. And I was horrified.

No other NBA player to that point, or since that point, has made me feel like that—at least not the way that Kobe did when he was at his most ferocious.[1] He was goddamn terrifying. What he could *do* was goddamn terrifying. So that's my first favorite Kobe Bryant memory: that he could inspire real, actual, palpable fear.

My second favorite Kobe Bryant memory happened during a separate game between the Spurs and the Lakers in San Antonio. He had just hit some big shot[2] late[3] in some big game[4] and was sort of jogging backwards up the court to get back on defense. And as he was doing so, he was holding his finger over his mouth, so as to shush the crowd because they'd been doing the "DE-FENSE [stomp] [stomp] DE-FENSE" chant in the moments before. But so he hit the shot, then told 18,000+ people to shut up as he glided backwards up the floor, looking very much like sassy evil incarnate. And it was a great villain moment. And then he tripped.

He somehow got his feet tangled up in themselves. He stumbled, fell down, ended up doing a backwards

---

1. Jordan had a similar impact on fans of opposing teams, I'm told. I never felt it, though, because I always found myself rooting for him.
2. Possibly not a big shot.
3. Possibly early.
4. Possibly an ordinary game.

roll thing, then popped back up. The arena, previously hissing, laughed at him. It was a great dork moment. So that's my second favorite Kobe Bryant memory. He was always interesting in a bunch of different ways, oftentimes in ways he didn't want to be, and when he wasn't intending to be.

▶

This chapter jumps back and forth between discussing Kobe being a dork and Kobe being a great player. It should be said, though, that he has a long history of doing things that are neither of those things. There's the time he (allegedly) ran Shaq out of LA; the time he (allegedly) ran Phil Jackson out of LA; the time he ran Andrew Bynum out of LA (he was caught on tape saying the Lakers needed to get him out of LA immediately so there's no need for an "allegedly" here); the time he told the police that Shaq cheated on his wife and paid hush money to the women he cheated on her with, which Shaq later claimed was the reason he ended up getting a divorce; the time he shouted a homophobic slur at an official during a game; and the time he was accused of rape by a 19-year-old Colorado girl, a charge that was eventually dropped in criminal court by the plaintiff but settled for an undisclosed amount in civil court.

▶

Here are a bunch of easy facts about Kobe Bryant, designated as either "cool" or "dorky":

Kobe Bryant was the first-ever guard drafted out of high school (cool). Kobe Bryant has more missed shot attempts than anyone in the history of the league (cool[5]). Kobe Bryant won five NBA championships during his career (cool). During the postgame press conference after he won his fifth, he was asked what it meant to him to have five championships and his response was, "I just got one more than Shaq," referring to Shaquille O'Neal, a former teammate that he, at times, appeared to hate playing alongside (cool). Kobe Bryant once scored 81 points in a game (cool[6]). Kobe Bryant was selected for 12 NBA All-Defensive Teams (cool). Kobe Bryant was the first-ever player to reach 30,000 points and 6,000 assists (cool). Kobe went to prom with R&B singer and actress Brandy (cool).

Kobe Bryant gave himself a nickname[7] (dorky). Kobe Bryant gave himself a second nickname and tried to pretend like someone else gave it to him because a lot of people made fun of him for giving himself his first nickname[8] (extra dorky). Kobe Bryant tried to be a rapper (super dorky) and in his first song he said the word "Italy" except he pronounced it "Eee-tah-lee"[9] (extra super dorky). Kobe Bryant one time did a photoshoot that accompanied a story on him in the *Los Angeles Times Magazine* and he let them dress him up in an all-white pilgrim costume and then he pretended like it was cool (dorky). Kobe Bryant ended his speech at the end of the final game of his career by saying, "Mamba out" (so fucking dorky). Kobe Bryant got two-pieced up by Chris Childs, and this one's dorky because, I mean, if you're gonna get beat up by a Knick, that's fine because that's kind of what Knicks had been doing for six or seven straight years by that point, but just don't let it be Chris Childs[10] (dorky, but I suppose in at least an understandable way).

---

5. Gunslingers are cool.

6. To be thorough, it was against the 2006 Raptors, which is like scoring 25 against a proper NBA team.

7. Black Mamba. I would pay any amount of money to see two things: (1) Derek Fisher's face the first time Kobe asked him to call him Black Mamba from now on, and (2) Kobe writing lyrics in a notebook during those couple of weeks when he thought he was gonna be a rapper.

8. In 2013, Kobe tweeted out that a friend (who he didn't name) gave him the nickname Vino, referring to his ability to get better with age. Kobe ended up missing 139 games over the final three seasons of his career after that. That does not sound like that great of a wine.

9. In a profile of Bryant in *Rolling Stone*, Anthony Bannister, a high school friend of Kobe's, said that Kobe would call him at 3 A.M. and they would write rhymes together. "You'd think it was Nas," Bannister said of Kobe's lyricism. I don't know Anthony Bannister, but I know that he's a liar. (In that same story, Kobe Bryant said he wanted to buy a tiger because he was friends with Mike Tyson and Tyson had three of them.)

10. Of course, the flip side of this is that Chris Childs immediately becomes one of the five coolest players in the league that year after the Kobe fight.

▶

HOW MANY YEARS WAS KOBE BRYANT THE BEST PLAYER IN THE LEAGUE?

Let's do some cleaning up first. Kobe Bryant played 20 seasons in the league. Of those 20 seasons, there are 10 seasons that we can automatically toss out of the discussion for one reason or another. We can get rid of

- **1997:** His rookie season. It certainly wasn't his best basketball season (7.6 points per game; only started six times), but it was definitely his best television season; between 1996 and 1997 he appeared on *The Rosie O'Donnell Show, Moesha, Arli$$, Sister, Sister, In the House,* and *Hang Time*. I feel like that's more impressive than the Lakers beating the Nets in the 2002 Finals.[11]
- **1998:** Nah.
- **1999:** The season only Spurs fans like to remember because everyone was out of shape and playing poorly because the lockout swallowed the first 32 games of the season.
- **2000:** Now it's getting interesting. He averages over 20 points per game for the first time in his career (22.5). He makes his first All-Defensive First Team and also his first All-NBA Second Team. More importantly, though, he has his first real all-caps SUPERSTAR MOMENT, taking over in the fourth quarter and overtime of Game 4 of the 2000 NBA Finals after missing all of Game 3 with an ankle injury, giving the Lakers a 3–1 lead on the Pacers in a series they'd eventually win in six.
- **2011:** LeBron owns the season, Dirk owns the playoffs.
- **2012:** Let's look at the advanced stats for LeBron, who was the league's best player this season, versus the advanced stats for Kobe, who was *not* the league's best player: [LeBron's Win Shares: 14.5; Kobe's Win Shares: 6.2] [LeBron's VORP: 7.6; Kobe's VORP: 2.4] [LeBron's PER: 30.7; Kobe's PER: 21.9] [LeBron's BPM: 11; Kobe's BPM: 2.3].
- **2013:** This was the last good version of Kobe anyone ever saw (27.3 points per game, 5.6 rebounds per game, 6.0 assists per game on the season; the

third highest True Shooting Percentage of his career; All-NBA First Team). He had to play with Dwight Howard on his team, though, which was so frustrating for Kobe that rather than finish out the season with Dwight, he decided it'd be better to rupture his own Achilles instead, which he did in an April game against the Warriors.

- **2014:** He only played six games due to injury. Flush it down the toilet.
- **2015:** The first time in his career since the 1998 season that he plays more than 30 games in a season and doesn't win any sort of All-NBA Team selection or All-Defensive Team selection.[12]
- **2016:** LOL.

That leaves us with the middle seasons of his career, which were easily his best seasons. But was he the *best* player?

To figure that out we can take a look at a bunch of different things, including personal accomplishments and accolades received during a season, personal accomplishments and accolades during the postseason, regular box score stats, advanced stats, team success during the regular season, and team success during the playoffs. If we take all of those and mush them all together, then we can figure out who the best player was for each of the seasons in question.

2001
All-Star / All-NBA Second Team /
All-Defensive Second Team / NBA Champion

Kobe begins to morph into a true terror.[13] The Lakers go 15–1 in the playoffs, winning their second straight title. Following Game 1 of the Western Conference Finals, in which Kobe scores 45, Shaq calls him "the best player in the league by far," even though it's pretty clear that Shaq is the best player in the league.[14] Kobe's shooting percentage drops from 46 percent in the regular season to 41.5 percent in the Finals; meanwhile, Shaq averages a gaudy 33-16-5-3 in the Finals and wins his second straight Finals MVP.

2002

All-Star (and ASG MVP) / All-NBA First Team /
All-Defensive Second Team / NBA Champion

Tim Duncan is the best player in the league during the regular season, Shaq is the best player during the playoffs.

2003

All-Star / All-NBA First Team /
All-Defensive First Team

Kobe averages 30 points per game for the first time in his career and he also beats Shaq in Win Shares for the first time, too. Tim Duncan is the runaway best player in the league, though, in both the regular season and the playoffs.[15]

2004

All-Star / All-NBA First Team /
All-Defensive First Team

Nope. Everything goes topsy-turvy because of Kobe's sexual assault case.[16] Kevin Garnett is the best player in the league.

2005

All-Star / All-NBA Third Team

Kobe (probably) gets Shaq traded and Phil Jackson decides not to return (reportedly because of Kobe). The Lakers go 34–48 and miss the playoffs for the first time in a decade. It's a toss-up for the league's best player. Choose between Garnett, Dirk, Shaq, and Nash.[17] An argument can be made for each of them.[18]

2006

All-Star / Scoring Leader / All-NBA First Team /
All-Defensive First Team

Here's the first tricky year to judge. It's the highest scoring average of Kobe's career (35.4), and it also happens to be the highest anyone's averaged since Jordan's 37.1 in 1987, earning Kobe his first scoring title. It's also the year that he scores 81 against the Raptors, marking the second highest game total in the history of the NBA, so he gets credit there for being historical. He's also selected to the All-NBA First Team and the All-Defensive First Team.

The bad side, though: Kobe does all of that and the Lakers only win 45 games, then explode into a ball of fire in the first round of the playoffs, ashing away a 3–1 series lead against the Suns. (The most memorable part of this was Kobe refusing to shoot in the second half

---

11. Interesting sidebar: The most points Kobe scored in any game during his rookie season was 24, which is what he ended up changing his number to in the off-season between the 2006 season and the 2007 season.
12. He played 35 total games, missing 47 on account of injuries.
13. If we're rounding, it's 29-6-5 in the season, 29-7-6 in the playoffs.
14. Iverson won the MVP that year. If we arrange him, Shaq, and Kobe for that season into rankings based on their VORP or their BPM or their Win Shares or their PER, the results are always the same: Shaq finishes ahead of both of them.
15. He leads the league in Win Shares, Playoff Win Shares, Playoff VORP, Playoff BPM, Playoff Net Rating; he's third in regular season PER, second in playoff PER; he's the league MVP and the Finals MVP; and the Spurs win their second championship. Plus, just for fun, he threw up 37–16 on the Lakers in Game 6 of their Western Conference Semifinals series, closing it out in LA.
16. I was in a casino in Louisiana when the news of his rape charge came out. I was in a different casino in Louisiana the night he scored 81 on the Raptors. I don't know what that means. I don't think it means anything. Also: Casinos in Louisiana are ugly.
17. If you want to add LeBron here, who was in just his second season but averaged 27-7-7 on the season and also led a closet full of brooms and mop buckets to 42 wins, then go ahead.
18. Probably not Nash, though.

THE ALPHA

WHO WAS THE BEST PLAYER IN THE LEAGUE EACH YEAR KOBE WAS IN THE NBA?

1997	MICHAEL JORDAN (MAYBE KARL MALONE)
1998	MICHAEL JORDAN (MAYBE KARL MALONE)
1999	KARL MALONE (MAYBE TIM DUNCAN)
2000	SHAQUILLE O'NEAL (MAYBE KEVIN GARNETT)
2001	MAYBE ALLEN IVERSON (BUT PROBABLY SHAQ)
2002	SHAQUILLE O'NEAL (MAYBE TIM DUNCAN)
2003	TIM DUNCAN (MAYBE KEVIN GARNETT)
2004	MAYBE KEVIN GARNETT (BUT PROBABLY TIM)

2005	KEVIN GARNETT (MAYBE DIRK NOWITZKI)
2006	DWYANE WADE (MAYBE LEBRON JAMES)
2007-2016	LEBRON JAMES (MAYBE TIM DUNCAN IN 2007)

(AND MAYBE KOBE IN 2008, MAYBE DWYANE WADE IN 2009, MAYBE KOBE IN 2010 BECAUSE OF HIS PLAYOFFS PERFORMANCE, MAYBE DIRK NOWITZKI IN 2011, MAYBE KEVIN DURANT IN 2012, MAYBE KEVIN DURANT IN 2013, MAYBE KEVIN DURANT IN 2014, MAYBE STEPH CURRY IN 2015, MAYBE STEPH CURRY IN 2016)

NOTE: THESE SELECTIONS WERE MADE BY TALLYING THE TOP FIVE PERFORMERS EACH SEASON IN WIN SHARES, PLAYOFF WIN SHARES, VORP, PLAYOFF VORP, PER, PLAYOFF PER, NET RATING, PLAYOFF NET RATING, BPM, AND PLAYOFF BPM. I WASN'T JUST PICKING THIS SHIT AT RANDOM. I JUST THOUGHT YOU SHOULD KNOW THAT.

of Game 7, which the Lakers lost by 31.) The all-around numbers say that Dirk and LeBron are battling for the designation of the league's best player, though Dwyane Wade owns the playoffs, tallying an NBA Finals statistically better than any Kobe's had up to this point (or even will have past this point).[19]

But, so, no: Kobe's not the best player for this season.

2007
All-Star (and ASG MVP) / Scoring Leader /
All-NBA First Team / All-Defensive First Team

Kobe changes his number to 24, which causes the creation of a bunch of fun theories about why he chose that particular number:

- He changed it because he wanted to be one better than Jordan (this is a deliciously petty thing that I really hope is true).
- He changed it because he wanted to rebrand himself after the sexual assault case, so he just took his original Lakers number and multiplied it by the number of championships he'd won to that point (3).
- He changed it as a callback to his high school days.

(He wore the numbers 24 and 33 in high school, and 24 wasn't available when he got to the Lakers because another player had it[20] and the number 33 was retired by the Lakers because Kareem Abdul Jabbar was a fucking badass.)

- He changed it to 24 because he really, really likes Jack Bauer.[21]
- He changed it to 24 to remind himself of how many seconds per each offensive position he should not pass the ball to any of his teammates.[22]

It's either LeBron as the best this season or maybe Dirk, though I'd lean toward LeBron because this is the season that Dirk's Mavs raced out to the best record in the NBA and then were upset by the eighth-seeded Warriors in the first round of the playoffs.

2008
All-Star / All-NBA Second Team /
All-Defensive Second Team / NBA Champion

Kobe's first trip back to the Finals following Shaq getting ousted. (Also worth mentioning that Pau Gasol arrives, which is important. He ends up being exactly what Kobe wants in a big man: basically someone who will get the fuck out of the way when people start talking about the Lakers.) Kobe charts the third highest Win Shares of his career and also the third highest VORP of his career (though Chris Paul and LeBron James beat him in both categories). If you were ever to argue that Kobe Bryant was the best player in the league, this is the season to do so, which is at least a bit ironic because his Lakers got crushed by the Celtics in Game 6 of the Finals to lose the series.[23] (The series swung toward the Celtics after the Lakers coughed up a 24-point lead in Game 4, letting the Celtics take what proved to be an insurmountable 3–1 lead.)

2009

All-Star (and ASG MVP) / Finals MVP / All-NBA First Team / All-Defensive First Team / NBA Champion

---

There are two reasons you can't call Kobe the best player in the league in 2009, the first post-Shaq championship of Kobe's career: (1) Pau Gasol beats out Kobe in Win Shares, VORP, and BPM for the season;[24] and (2) LeBron James goes fucking atomic.[25] He's the best player in the league.

One reason that maybe you can call Kobe the best: (1) He beat Dwight Howard in the NBA Finals, and I am 100 percent in favor of calling anyone anything they want me to call them if they beat Dwight Howard. It doesn't even have to be the Finals. If you beat Dwight

Howard in a regular season game or even a preseason game, then fuck it, you're the best player in the league.

So no, Kobe wasn't the best player the league in 2009, but by virtue of the Beat Dwight Howard Rule he was, you know what I'm saying?

2010

All-Star / Finals MVP / All-NBA First Team / All-Defensive First Team / NBA Champion

---

This was my personal favorite version of Kobe. It was the first time I watched him and felt like he wasn't doing (a) his best Michael Jordan impersonation or (b) his best villain impersonation.[26] He was just existing and playing basketball. Still, sentiment aside, he finished outside of the Top 5 in just about every major statistical category, advanced or otherwise. LeBron's the best during the regular season, Kobe is *MAYBE* the best during the playoffs.

▶

Is Kobe Bryant a dork?
    Yes.
How many years during his career was Kobe Bryant the best player in the league?
    Zero. Possibly one. Potentially two.

---

19. John Hollinger of ESPN.com, writing about Wade's 2006 Finals: "Overall, Wade's 33.8 PER is easily the best of any Finals performer since the merger. While it seems strange to have somebody besides Michael Jordan in the top spot, the truth is Jordan never dominated a Finals to this extent."
20. This is correct but also incorrect: George McCloud wore 24 during Kobe's rookie year, but he actually wasn't acquired until mid-season, so Kobe could have chosen 24. The season before Kobe's rookie year, it was worn by Fred Roberts, who was waived in July of 1996, the month after Kobe was acquired and several months before Kobe's rookie season began.
21. I made this up, but there's at least a 15 percent chance this is true. He watched *Kill Bill: Vol. 2* and decided he wanted to tell everyone to call him Black Mamba. There's no way you can convince me that it's impossible that he watched *24* and then decided he wanted that to be his number.
22. I also made this up. It's also probably true, too.
23. Possibly interesting: Kobe's Lakers suffered four losses by 28 or more points in elimination games. That said, Kobe played in 17 elimination games as a starter and was 9–8 in them. (Jordan was 6–7 in his 13 elimination games.)
24. Possibly interesting: Kobe never led a championship team in Win Shares for the season.
25. LeBron's VORP that season remains the best ever among all seasons and all players who are not Michael Jordan.
26. His whole 2006 season was like some Daniel Day-Lewis method actor shit.

WHAT ATTRIBUTES MAKE FOR THE
BEST BASKETBALL VILLAIN?

(AND ALSO: WHO'S A FIRST-BALLOT SELECTION
FOR THE BASKETBALL VILLAIN HALL OF FAME?)

I was playing Mortal Kombat II not that long ago, and the way the game is set up (and the way most fighting games are set up) is you pick a fighter, then you fight your way through a bunch of other fighters until you get to the boss. In the early editions of the MK series,[1] the fighters you had to face were arranged in a literal tower, bottom to top, in order of ascending difficulty. So the first person you fought was at the bottom of the tower and he or she was always super easy to beat, and then after you'd beat that person, you'd move up a level and fight the next person, who was slightly harder to handle. It looked like this (imagine the equal signs are fighter faces):

[=] (last person: hardest fight)

[=]

[=]

[=]

[=]

[=]

[=]

[=] (first person: easiest fight)

There were either more or less people in the tower depending on the game, but you get it. That's how it worked.

Now, and I'm slightly embarrassed by this, but I have to tell you a thing: This kind of doesn't have anything to do with this chapter. I mean, in a sense, yes, it does, but in a different sense it doesn't.

The chapter is about basketball villains, which are great, and also the Tower of Villains, which is a thing I just made up right now. It's similar to what you had to face in those Mortal Kombat games, in that it's a tower, but it's also not similar to what you had to face in those Mortal Kombat games, in that we're not talking about fighting them here. Mostly, all we're doing is (1) identifying the attributes a good basketball villain has and (2) identifying some players who belong in the Basketball Villain Hall of Fame.

That's just the way these things go sometimes.

▶

WHAT ATTRIBUTES MAKE FOR THE BEST BASKETBALL VILLAIN?

There are 13 of them. When determining the excellence or non-excellence of a basketball villain, you have to ask yourself:

1. **Is he very smart?** Big, strong, dumb villains are rarely ever as big-picture dangerous as smart, poised, composed villains. It's why Godzilla was never as scary as Anton Chigurh. So, are you talking about (a) someone who is just going to clobber you upside the head for no reason other than to clobber you upside the head, like what Brad Miller did to Shaquille O'Neal in 2002 when Shaq tried to post him up in the lane? Or are you talking about (b) someone who has concocted a master plan to unravel your team's whole everything, and the first step in that master plan is to clobber you upside the head, like what Kevin McHale did to Kurt Rambis in the 1984 Finals?

2. **Does he revel in the idea of his own villainy?** This one is important. For a guy to be a truly elite basketball villain, he has to want to be a basketball villain. He has to want to slit the sports-throats of his opponents and, in the case of a few, also the sports-throats of the fans of his opponent. It's what separates someone like Dwight Howard, who appears to hate the idea of people not liking him, from someone like Shaq, who appeared to thrive on it.

3. **Is he willing to taunt people?** For this category, we're talking about instances like when Reggie Miller hit a game-winning shot against the Bulls in Chicago during a game in 1994 and then bowed to the crowd as his team celebrated around him. (Bowing in an opposing stadium is such a dope move.) (Of course, it'd have been even doper if the shot had actually won the game for the Pacers. What happened was it put the Pacers up two with 0.8 second left. On the next play, Toni Kuko hit a three at the buzzer to

---

1. Mortal Kombat II is the best version of the game. After that it's Mortal Kombat, then Mortal Kombat III, then Ultimate Mortal Kombat III: Tournament Edition.

win the game for the Bulls. The next time the teams played, a game the Bulls won in Indiana, Scottie Pippen bowed to the crowd after the final buzzer. Scottie Pippen remains wildly underrated.)

4. **Is he a contributing player?** For a basketball villain to have any real heft or weight to his villainy, he has to be action-involved. He has to be in the game doing things.

5. **Is he a contributing player on a good team?** Draymond Green makes for such a great basketball villain because he's an important player on an important team. If a lesser player on a lesser team did all of the same things Draymond has done, we wouldn't look at that player as a villain. He'd just be a dick.

6. **How far outside of the rules is he willing to step during warfare?** Will he trip someone when he thinks no one is looking like what Bruce Bowen did to Chauncey Billups in Game 7 of the 2005 NBA Finals? Will he clothesline someone when he knows everyone is looking like what Raja Bell did to Kobe Bryant in the 2006 playoffs?[2] And so on.

7. **Is there a team that he just really looks to love giving the business to?** Larry and the Lakers, Magic and the Celtics, Jordan and the Pistons, Latrell Sprewell and the Knicks, Shaq and the Kings, Allen Iverson and the Cavs, John Wall and the Celtics, etc.

8. **If yes to the above question, then does he have a good reason for it?** Did he get traded away after tension between him and those in charge grew too big to ignore? Was he overlooked on draft night? Did it start out as a hatred for one of the players on the other team and then it just eventually spread to everyone else on the team?

9. **Is there a player that he just really looks to love giving the business to?**

10. **If yes to the above question, then does he have a good reason for it?** A lot of times when we see this one it's because one guy played the same position as the guy he hated and so people were always comparing the two and he hated it. Another reason is both guys belonged in the Top Ten Players in the League This Year grouping for more than a couple seasons together so they just developed a dislike for one another. Another reason is the two players were on the same team and their relationship soured and then one got traded away. Another reason is personal stuff that isn't at all basketball related, like the time [redacted] [redacted] a player's [redacted], or the time [redacted] [redacted] a player's [redacted], or the time [redacted] [redacted] a player's [redacted].

11. **Does he possess a discernible amount of mystery in his bones?** Complicated basketball villains are ideal. What's his motivation? What's his purpose? Why does he exist?

12. **Does he have a "look"?** Can you identify him just by his shadow, or maybe just by his arms, or maybe just by his smile, or maybe just by the way he walks? I have a guy in my head right now that I'm thinking of that I hate from high school and if you took him and literally everyone else in the world and had them walk behind a sheet with a light shining toward them so that all I could see was the outline of the way they walked, I could absolutely pick that fucker out of the seven billion other people.

13. **Was he ever slain?** Bill Laimbeer is the greatest basketball villain of all time, and a big part of the reason is because there's an arc to his existence. He has an identifiable beginning to his reign (when the Bad Boys–era Pistons became dominant) and also an identifiable end to his reign (after Jordan and the Bulls knocked the weapons out of their hands in the 1991 playoffs). Villains who are impossible to beat are fine. But villains who are mortal are way better.

The more of these attributes a person possesses, the greater the basketball villain he is. That's how you figure out who belongs where in the Tower of Villains. A player who only possesses one or two of them can be a villain, sure, but just barely. He'd belong at the bottom of the tower. Someone who possesses all of them, however—well, now you're talking about a first-class

---

2. What's crazy about this example is it was actually Kobe Bryant who was the villain that series, and also that play.

villain. A top-level villain. An iconic basketball villain, of which there are only four, maybe five.

▶

THREE QUESTIONS ABOUT BASKETBALL VILLAINY, AND ONE QUESTION ABOUT THE TOWER OF VILLAINS

1. If a player is a villain, does he always remain a villain? Is that just who he is for his entire career? Or can he move in and out of villainy?
Villainy is not a state of permanence. There's always redemption to be had. The most straight-line example of this is LeBron James deciding to leave Cleveland via an hour-long televised announcement in 2010, immediately becoming a villain, staying a villain for the four years he was in Miami, and then wiping away his villain status after he returned to Cleveland for the 2015 season. He and the Cavs eventually lost in the Finals that year, but he offered so much of himself during that run that it became impossible to view him as a villain anymore.
2. What about for players who weren't in that sort of circumstance? How do they redeem themselves?
Well, it's just a matter of balance, really, and I mean that literally. Think on it like it's one of those scales with weights on both sides. On the left side, you've got all of the villainous and dastardly things a player did. If, following his heel turn, he's able to amass enough good things to stack up on the right side so as to counterbalance the bad things, then that's how he redeems himself.

A fun way to approach villain redemption—and I mean villainy in general, not just basketball villainy—is to say, "Okay. If [NAME] were on a cruise ship and the cruise ship all of a sudden sunk, how many people would he [or she] have to save before I considered them to be a good person now?" If we stick with LeBron, then he probably would've had to save a good eight, nine people's lives on that boat before Clevelanders would've been like, "Maybe he ain't that bad after all." Meanwhile, someone like Rick Barry, a historic mega-prick, he'd have to save everyone on the cruise, then he'd have to swim to the bottom of the ocean, retrieve the ship, fix it, then load everyone back on it so they

could resume their vacations. That's what he'd have to do to redeem himself.
3. That's fun. Can we do that for more basketball villains? How many people would _____ have to save from a sinking ship before we consider him to be good?
No.
4. How do you know who belongs where in the Tower of Villains?
Easy. It's an attributes-based thing. There are five levels in the Tower of Villains. The bottom level (Level 1) is made up of the weakest villains. The top level (Level 5) is made up of the strongest villains. And the middle section increases as you'd expect it to.

People who end up in Level 1 are those who possess one to three of the basketball villain attributes. (Unofficially, this is the Arnold Schwarzenegger as Mr. Freeze in *Batman & Robin* level.) People who end up in Level 2 possess four to seven. (This is the Colin Farrell as Bullseye in *Daredevil* level.) People in Level 3 possess eight or nine. (This is the Chong Li in *Bloodsport* level.) People in Level 4 possess ten or eleven. (This is the *Jaws* level.) And people in Level 5 possess twelve or thirteen. (This is the Hannibal Lecter level.)

▶

THE BASKETBALL VILLAIN HALL OF FAME FIRST-BALLOT PICKS, ARRANGED BY VILLAINY

1. **Bill Laimbeer,[3] 1981–1994 (Level 5):** The alpha villain. My favorite thing about him is that he was punched by so many people. He was punched by Charles Barkley, Michael Jordan, Robert Parish, Alonzo Mourning, Bob Lanier, Larry Bird. Even Isiah Thomas punched him. That's basically the starting lineup of an All-Star team. There was even a time when Benny the Bull, the mascot for the Bulls, beat up a life-size Bill Laimbeer doll during a stoppage in game action.
2. **Reggie Miller, 1988–2005 (Level 5):** The second-greatest basketball villain of all time. He checks off literally every box for the categories mentioned earlier.
3. **Kevin McHale, 1981–1993 (Level 5):** (I think I'm

supposed to not like Kevin McHale, but I actually really, really like him. I watched a bunch of his interviews while researching for the book, and also he had a run at head coach for the Rockets while I lived in Houston, and he was always just very charming and affable. Sorry.)

4. **Vernon Maxwell, 1989–2001 (Level 4):** (I talked about all of his things during the Purge chapter.)[4]

5. **Rick Barry, 1966–1980[5] (Level 4):** His most heinous act: being Rick Barry.

6. **Dennis Rodman, 1987–2000 (Level 4):** An all-world irritant.[6]

7. **Karl Malone, 1986–2004 (Level 3):** His most heinous act: splitting Isiah Thomas's face open in 1991 with an elbow.

8. **Latrell Sprewell, 1993–2005 (Level 3):** His most heinous act: choking his coach during a practice in 1997.[7] His second-most heinous act: turning down a three-year 21-million-dollar contract in 2004. When asked why, he said, among other things, that he had "a family to feed." That's beautiful.[8]

9. **Danny Ainge, 1982–1995 (Level 3):** During Game 3 of the 1994 Western Conference Semifinals, Mario Elie made an and-one floater over Danny Ainge, then hollered in his face about it. Later in the game, after Hakeem Olajuwon dunked it in the final seconds (of a blowout, mind you), Ainge, who'd been tossed the ball by the ref, cocked it back and then rocketed the ball 100 miles per hour into Mario Elie's face as he celebrated with Hakeem. It's not the only instance of Danny Ainge being a bastard, but it's definitely the best[9] one.[10]

10. **Bruce Bowen, 1997–2009 (Level 3):** An all-world dirty player.

11. **Kevin Garnett, 1996–2016 (Level 2):** His most heinous act: One time, during a game in 2010, he (reportedly) called Charlie Villanueva a "cancer patient." He (reportedly) did so because Villanueva has alopecia universalis, a skin disease that prevents hair growth. Garnett tried to clean it up in a statement afterward, saying that what he actually said to Villanueva was, "You are cancerous to your team and our league."

12. **Kermit Washington, 1974–1988 (Level 2):** Kermit ends up backing his way into the BVHOF off the strength of that Rudy Tomjanovich punch he threw in 1977. It's an unfair designation, but one he gets nonetheless.

13. **Metta World Peace, 2000–Present[11] (Level 2):** How's this for a villain origin story: In 2009, following an especially chippy game between Artest's Rockets and Kobe's Lakers, Artest talked about how it actually wasn't a chippy basketball game at all—that one time when he was growing up, he watched a guy die at a game because someone else broke off a piece of a table leg and threw it through the guy's heart like the fucking deadliest javelin of all.

---

3. I just made up a rule right now where only one player per team can make it per ballot. Isiah Thomas loses his spot to Buffalo Bill.
4. See page 82.
5. I was not intending on including anyone here that didn't play after 1980, but after watching several old Rick Barry interviews and reading several Rick Barry stories, I couldn't help myself.
6. Draymond Green is right here, too.
7. In an interview with *60 Minutes* Sprewell explained, "It's not like he was losing air or anything."
8. Sprewell had a year left on his contract at that point, and he wanted to sign an extension. The extension never happened, and so Sprewell played out that final year of his contract and then never played again.
9. Zach Lowe ran a story at ESPN in 2016 about Ainge eating lunch at Chipotle seven days a week, and sometimes following up his lunch with dinner there, too. "I have to admit, there are days I eat there twice." I don't know why this is so extremely weird to me, but it absolutely is.
10. One time he made Tree Rollins so mad that, during a scuffle, Rollins bit his finger all the way down to the tendon.
11. For all intents and purposes of this book, I'm defining "present" as the spring of 2017.

SHOULD WE DO A CHAPTER THAT'S
JUST A BUNCH OF LISTS?

For all of the other parts of this book, each chapter is treated as a single question, and each answer for each question is carefully considered and worked through thoroughly. It was important to me for the book to move that way because in situations like these—situations where you're trying to convince someone of something—people are far more receptive to receiving an answer (even one that they might disagree with) if they can see how you arrived at your conclusion.

It would be disingenuous, though, for me to pretend like talking about basketball (or any subject, really) in that manner is a natural thing for me or a regular thing for me. Truth be told, it rarely works that way. More often than not, the flow of that kind of conversation is me (a) saying a thing while offering no real evidence to substantiate my claim, and then (b) calling the person disagreeing with me an unfavorable name when they inevitably buck back.[1] Now, to be sure, I of course wish I were smarter and that that were not the case. I wish that I was consistently fluid and that all of my responses to questions were measured and thoughtful. But I am not, and they are not. And so I'm mildly sad about that, sure. But the thing of it is, that's how it goes for most people, I'm guessing—or, at least, that's how it goes for most of the people that I talk to about basketball (or any subject, really).

As such, the rest of this chapter is the inverse of all the other parts of the book. Rather than it being one question answered rigorously, it's 18 questions answered without any more info given beyond the answer itself. It's just how arguing goes sometimes. Getting that into this book was important to me, too.

▶

WHO ARE THE 10 GREATEST BASKETBALL PLAYERS OF ALL TIME?

1. Michael Jordan
2. Kareem Abdul-Jabbar
3. LeBron James
4. Magic Johnson
5. Tim Duncan
6. Bill Russell
7. Wilt Chamberlain
8. Larry Bird
9. Hakeem Olajuwon
10. Shaquille O'Neal

WHAT ARE THE 10 GREATEST BASKETBALL REFERENCES FROM RAP SONGS?

1. "I'm slammin' niggas like Shaquille." —The Notorious B.I.G., "Gimme The Loot"
2. "And you can live through anything if Magic made it." —Kanye West, "Can't Tell Me Nothing"
3. "If Jeezy's paying LeBron, I'm paying Dwyane Wade." —Jay Z, "Empire State of Mind"
4. "The height of Muggsy Bogues, complexion of a hockey puck." —Phife Dawg of A Tribe Called Quest, "Steve Biko (Stir It Up)"
5. "Basketball is my favorite sport / I like the way they dribble up and down the court." —Kurtis Blow, "Basketball"
6. "I got more foreign shooters than the Sacramento Kings." —50 Cent, "Follow Me Gangster"
7. "See, I've got heart like John Starks." —Mike D of The Beastie Boys, "Get It Together"
8. "With my hair slicked back I look like Rick Pitino."[2] —Action Bronson, "NaNa"
9. "One minute you hot, next minute you not / Remind me of the New York Knicks with they jump shots." —Ghostface Killah, "Barbershop"
10. "Coupe is on Manu Ginobilis / But the truck is on Kobes." —Fabolous, "I'm The Man"

---

1. "You're a fucking idiot," is my main one.
2. He has another line on that same song where he says, "I got a team of hoes like Pat Summitt," and then also, "I had the full Bulls warm-up with the Pippens on."

CHAPTER 26

WHO ARE THE 10 GREATEST POINT GUARDS OF ALL TIME?

1. Magic Johnson
2. John Stockton
3. Oscar Robertson
4. Isiah Thomas
5. Jason Kidd
6. Steve Nash
7. Chris Paul
8. Steph Curry
9. Walt Frazier
10. Gary Payton

WHAT ARE THE 10 GREATEST HAIRSTYLES IN BASKETBALL HISTORY?

1. Bill Walton's hippie ponytail that he would wear with a headband, so then by, like, the second quarter of every game he looked like a large white woman after a long day at Coachella.
2. Allen Iverson's cornrows.
3. Artis Gilmore's Afro (or Dr. J's Afro, if you want).
4. Latrell Sprewell when he had the pigtails.
5. Chris Mullin's flat top (or Dwayne Schintzius's flat top mullet, if you want).
6. One time Scot Pollard wanted to wear his hair in a ponytail, but it wasn't quite long enough so he did a thing where he had one ponytail at the top of his head and then one ponytail near the nape of his neck. It was double fucking ponytails, is what I'm saying.
7. When Anthony Mason had "KNICKS" shaved into the side of his head.
8. Kenny Walker's high top fade.
9. That time Lou Amundson cut his hair like Jennifer Aniston had it in *Friends*. (Google this.)
10. That time Brandon Jennings had the Gumby fade.

WHO ARE THE 10 GREATEST SHOOTING GUARDS OF ALL TIME?

1. Michael Jordan
2. Kobe Bryant
3. Dwyane Wade
4. Jerry West
5. Allen Iverson
6. Clyde Drexler
7. George Gervin
8. Reggie Miller
9. Ray Allen
10. Tracy McGrady

WHO ARE THE 10 NBA PLAYERS WHO SEEMED THE MOST LIKELY TO LIE TO YOUR FACE ABOUT SOMETHING UNIMPORTANT?

1. Dwight Howard in 2016
2. Christian Laettner in 1998
3. Isiah Thomas in 1986
4. Kris Humphries in 2012
5. Kevin Johnson in 1993
6. Kelly Tripucka in 1988
7. Kobe Bryant in 2009
8. Danny Ainge in 1991
9. Sasha Vujacic in 2008
10. D'Angelo Russell in 2016

WHO ARE THE 10 GREATEST CENTERS OF ALL TIME?

1. Kareem Abdul-Jabbar
2. Bill Russell
3. Wilt Chamberlain
4. Hakeem Olajuwon
5. Shaquille O'Neal
6. David Robinson
7. Moses Malone
8. Bill Walton
9. Patrick Ewing
10. Dikembe Mutombo

WHAT ARE THE 10 GREATEST NBA CONSPIRACY THEORIES?

1. That Paul Pierce pooped himself during the 2008 Finals and so that's why he pretended like he hurt his knee.
2. The NBA rigged the 1985 draft lottery so that the Knicks could get Patrick Ewing.
3. Michael Jordan didn't actually want to retire for those two years in the middle of his career—it was just that the NBA forced him to as a punishment for gambling.
4. Michael Jordan made sure the Wizards traded Richard Hamilton to the Pistons in 2002 because he wanted the Pistons to beat the Lakers in the 2004 Finals to help slow down Kobe from catching him in championships. He did the same thing with the Bobcats in 2012 when he had them waive Tyson Chandler, who then went to the Mavs, who beat the Heat in the Finals, preventing LeBron from getting his first ring. Then, in 2013, he made the Bobcats waive Boris Diaw. Diaw went and played for the Spurs, who beat the Heat in the Finals in 2014, preventing LeBron from collecting another championship ring.
5. The NBA told the refs to make sure that the Lakers didn't lose Game 6 against the Sacramento Kings in the 2002 Western Conference Finals.
6. The NBA rigged the 2012 draft lottery so that the New Orleans Hornets could get Anthony Davis.
7. The NBA told the refs to make sure the Bucks lost to the Sixers in the 2001 Eastern Conference Finals because nobody wanted to see the Bucks in the Finals, not even people from Milwaukee.
8. Russell Westbrook gets injected with wolverine blood before every game.
9. Wolverines get injected with Russell Westbrook blood before every hunt.
10. LeBron James left Cleveland for Miami in 2010 so that they could be terrible and draft good players for him to play with when he returned to Cleveland in 2014. He set it all in place before he announced his intention to leave Cleveland via The Decision.

WHO ARE THE 10 GREATEST SMALL FORWARDS OF ALL TIME?

1. LeBron James
2. Larry Bird
3. Kevin Durant
4. Scottie Pippen
5. Julius Erving
6. Elgin Baylor
7. James Worthy
8. Rick Barry
9. Dominique Wilkins
10. John Havlicek

WHAT ARE THE 5 BEST PLAYOFF BUZZER BEATERS OF ALL TIME?

1. I don't know, but not the 0.4 shot Derek Fisher hit against the Spurs in 2004. That one was stupid.
2. I don't know, but not the 0.4 shot Derek Fisher hit against the Spurs in 2004. That one was stupid.
3. I don't know, but not the 0.4 shot Derek Fisher hit against the Spurs in 2004. That one was stupid.
4. I don't know, but not the 0.4 shot Derek Fisher hit against the Spurs in 2004. That one was stupid.
5. I don't know, but not the 0.4 shot Derek Fisher hit against the Spurs in 2004. That one was stupid.[3]

3. The actual 10 best playoff buzzer beaters of all time: 1. Michael Jordan's series-winning jumper over Craig Ehlo in Game 5 of the 1989 matchup between the Bulls and Cavs. / 2. Gar Heard's turnaround 20-footer to send Game 5 of the Celtics–Suns Finals into triple overtime. / 3. Robert Horry's three to win Game 4 of the 2002 Western Conference Finals between the Lakers and Kings. / 4. Jerry West's 60-footer to tie Game 3 of the 1970 Finals between the Lakers and Knicks. / 5. Derek Fisher's 0.4 turnaround to win Game 5 of the 2004 Western Conference Semis between the Lakers and Spurs. / 6. John Stockton's series-winning three against the Rockets to send the Jazz to the 1997 Finals. / 7. Alonzo Mourning's series-winning 20-footer in Game 4 of the Hornets–Celtics series. / 8. Ralph Sampson's series-winning turnaround flip shot against the Lakers that sent the Rockets to the 1986 Finals. / 9. Kobe Bryant's jumper to win Game 4 of the Lakers–Suns first-round series in 2006. / 10. LeBron's three to win Game 2 of the 2009 Eastern Conference Finals between the Cavs and the Magic.

WHO ARE THE 10 GREATEST POWER FORWARDS OF ALL TIME?

1. Tim Duncan
2. Dirk Nowitzki
3. Karl Malone
4. Charles Barkley
5. Kevin Garnett
6. Kevin McHale
7. Elvin Hayes
8. Dennis Rodman
9. Chris Webber
10. Shawn Kemp

WHAT ARE THE THREE MOST INTERESTING PHILOSOPHICAL QUANDARIES TANGENTIALLY CONNECTED TO A CARMELO ANTHONY CAMEO IN A MOVIE OR TV SHOW?

1. In 2016, Carmelo was in the movie *Teenage Mutant Ninja Turtles: Out of the Shadows.* A lot of people disliked it, and I guess maybe I did, too, but I also thought it was good, because one piece of it presented a very advanced philosophical question: As part of the movie's plot, two guys accidentally get mutated into a giant warthog and a giant rhinoceros. As soon as they realize it's happened, the first thing they do is look at their new animal dicks. I was struck by that moment. At first, I thought it was ridiculous that that was their response, but the more I thought about it, and the more I think about it, the more reasonable it's starting to become. Is looking at your new dick one of the first things any man who happened to get transformed into something else would do? I remember it happening in that movie *Big*, too, where Young Josh Baskin woke up as Grown Josh Baskin. And part of me wants to say it also happened in *Captain America: The First Avenger* after Steve Rogers got transformed into a superhero, though that can't

possibly have been the case.[4] But so, again: Is looking at your new dick one of the first things any man who happened to get transformed into something else would do?

2. In 2004, Carmelo was on a TV show called *Punk'd*, the premise of which was: Let's put famous people in bad spots and record how they react. Mostly, it was harmless pranks that were pulled on celebrities, stuff like, "Oh, no, your waiter is very rude," or, "Oh, no, someone parked too close to your car." When Carmelo was on there, though, what they did is they trashed his hotel room while he was out and then, when he got there, they sent an underage girl in to say she had left her purse there, then the authorities show up, then she tells them she was partying with Carmelo, and so Carmelo's prank is that he's being accused of inappropriate contact with an underage girl. There's actually no real philosophical dilemma attached to this one. I just wanted to mention it because it was insane.

3. In 2014, Carmelo was on a TV show called *Sons of Anarchy*. The show was about a motorcycle gang (they were the Sons of Anarchy) that did many, many bad things, several of which were secretly good things. Carmelo was part of a rival crew that was torturing one of the Sons (a character named Bobby Munson) to get information out of him. During the torture, one guy carved Munson's eye out with a grapefruit spoon. As retaliation, that guy later had his own eye yanked out of his head by the president of the Sons. It was an eye-for-an-eye situation in the most literal sense possible. The quandary: Is retribution as punishment a morally stable foundation? It seems like no, but it also seems like yes.

---

4. Captain America probably has the best dick of all the Avengers. It's him or Thor. Definitely.

WHO ARE THE 10 NBA PLAYERS WHO WERE THE BEST AT WEARING TALL SOCKS?

1. Manute Bol
2. George Gervin
3. Jason Terry
4. Adrian Dantley
5. Clyde Drexler
6. Tom McMillen (Google this guy. Look for pictures of him when he played with the Washington Bullets at the end of his career. He was in his early 30s at the time but he looked, like, at least in his 60s.)
7. Keith Van Horn
8. Michael Cooper
9. Jack Sikma
10. Shaun Livingston

WHAT ARE THE 15 BEST "10 BEST" RANKINGS THAT DIDN'T MAKE IT INTO THIS CHAPTER OF LISTS BECAUSE YOU RAN OUT OF SPACE?

1. Who are the 10 Best "He should've had a cameo in a *Fast and the Furious* movie" Players Picks?[5]
2. What are the 10 Best Wilt Chamberlain Things?[6]
3. What are the 10 Best Announcer Play Calls That Happened During Big Games?
4. What are the 10 Best Alley-Oops?
5. Who are the 10 Best Coaches of All Time?
6. Who are the 10 Best Courtside Celebrity Fans?
7. What are the 10 Best Team Logos?
8. What are the 10 Best Arena Nicknames That Would Also Make for Good Nicknames of the Room in Your House Where You Most Often Have Sex?[7]
9. What are the 10 Best Finals Games?
10. What are the 10 Best Post-Shot Celebrations?
11. What are the 10 Best Arena Foods to Eat during a Game?
12. What are the 10 Best Accessories Players Have Worn during Games?
13. What are the 10 Best Jersey Numbers?
14. What are the 10 Best Referee Signals for Infractions?
15. What are the 10 Best "Short Player Blocks Big Player" Moments?

WHAT ARE THE 10 BEST DUNK CONTESTS?

(The participants are listed. The winners are bolded.)
1. **2016:** **Zach LaVine (Timberwolves)**, Will Barton (Nuggets), Andre Drummond (Pistons), Aaron Gordon (Magic).
2. **1988:** Jerome Kersey (Blazers), Greg Anderson (Spurs), **Michael Jordan (Bulls)**, Dominique Wilkins (Hawks), Spud Webb (Hawks), Clyde Drexler (Blazers), Otis Smith (Warriors).
3. **2000:** **Vince Carter (Raptors)**, Tracy McGrady (Raptors), Steve Francis (Rockets), Larry Hughes (Sixers), Ricky Davis (Hornets), Jerry Stackhouse (Pistons).
4. **1986:** **Spud Webb (Hawks)**, Terry Tyler (Kings), Roy Hinson (Cavs), Dominique Wilkins (Hawks), Paul Pressey (Bucks), Jerome Kersey (Blazers), Terence Stansbury (Pacers), Gerald Wilkins (Knicks).
5. **1985:** Michael Jordan (Bulls), Orlando Woolridge (Bulls), Clyde Drexler (Blazers), **Dominique Wilkins (Hawks)**, Terence Stansbury (Pacers), Julius Erving (Sixers), Darrell Griffith (Jazz), Larry Nance (Suns).
6. **2008:** **Dwight Howard (Magic)**, Jamario Moon (Raptors), Gerald Green (Timberwolves), Rudy Gay (Grizzlies).
7. **2011:** JaVale McGee (Wizards), Serge Ibaka (Thunder), DeMar DeRozan (Raptors), **Blake Griffin (Clippers)**.
8. **1991:** Blue Edwards (Jazz), **Dee Brown (Celtics)**, Rex Chapman (Hornets), Shawn Kemp (Sonics), Kenny Smith (Rockets), Kendall Gill (Hornets), Kenny Williams (Pacers), Otis Smith (Magic).
9. **1987:** Gerald Wilkins (Knicks), Tom Chambers (Sonics), **Michael Jordan (Bulls)**, Jerome Kersey (Blazers), Clyde Drexler (Blazers), Johnny Dawkins (Spurs), Terence Stansbury (Sonics), Ron Harper (Cavs).
10. **2003:** Desmond Mason (Sonics), Amar'e Stoudemire (Suns), **Jason Richardson (Warriors)**, Richard Jefferson (Nets).

WHO ARE THE 10 PLAYERS MOST LIKELY TO ADOPT A KID IN A *LIKE MIKE* SITUATION?

1. David Robinson (any year)
2. Matt Bullard in 1996
3. Tim Thomas in 2005
4. A.C. Green in 1987
5. Steph Curry (any year)
6. Grant Hill in 1995
7. Mike Conley in 2011
8. Rik Smits in 1991
9. Sean Elliott in 1998
10. Dirk Nowitzki in 2005

WHAT ARE THE 10 BEST FREE THROW RITUALS OF ALL TIME?

1. That thing Richard Hamilton would do where he'd dribble twice forward and then once off to his right before shooting.
2. That thing Alonzo Mourning would do when he'd tap his wristband to his chin and then forehead before shooting.
3. That thing Amar'e Stoudemire would do after he started wearing goggles where he'd move his goggles up to his forehead before shooting.
4. That thing Karl Malone would do where he'd speak in tongues before shooting.
5. That thing Kevin Durant does where he shakes his right shoulder twice before shooting.
6. That thing Jeff Hornacek would do where he'd rub his face a couple times before shooting.
7. That thing Shaquille O'Neal would do where he'd miss 47 percent of all of the free throws he shot during his career.
8. That thing Dirk Nowitzki would do where he'd sing a David Hasselhoff song to himself before shooting.
9. That thing Gilbert Arenas would do where he'd pass the ball around his waist three times before shooting.
10. That thing Jerry Stackhouse would do where he'd do a deep squat before shooting.

WHAT ARE THE 10 BEST IN-ARENA ENTERTAINMENT THINGS?

1. The Kiss Cam.
2. The half-court shot to win something.
3. The T-shirt gun.
4. When they do the baby races.
5. The thing when everyone gets some sort of free food if the home team breaks 100 points or whatever.
6. The thing when everyone gets some sort of free food if a player on the away team misses two free throws in a row.
7. The Simba Cam. (They play the music from the beginning of *The Lion King* and parents hold their children up like how Rafiki held Simba up.) (This is a real thing.)
8. The thing where they show people on the jumbotron and the people dance for whatever reason.
9. The thing where the mascot has sides of the arena cheer at different times to see who's the loudest.
10. The thing where the mascot spills something on someone in the opposing team's jersey.

---

5. J. R. Smith absolutely should've been in a *Fast and the Furious* movie.
6. My favorite Wilt Chamberlain thing was when he claimed that he one time killed a mountain lion with his hands when it attacked him at a roadside rest stop.
7. The Highlight Factory. The Palace. The Roaracle. The Thunderdome. The Grindhouse (my favorite).

This chapter and the one that follows are both (a) structured the exact same way, and (b) about pickup basketball, which is the best version of basketball:[1] There's a sentence with a fill-in-the-blank in it ("Am I allowed to _____ during pickup basketball?") and then there are a bunch of different things that get plugged into the blank. ("Am I allowed to try and take a charge during pickup basketball?" and "Am I allowed to call a foul during pickup basketball?" Things like that.) The answer to all the questions in this chapter is yes. The answer to all the questions in the next one is no.

▶

The first person who ever tried to fight me over something I'd done or said on a basketball court was a monster named Saul. In the neighborhood where I lived, he was one of the tougher kids. He and I were in the same grade, but he was, like, maybe 10 or 12 years older because he'd been held back a bunch of times because nobody ever bothered to teach him how to read.[2] He used to play basketball in Dickies, that's the kind of kid he was. And let me be clear: I don't mean Dickies shorts. I mean Dickies work pants. He was navigating pick and rolls in some fucking factory worker pants. He was dropping off perfect assists in the same pants as guys who were putting bumpers on Chevys. Do you even understand how hard of a person you have to be to run a fast break in the same pants as a Detroit assembly-line worker?

Here are five things I remember about Saul: (1) He used to slick his hair straight back. (2) Sometimes he wore a hairnet over his slicked-back hair. (3) He had a couple of tattoos, and that maybe doesn't seem like a strange thing because you're an adult and so maybe you're picturing another adult in your head, but let me please just remind you that this was when we were in *middle school*. Having tattoos in middle school is basically the same thing as having a couple bodies on you in prison. (4) He had an older brother who'd gotten sent to prison either for robbing a convenience store owned by Asian people or for robbing Asians in a convenience store.[3] (5) There was a rumor that he'd at one time beaten up a bus driver for failing to pick him up for school one morning. I don't know how true it was, but that's not the point. The point is that Saul was not the person you wanted to get in a fight with at a basketball court. And yet, at 12 years old, that's where I was.

When it happened, Saul was already mad because his team was losing and I was letting him hear about it. But he'd gotten even madder because he'd called a foul and I made fun of him for it. I don't recall exactly what I said to him, but I know his response was to shove me to the ground and shout, "You talk too fucking much," to which my response was to just sit there on the pavement and do that thing where you try not to blink or talk because you know if you do you're going to start crying.

But listen, here's the whole reason I'm telling you this: There are things you are allowed to do in a pickup basketball game, and there are things you're not allowed to do in a pickup basketball game. Calling a foul is a thing you're not supposed to do.[4] (More on this in a moment.) Saul's response to being hacked across the arms was reflexive, but so was my response to his response. When Saul called that foul, I suspect he knew immediately that it was a thing he wasn't supposed to do. That's (probably) why he got so mad when he got called out for it. Or I don't know, man. Maybe he actually didn't

---

1. The NBA is the second-best version of basketball. Third-best is NCAA Basketball. Fourth is And1 Basketball. Fifth is NERF Basketball. Sixth is Middle School Basketball. Seventh is Hallway Basketball (where you slap a doorjamb or a sign to indicate a dunk). Eighth is SlamBall. Ninth is Trash Can Basketball. Tenth is Movie Basketball. Eleventh is High School Basketball. Twelfth is Video Game Basketball. Thirteenth is YMCA Kids Basketball. Fourteenth is Swimming Pool Basketball. Fifteenth is YMCA Adult Basketball. Sixteenth is Harlem Globetrotters Basketball. And seventeenth is whatever version of basketball the Philadelphia 76ers were playing in the 2015 season.
2. I'm assuming.
3. The exact details were always hazy in that way that neighborhood folklore generally is. The only things everyone seemed to agree on were that the robbery took place in a convenience store and two Asian men were present.
4. Incidentally, making fun of someone for calling a foul *is* a thing you are supposed to do.

know he wasn't supposed to call fouls. Maybe nobody ever taught him that, same as nobody ever taught him to read.[5]

▶

Am I allowed to _____ during pickup basketball?

. . . talk shit . . .

Yes. Of course. Absolutely. For sure. It's one of the very best parts of basketball, I think. The only thing better than blocking a shot during a game is blocking a shot and shouting "Get that shit outta here!" as you do so. It feels SO good. I am 100 percent in favor of it. The only time I ever talked shit to someone and regretted it afterward is one time I was playing at this park and I think I'd scored three or four times in a row on a guy. We were coming back down the court and I was letting everyone know he couldn't guard me and so I said something close to "You better call your mom to help you guard because you sure as shit can't do it by yourself." He said something close to "My mom passed away in 2009." And so what I should've said there was either (1) "Ay, my bad, I didn't know," or (2) nothing at all. But neither of those are what I chose. Instead, I responded—and I'm so sad and embarrassed remembering this—but instead I responded, "I guess it's gonna be a long-distance call then." ☹

. . . stand in the paint on offense . . .

This one is in reference to the three-second rule, which says you're not allowed to stand in the paint for three or more seconds during an offensive possession without reestablishing your possession. That's for proper basketball, though. In pickup basketball, yes, of course you can stand there for three seconds. You can stand there for three days, if you want. Doesn't matter. Build a small townhome and live in that bitch. You're completely within the rules of pickup basketball.

. . . stand in the paint on defense . . .

This one is in reference to the defensive version of the three-second rule, which says you're not allowed to stand in the paint for three or more seconds during a defensive possession without reestablishing your possession if you're not guarding someone. You're safe here same as you are on offense. Really, it's a smart play to just camp someone out down there, especially if you're playing on an outside court because it's way harder to shoot jumpers outside so people drive to the basket a bunch more.

. . . take a heat check shot . . .

A heat check shot is a shot that comes after a person has made one or two shots in a row. The way it typically works is a guy will hit an open jumper, then he'll hit a second open jumper, then his chest will fill with courage as he realizes, *Oh, fuck. I'm the new Steph Curry.* Then he'll come down and chuck up a fadeaway 27-footer. Foolhardy and shortsighted as this may seem, it is okay to do (and usually encouraged, really). You just keep on tossing that ball up there until you miss, each shot getting more and more ridiculous. You make a 27-foot fadeaway, you try a 31-foot hook shot. You make a 31-foot hook shot, you try a runner from half court. You make a runner from half court, you make sure your hair looks good for when they make the statue they're going to build of you in the center of downtown.

. . . hang on the rim if I dunk it . . .

Three things here:

1. You can absolutely hang on the rim if you dunk it, yes. You've earned it.

2. When I was in high school there was this guy during gym class who, while on a fast break, jumped and tried to dunk it and he did manage to dunk it, but he was going so fast that his feet swung out from under him and he lost his grip on the rim and fell backward and put his arm back to try to blunt the fall and ended up snapping that bitch right in half. It remains the worst injury I've ever seen in person during a basketball game.

---

5. I'm still assuming.

It was gruesome. For, like, the next two months I refused to jump for any reason at all. I wouldn't even stand up. I just fucking crawled everywhere for fear of falling.

3. I've never dunked a basketball on a regulation goal. Matter of fact, I've only ever slapped the back-board twice in my whole life.[6] A regular dream I have while sleeping is that I can jump high enough to dunk it. It's my favorite kind of erotic dream.

...win a game by one point...

You're playing to 11. The score is tied 10–10. Your team scores. Then that means your team wins. That's how it works. Sometimes someone will shout out "Deuce," which means that the game now has to be won by two points, not one. Deuce is for cowards.

Sidebar: There's another thing that happens during pickup basketball sometimes, when a team can win by one point BUT they can't win with a two-point shot. What I mean is, okay, so let's say you're playing to 11 and the score is their team has 10 and your team has 9. Your team has the ball. The "Can't Win on a 2" rule says that in this particular case, even if your team manages to make a two-point shot, which would technically give them 11, it's a conditional 11 points. You have to score another basket before the other team does to win. It's the dumbest thing. It's a way for someone to call Deuce without having to actually call Deuce.

...ignore the guy who shoots it every time he touches it...

Yes. Unless he's in the middle of a heat check thing, in which case you are obligated to pass him the ball every time until he misses it.

...foul as many times as I want...

Definitely, but just know that the more you foul the more contentious things are going to get. You are within your pickup basketball rights to pretend to be Charles Oakley if you so choose, but that means you're going to end up in some Charles Oakley-type situations, and let me tell you a secret: You ain't Charles Oakley. So exercise this one judiciously. I always recommend one good hard foul at the beginning of the game and then you chill and then it's free reign if you end up in a spot where the other team has Game Point. Go nuts. It's jungle law at this point. Everyone understands.

---

6. I'm the Vince Carter of grabbing the net.

AM I ALLOWED TO
                    DURING

Part 1 of this double chapter started with an anecdote about the first person who'd ever tried to fight me over something I'd said or done on a basketball court, so I'm going to start this one with an anecdote about the last person[1] who ever tried to fight me over something I'd said or done on a basketball court. Mostly I like for things to end in just this misty or nebulous manner, but sometimes I like when things tie themselves together neatly, too. So:

It happened when I was 25 years old. I was playing in this nighttime rec league with some guys from the place where I was working at the time. We were playing a game against a team everyone assumed was going to crush us, but it was late in the third quarter or early in the fourth and we were ahead by a few points. The guy I was guarding was probably, say, 7 or 8 inches taller than me and stronger than me and more handsome than me and was otherwise way better than me at basketball, but he was having a very bad game, and so I was reminding him of how bad he was playing every time I took a breath, which he was not especially happy about.

Someone shot a long shot, missed, and so the ball bounced high into the air and out near the three-point line, where we were both standing. There was no chance I was ever going to be able to out-jump him to get the ball, so right before he was about to leap into the air I just sort of crabbed my way backwards into his legs real fast and hard, uprooting him from his launch-pad. I didn't even have to jump. The ball landed right in my hands. It worked out perfect. I turned to see up the court, but before I could dribble or pass or do anything I felt a big ***whop*** across the side of my face.

I stumbled back a bit, insta-realized I'd been hit, felt my body turn into a volcano, then charged at him so we could fight. It only lasted a handful of seconds before we got separated. I shouted some not nice things as they dragged us apart ("I'm gonna kill you, you motherfucker," things like that), he shouted some not nice things ("Fuck you, little bitch," things like that). We both got ejected and that was that. That was the end. That was the fight.

Now, to be thorough, I will tell you that the guy and I ended up talking about everything after the fact and he said that he didn't intend to hit me, he was just trying to get the ball. I will also tell you that I didn't believe him then and I still don't believe him now. I think he was mad because I was running my mouth, which is completely understandable because that's sort of the whole point of talking shit to someone during basketball.[2]

You're allowed to talk shit while you play pickup basketball. You're also allowed to ***whop*** someone in the head if they talk too much shit while you play pickup basketball. It's all part of it. I love it all, even if it occasionally ends in a less than ideal manner.

▶

---

1. I feel confident in describing the guy in the fight here as "the last person" because I know I'm never going to get in a fight on a basketball court again. As I'm writing this, I'm 35 years old. By the time this book comes out I will be 36 years old. 36-year-olds don't fight during pickup basketball games. There's for sure yelling. And there's definitely pre-fight theater. But that's it. The older you get, the more invested you become in just yelling at people. The amount of time you spend yelling goes up and the amount of time you spend fighting goes down. When you're 20, the pre-fight conversation is super short. One guy fouls someone too hard and the other guy goes, "What the fuck, man?" and then that's it. The fight starts. When you're 36, the pre-fight conversation is endless. One guy fouls someone too hard and the other guy goes, "What the fuck, man?" Then the first guy goes, "What, bitch?" and takes a step forward. Then the second guy goes, "What the fuck did you just say?" and he takes a step forward, too. Then the first guy goes, "You heard me." Then the second goes, "Say it again. Make your mouth say it again and I'ma kill everyone in this bitch." Then the first goes, "I. Said. *What. Bitch.*" Then the second guy goes, "Oh, you really said that shit again, huh?" And the first guy nods. Then the second guy nods. Then it's 10 minutes later and they've both threatened to burn the other one's house down or whatever. And it just goes on and on and on and on. I'm glad to finally be at that stage of my pickup basketball career. Threatening to burn someone's house down is just as fulfilling as fistfighting him. That's the sort of thing only time and experience can teach you.
2. Or in life, really.

Am I allowed to _____ during pickup basketball?

...take a charge...

No. 100 percent no. Really, they shouldn't even call charging in the NBA, so you sure as shit shouldn't call it during a game at the park or whatever.

...call a foul...

The answer to this one is no and also yes, and I don't want you to think that that's a clever way to step around this question, because it's not. It's just that there's a clear and definite time when you're allowed to call a foul and a clear and definite time when you're not.

NOT ALLOWED: You're not allowed to call fouls during pickup basketball if you're the aggrieved party. That's just not a thing you should do. If you get hit on a jumper or whacked on a drive to the basket, then that's just some shit that happened to you. Have you ever heard of Floyd James Thompson? His plane was shot down during the Vietnam War. His body was burned, his back was literally broken, he took a bullet to the face. But he survived the crash. And his prize for surviving all that was getting to spend nearly nine years in enemy incarceration as a prisoner of war where he was regularly tortured and intermittently starved. That's the longest POW prison term in American history. And do you know what happened after those nine years? He came home to America, that's what. That's it. That's all. He survived all that with nary a peep and you're telling me you can't survive a slap on the wrist during a layup without demanding retribution? Unacceptable. If you rise up to shoot a three during a game and your defender busts you in the side of the head with a two-by-four, you don't say a goddamn word. You just lie right there on the floor and let your brain ooze out of your head.[3]

YES ALLOWED: You're allowed to call a foul if you're the person who committed the foul. That's the proper way the game should work. You clobber your guy on a

shot, you just say something like, "Aye, I got him," and then your team gives the other team the ball back and there you go. That's a little thing called having some integrity and also some honor. That's civility. That's nobility. George Washington admitted when he fouled someone during pickup basketball. John Adams did, too. Thomas Jefferson, James Madison, Alexander Hamilton— they were all good for it. It's right there in the Bill of Rights: "No pickup basketball player shall, during a game or even at game point, commit a substantial foul without admitting to it, in a manner prescribed by law." That's from the Third Amendment. James Madison wrote it in 1789. Still holds true today.

...call a three-second violation...

What the fuck? This is even worse than trying to take the charge because at least with taking a charge it requires some sort of physical dedication to the call. With a three-second call, literally all you did was count to three. Offensive three seconds, defensive three seconds—it doesn't matter. A three-second violation is the most egregious of all calls. In order, it's followed by

- **The five-second violation.** I guess at least this time you counted to five, which is almost twice as hard as counting to three.
- **Carrying.** Chill out. They don't even call this in the NBA. Allen Iverson earned over 200 million dollars carrying the ball.
- **Personal foul.** See above.
- **Shouting "First!" during a tie-up situation.** Ridiculous. In the NBA, tie-ups are settled with a jump ball. In the NCAA and middle/high school basketball, they're settled with a possession arrow. In pickup basketball, the ball always goes to the defense on a tie-up. It's the reward for the bravery one must exhibit in forcing a tie-up. Shouting "First!" during a tie-up and getting the ball for doing so is like shouting "I win!" during a 100-yard dash and being given the first-place trophy.
- **Traveling.** Only the most appalling traveling calls can

---

3. I wrote an article called "The NBA Fan's Guide to Talking Trash During Pickup Basketball" when I was working at *Grantland* in 2014.

be made. It's gotta be one of those situations where after the guy travels everyone just starts laughing at how terrible it was. Anything else is a play-on.

...play by 2s and 3s...

Eww. You're not in the league, my dude. Relax. In pickup basketball, two-point shots are worth 1 and three-point shots are worth 2 and that's just how it goes. And I know there's been this quasi push in recent years to change this because of the way advanced analytics and metrics have been absorbed into basketball and basketball thinking, and so people all of a sudden realized that playing by 1s and 2s means that some shots are worth twice as much as other shots, but the thing of it is: That's how it should be. And I don't just mean it as a romantic or nostalgic tie to the past. Have you ever even tried to shoot a three-pointer outside on a double rim? You gotta be a top-tier assassin to get one of those to drop. It should absolutely be worth double.

...suggest we play zone defense...

I need you to go home, okay.

...inbound the ball from the sideline or under the basket if it gets knocked out there...

No. Go away. You always bring the ball up top and start play from there. And while we're at it, you also have to pass the ball into play to start. You can't just dribble it in after you've checked it. I don't know what kind of lonely childhood you had where you didn't have anyone to pass the ball to, but that shit's not proper, man. Pass it in.

...cherry-pick...

No. The rule is if you don't make it past the half-court line on defense, then you're not allowed to score on the next offensive possession.

...leave the court after a game...

You're not allowed to leave the court if your leaving means someone else has to sit out a game, too. So, say, there are 10 people at the court. If you stay, that means everyone gets to play 5-on-5. If you leave, now they gotta play 4-on-4 and that ninth player has to sit until the next game. And maybe he or she deserves to sit out for being the ninth best player, but that's not the point.

...suggest we don't play make-it-take-it...

Half court = make-it-take-it.

Full court = alternating possessions after made buckets.

...question the local rules...

In 2013, I was visiting a friend of mine in Austin. I was there for a couple days, and so on one of those days we ended up at the basketball court in his apartment complex. Some people were already there playing 21 and they were on the only court there that actually had a rim still attached to the backboard so we just jumped in on their game.

Now, these guys must've been some fucking *Good Will Hunting*–type math geniuses or something because they were playing this bizarre version of 21 where if someone tipped you (caught a rebound in the air and then tipped the ball in the hoop before his feet touched the ground), then the person who tipped you was awarded whatever points you had *plus* the two points for the basket he just scored. What's more, if the sum total of the tipping player's current points plus the points he stole from you was higher than 21 then his score defaulted to 17, unless he was already at 17, 18, or 19, in which case he was allowed to decide between (a) automatically being declared the game's victor, or (b) moving everyone else's score back by up to 10 points. It was the most ridiculous shit of my whole life. I'd never heard of 21 played in that manner before, and I haven't heard of it played that way anywhere else since. But that's the way I played that day because those were the home team's rules. You're never allowed to question the local rules, even if they are absolutely psychotic.[4]

---

4. All the things mentioned in this chapter notwithstanding.

There are nine legit contenders for the The Greatest Big-Name Game Under Duress title.

In chronological order, there's George Mikan's Cast Game (April 11, 1949), Willis Reed's Broken Leg Game (May 8, 1970), Bernard King's Flu and Fingers Game (April 27, 1984), Isiah Thomas's Sprained Ankle Game (June 19, 1988), Larry Bird's Cracked Cranium Game (May 5, 1991), Michael Jordan's Flu Game[1] (June 11, 1997), Kobe Bryant's Sore Ankle Game (June 14, 2000), Derek Fisher's *Taken* Game (May 9, 2007), and LeBron James's Hurt Feelings Game (June 13, 2016). Of those nine, we can eliminate one on a technicality, two because the player's game wasn't quite good enough, one out of good taste, one because the stakes weren't high enough, one because it got eaten up by history, and one because the duress in question (probably) wasn't really all that bad.

THE TECHNICALITY: We lose George Mikan's Cast Game here. Mikan broke his wrist during Game 4 of the 1949 Finals, then played Game 5 while wearing a cast (he scored 22 points). That's pretty impressive, but it also happened in the BAA (Basketball Association of America), not the NBA, so it gets tossed out.

THE TWO THAT JUST WEREN'T QUITE GOOD ENOUGH: First, we lose Kobe's Sore Ankle Game. He'd sprained his ankle during Game 2 of the 2000 Finals, missed all of Game 3, then played 47 minutes in Game 4, the most crucial of which being the last three or so minutes of overtime after Shaq had fouled out. He scored six points over that stretch, including an offensive rebound and putback that put the Lakers up three for good. Had he done it all in the same game as the one when he actually sprained his ankle, this game probably would've squeaked its way into the final four. Since he didn't, though, it doesn't.

Second, we lose Willis Reed's Broken Leg Game. Two reasons here: (1) While Reed's willingness to play in the game was obviously a very big emotional lift to his team, Reed ended up only scoring four points that night.[2] He made for a great totem, then, but that was about it. (2) As the years have gone on, the Willis Reed Broken Leg Game has grown a bigger and bigger shadow, as it should, because playing basketball with a broken leg is incredibly unbelievable. The thing of it is, though, Reed didn't actually have a broken leg. He had a torn muscle in his leg.

THE ONE THAT GETS CUT FROM THE CONVERSATION OUT OF GOOD TASTE: We trim away Derek Fisher's *Taken* Game here. It happened during Game 2 of the Conference Semis of the 2007 playoffs. Fisher was playing with the Jazz at the time and they were matched up against the Warriors. He'd missed almost all of the game because he'd been in New York with his family while his 10-month-old daughter underwent eye surgery to treat a form of cancer. Following the surgery, he flew to Utah, showed up to the arena in the third quarter, then eventually hit a dagger three in overtime to help the Jazz win. His daughter was in danger. He was there for her. Then he (metaphorically) killed some guys. That's basically *Taken*, so that's why I'm calling this the Derek Fisher *Taken* Game. We can cut it from the silliness of this chapter's discussion just as a matter of respect.[3]

THE ONE WHERE THE STAKES WEREN'T HIGH ENOUGH: Game 5 of the first round of the 1991 playoffs. While diving for a loose ball late in the first half, Larry Bird all-caps *SLAMMED* his face on the floor. He stayed down on the court for a bit, definitely broken, possibly dead, then peeled himself up and disappeared off to the locker room. Dread filled the Garden. He returned in the third quarter and fucking dominated. He

---

1. For all of this chapter, let's 100 percent believe that Jordan actually did have the flu and not that he was hungover (as a popular conspiracy theory asserts) or that he was food poisoned (as his trainer asserts) or that he wasn't near as sick as he was said to have been (as Jerry Sloan, coach of the Jazz, asserts).
2. The first two field goals of the game for the Knicks, actually.
3. Another game that fits into this category: Jordan's Father's Day Game. It was Game 6 of the 1996 Finals. The Bulls clinched the title. Afterward, Jordan laid on the floor in the locker room alone and cried. It was his first championship since his father's murder in 1993.

finished the game with 32-9-7. The Celtics won by three. His legend won by a billion.

THE ONE THAT GOT EATEN UP BY BIGGER HISTORY (TWICE): The Knicks and the Pistons met in the first round of the 1984 playoffs. In the elimination Game 5, Bernard King, playing with a dislocated middle finger(!) on each hand(!!) and also the flu(!!!), put up 44–12(!!!!) to push the Knicks to victory, which is incredible because one time I had a hangnail and I briefly considered just cutting off my hand and being done with it. Bernard's game got overshadowed by (1) Isiah Thomas, who scored 16 points in 93 seconds to send it into overtime, and (2) Jordan's bigger, badder, sexier Flu Game. (I love Bernard's Flu Game a whole bunch. Poor Bernard. He never gets his due.)

THE ONE WHERE THE DURESS WASN'T ACTUALLY REALLY ALL THAT BAD: In the postgame press conference following Game 4 of the 2016 Finals, Klay Thompson, reacting to LeBron getting extra mad at Draymond Green during the game, implied that LeBron overreacted to Draymond's barbs, then finished by saying, "I guess his feelings just got hurt." LeBron, intent on etching the Hurt Feelings Game into the canon, responded in Game 5 by throwing up 41-16-7, which is just so, so gross. The Cavs won that game, and eventually won the series. I don't want to say that playing with hurt feelings is heroic, but I also don't want to not say that, you know what I'm saying?

But so that leaves us with just two games:[4] Isiah Thomas's Sprained Ankle Game (1988) vs. Michael Jordan's Flu Game (1997). One of those is The Greatest Big-Name Game Under Duress of all. Which one, though?

Let's sort through the five main parts of the games and their surrounding lore, choose a winner for each category, then add up the wins and see which game was the greatest.

▶

1. WHOSE STAKES WERE THE HIGHEST?

The difference here is really on a granular level. Both games happened in the NBA Finals (Isiah's was the 1988 Finals, Jordan's was the 1997 Finals). Both games happened on the road (the Pistons were in LA, the Bulls were in Utah). Both games happened against teams that were genuinely good (the Lakers won 62 games that season, they were the defending champs, and they would return to the Finals the following season for a rematch with the Pistons; the Jazz won 64 games that season, Karl Malone was the league's MVP, and the Jazz would return to the Finals the next year for a rematch against the Bulls). And both games happened late in each respective series (Isiah's was Game 6 of a series they led 3–2, Jordan's was Game 5 of a tied series). So, like I said, it's really very close.

THAT SAID, there *is* a difference here, and it's on account of two things:

(1) Had the Bulls lost Game 5, they'd have returned home for Game 6 and Game 7, and that would've likely worked out well for them given that (a) they were 39–2 at home that season, and (b) they'd already beaten the Jazz in Chicago in Game 1 and Game 2. So there's that. Also, and this is just fodder, but the Jazz were 38–3 at home that season. Them winning all three of the games there wouldn't have been terribly surprising. "That's what they were supposed to do," Phil Jackson probably would have said, because Phil Jackson is a master of undermining things other teams do.

(2) There weren't really any residual effects on Jordan from The Flu Game. I mean, people said that there were, and maybe if you squinted you see him a tiny bit below 100 percent, but still, 94 Percent Michael Jordan is still basically unbeatable. He put up 39-11-4 to end the series in Game 6.[5] For Isiah, on the other hand, he knew that he wasn't going to be right in Game 7. As a

---

4. Ignoring Rondo's Dislocated Elbow Game, Dirk's Flu-like Symptoms Game, MJ's Father's Day Game, Kobe's Flu Game, Dwyane Wade's Flu Game, and Iverson's Swallowing Blood Game. (Iverson had gotten hit in the mouth near the end of a close Sixers–Bucks game. He wasn't able to stop the bleeding during a timeout and so, afraid that the referees might not let him play, he simply closed his mouth and started swallowing blood. Over the next two minutes, Iverson made a layup, stole the ball, and hit five of six foul shots.)

5. These numbers very much fall into the GTFOH range for stat lines.

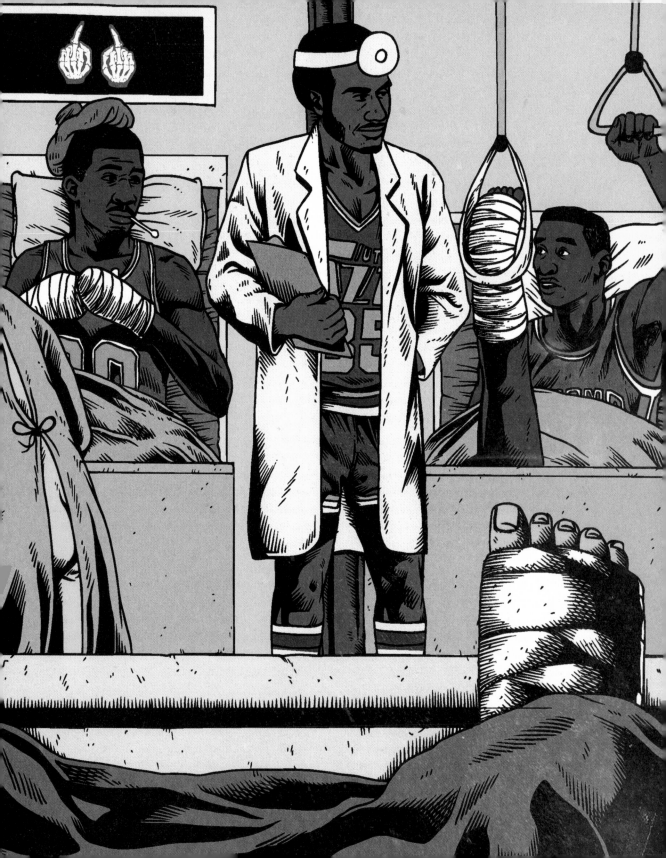

matter of comparison: Thomas had 43 points, 8 assists, and 6 steals in Game 6. In Game 7, just two days after the sprain, he had 10 points, 7 assists, and 4 steals. But so what I'm saying is he knew it was either the Pistons win the championship in six or they lose the championship in seven. There weren't any other ways around it.

Winner: Isiah gets the nod here. It's by a tiny amount, but it's still an amount.
Tally: 1–0, Isiah

2. DID THE PLAYER ACTUALLY WIN HIS GAME?
Jordan and the Bulls won by two, 90–88. Isiah and the Pistons lost by one, 102–103.

Winner: Jordan
Tally: 1–1
Sidebar: The Lakers were down one in the final seconds of the Sprained Ankle Game and so Kareem had the ball. He turned to let fly a hook shot over Laimbeer. The shot clanked off the rim but Laimbeer was called for a foul. Replays showed that Laimbeer didn't touch him.[6] Kareem made both free throws,[7] the Lakers won by one, then they won the title in Game 7. The next year, the Pistons beat the Lakers to win the title, and then they won it again the year after that. So you could make a pretty good argument that the Pistons were one bad call away from three-peating, which is crazy.

3. WHAT POST-INJURY POSE IS THE MOST ICONIC?
This is an important category because the poses are the images that grow into myth. Figuring out who the winner is here is just a matter of looking to see which guy looked the most broken during the moment that people most remember from the game.

For Jordan, it was Pippen basically carrying him back to the bench after the Bulls had taken a three-point lead with just 6.2 seconds left following an especially rigorous few possessions.[8] Jordan looked all the way cooked there. He looked like a deflated balloon, or like a bag of sand Pippen was dragging through an airport.[9] It was great.[10]

For Isiah, it was him, his right ankle completely useless by this point, trying to sprint back to the defensive end of the floor after he'd made a layup that capped an 11–1 run that had finally, magically, mystically, unbelievably given the Pistons the lead. It's a fantastic clip, that one of him trying to run back up court on one leg. There's lots and lots of motion and very little movement. He looks like a dirt bike in the mud trying to throttle its way out of a rut. It was, same as the Jordan one, also great.

Winner: It has to go to Jordan, right? I love Isiah trying to tumble his body forward to get back into that play during his game. And I love all of the parts that exist within that specific moment. But I can't get past Jordan looking like death as Scottie held him up. It might've maybe been a little exaggerated, and it might've maybe even been a little TOO perfect. But I think what it ends up being is: Isiah looked like he was ready to give his life to win that game as he tried to sprint back up the floor. Jordan looked like he'd already given his. Jordan wins here.
Tally: 2–1, Jordan

4. WHAT PERFORMANCE INSPIRED THE BEST IN-GAME CALL FROM ONE OF THE GAME'S ANNOUNCERS?
This is a tinier category than the rest, but it still matters. The best thing anyone said during Jordan's game was when Marv Albert, following Jordan's near-end-of-game three, marveled, "He looks like he's a boxer just hanging on along the ropes, but able to hit for a three-point Chicago lead."[11]

The best thing anyone said during Isiah's game happened at the end of his third-quarter run. By that point, it was all the way clear that he had been touched by whomever it is that controls the universe, and so there really wasn't much left to do except watch him flame-throw the Lakers into the Pacific Ocean. His 24th and 25th points came as the quarter was ending. He caught the ball in the left corner, gave the much taller Michael Cooper a tiny dribble move to create a hair's worth of space between the two, then threw up a rainbow fade-away that scraped the ceiling in the Forum. The ball swished through the net, and all the color commentator Billy Cunningham could think to do was shout "Again!" and he did it with such fervor, with such joy, with such disbelief, that there's really no way to put Marv's (albeit considerably more poetic) call above it.

Winner: Isiah.
Tally: 2–2

5. WHICH PLAYER HAD THE BETTER ACTUAL STAT LINE? Both were gigantic.

Jordan put up 38 points (13/27), 7 rebounds, 5 assists, 3 steals, 1 block, and 3 turnovers in his game. Isiah put up 43 points (18/32), 3 rebounds, 8 assists, 6 steals, 1 block, and 5 turnovers. Those are goofily close,[12] so I guess maybe the most appropriate thing to do would be to look at each player's Game Score, which is an advanced stat that was created by John Hollinger that gives a designated score for each player based on how well or poorly he played in a given game.

On Hollinger's Game Score scale, anything up near a 40 is exceptional and anything down near a 10 is pretty average. For the Flu Game, Jordan's Game Score was 29.4. For the Sprained Ankle Game, Isiah's Game Score was 34.0. So there's that.

BUT ALSO, we should probably give Jordan a few extra points because he played the entirety of his game under duress, while Isiah didn't sprain his ankle until halfway through the third quarter.

BUT ALSO, we should probably give Isiah a few extra points because his third-quarter atomization of the Lakers, during which he scored 25 points, is still an NBA Finals record.

BUT ALSO, we should give Jordan a few extra points because, really, *technically*, Isiah only scored 11 points in the third quarter after his ankle sprain; meanwhile, Jordan had 17 flu-ridden points in the second quarter of his game.

BUT ALSO, we should give Isiah a few extra points because he was being guarded mostly by Michael Cooper, and Michael Cooper was selected to the NBA All-Defensive First or Second Team every year from 1981 to 1988 and also he won the 1987 Defensive Player of the Year Award; meanwhile, Jordan was mostly being guarded by Bryon Russell, whom Jordan regularly slayed.

So, I mean, I don't know. It's close. It's all very close. It's all very, very close. There are just so many pieces here. If I squint, though—if I make my eyes as tight and as focused as they can get—it looks a lot like this category has to go to . . .

Winner: Isiah
Overall Winner: Isiah Thomas's Sprained Ankle Game proves better than Michael Jordan's Flu Game, 3–2.

---

6. In 2014, Pat Riley acknowledged that there'd not been a foul. Pat Riley waiting 26 years to admit a thing everyone saw as soon as it happened is an extremely Pat Riley thing to do. I respect his dedication to the hustle.
7. In his 1993 book, *The Winner Within*, Riley said of Jabbar making those two very, very, very pressure-filled free throws: "Later, I asked Kareem what he had been thinking when he made those two shots. He said, 'I like to get paid.'" I love that.
8. Jordan shot two free throws. He missed the second but got his own rebound. After stalling a bit, the Bulls initiated their offense. It ended with Jordan hitting a three, putting the Bulls up three. The Jazz came down, ran a quick play, got a dunk, then totally panicked. Rather than fouling (there were about 15 seconds left in the game and they were down one), they played regular full-court defense. It resulted in a Chicago dunk. Following his initial three, Jordan just sort of wandered around the court in a daze.
9. I don't know which airline is letting people carrying bags of sand onto planes. Probably Southwest.
10. I think my favorite thing about it is that Pippen, ever brilliant, absolutely understood the mythology that was going to be built into that moment, which you can tell because there's a brief moment where he flashes a big smile as he holds Jordan up.
11. The second-best call of the game happened at the very end of it. The Bulls, who had a one-point lead, were inbounding the ball with 15 seconds left in the game. Luc Longley threw it to Scottie Pippen, and Pippen paused a bit because he was waiting for Karl Malone (who was guarding him) to foul him, because that's what was supposed to happen in that moment. Malone, though, panicked, and so rather than foul Pippen, he just stood by him for a few seconds. Bill Walton, who was helping call the game, started shouting over everyone, "You gotta foul right now! You gotta foul! Karl Malone! What are you doing?!" I'm sure it's a call that haunts Jazz fans, but for me, I loved every bit of it and still love every bit of it.
12. Writing for ESPN, Kevin Pelton had Jordan's Flu Game ranked as the eighth greatest Finals game of all time, and then had Isiah's Sprained Ankle Game as the seventh greatest.

Following the 1995 NBA Finals, Shaquille O'Neal, whose Magic lost the series 4–0 to Hakeem Olajuwon and the Houston Rockets, wrote a typed note to Olajuwon. The note very simply read:

```
    Hakeem-
   The series may be a done deal,
   but it ain't over between you and me.
   Sure, you're pretty good with your team
   behind you, but I want you one on one.
                                   —Shaq
```

That was the entire note. I happened across it while I was rummaging around through the old *Sports Illustrated* archives. There are some quick questions that come along when something like this comes up. To wit:

- Were typewritten notes very popular in 1995? Is that just what was happening back then? People were typing up tiny notes like that and sending them to each other? Because that sounds like the shittiest version of Twitter I have ever heard of.
- Beyond just person-to-person notes, were post-Finals notes a common thing among NBA superstars? Are they a common thing now? Is it some long-standing tradition that the public at large is just unaware of? Did Bill Russell write one to Wilt after the Celtics beat the Lakers in 1969? Did Jordan write one to Malone after the Bulls beat the Jazz in 1997?[1] Did LeBron write one to Steph after the Cavs beat the Warriors in 2016?[2]

- Did Shaq own his own typewriter? Because that's fun to think about. It seems more likely that he was just sitting there and shouted out, "Aye, someone bring me a typewriter right now," and then someone brought him a typewriter. But maybe not. Maybe he was actually a typewriter enthusiast back then. Maybe he has a very literature-romantic side to him that nobody talks about.[3] Maybe he sat there at the typewriter while in a bathtub, a cigarette in one hand, his own wit in his other, tapping away at it like Dalton Trumbo.[4]
- If Shaq did own a typewriter, I wonder if it was a giant typewriter. I seem to remember reading a thing when he was going through a divorce where his monthly expenses were made public and he was spending $24,300 a month on fuel for all of his cars. I bring that up to say it doesn't seem that unreasonable that he would've commissioned someone to build him a giant typewriter to accommodate his giant ham hands.

There are a lot more questions that can be asked, really.[5] But there's only one that I want to get answered in this chapter:

The note (apparently) was the first of all the pieces of what was to be a remarkable event: Three months after the Finals, Shaq and Hakeem were going to play one-on-one live for $1,000,000. It was called The War on the Floor and it was sponsored by Taco Bell, if you can even believe that, which you should, because the '90s were super fucking weird. The day before the game, though, Hakeem pulled out, saying he'd injured his back lifting weights and couldn't play.[6] The game got

---

1. "Hey, Karl. Fuck you. —MJ" (Charles Barkley actually one time did send a not to Bill Laimbeer before a game in 1990. It very simply read: "Dear Bill. Fuck you. Love, Charles Barkley." That's not a joke. He really did that.)
2. "Congrats on your back-to-back MVPs, though. —LBJ"
3. A typewritten note is easily the most romantic of notes. The second-most romantic kind of note is one written on parchment paper with one of those quills you dip in the ink. The last-place romantic note is if you key the words "Eat shit" into the hood of an ex's car.
4. There is maybe a tiny chance that this Dalton Trumbo reference has made me appear more cultured and intelligent than I actually am. To be clear, the only reason I know who he is today is that there was an episode of *Modern Family* one time where one of the characters dressed up as him for Halloween.
5. The one I spent the most time thinking about: How did Shaq deliver the note to Olajuwon? Shaq doesn't seem like the post office type. I hope it was like in those old karate movies where one guy is challenging another guy to a duel and so some guy shows up with a big scroll and he unrolls it and then reads it to the person who the message is for.

canceled, then some possible names came up as replacements,[7] then the whole thing was eventually just outright canceled. There was never a follow-up or anything.

But so then the question here is obvious: If Shaq and Hakeem *had* played that game, who would've won?

▶

As foreign as the idea of two basketball superstars playing against each other for money in games of one-on-one may sound today, there was actually precedent for exactly that sort of matchup. The five best examples: **(5)** In 1990, eight potential members of that year's NBA Draft class played in a one-on-one tournament called the One-on-One Collegiate Challenge. Bo Kimble beat Gary Payton in the final game, winning himself $100,000.[8] **(4)** In 1972, there was an actual one-on-one tournament sanctioned by the NBA. The winner received $15,000. **(3)** In 1988, there was a video game that came out called Jordan vs. Bird: One on One, and I know that's not real life, but that game meant a whole lot to me so that's why I included it here.[9] **(2)** In 1992, six retired NBA players played in a pay-per-view one-on-one tournament called "Clash of the Legends." Kareem was there. Dr. J was there. George Gervin, Connie Hawkins, Rick Barry, Tiny Archibald were all there. Kareem ended up beating Dr. J in the final round. The whole thing may, as you're reading those names, sound like it was a good and fun thing, but mostly it was not.[10] Mostly it was just a bunch of old guys shooting hook shots and layups. **(1)** In 2011, rapper Bow Wow challenged Kobe Bryant to a game of one-on-one for $1,000. (Bow Wow starred in *Like Mike* so I'm counting him as a "basketball superstar.") It was a bloodletting. The game ended with Bow Wow, exhausted, lying on the floor of the gym. "I don't ever wanna go to the NBA," he said, smiling, but smiling the way you smile when you're just glad a horrible thing is over. "Everything that [Kobe] does on [the video game NBA] 2K, that shit is real."

▶

These are guidelines for how the Shaq vs. Hakeem one-on-one game was supposed to be played and governed:

- The game would be organized as such that, rather than play a single game to 15 or 21 or whatever for the $1,000,000, they would play 10 separate 2-minute rounds, each worth $100,000.
- The 2-minute rounds would have a 12-second shot clock per possession.
- For any round that ended in a tie, the money and the victory for that round would just get rolled over to the next round.
- Scoring would be done same as the NBA (two points for baskets made inside the three-point line, three points for baskets made outside of it), with one big exception: Any shots made from 32 feet and beyond would be worth six points.

A few other things about the event that are interesting to know but aren't explicitly part of the rules or structure:

- The game was going to be shown on pay-per-view. It was going to cost between $19.95 and $29.95 to watch it. That seems like a remarkably low price to me. I mean, these were the two main guys from the two NBA teams that had just met in the Finals. Right now, as I write this book, it's 2017. So that means if we had the today version of this game, it'd be LeBron vs. Steph.[11] I can't think of an amount of money I wouldn't pay to watch that.
- There were two undercard matches that were to precede the Shaq and Hakeem game: Lakers guard Nick Van Exel was going to play one-on-one against Nets guard Kenny Anderson, and Joe Smith, then an unsigned rookie but the number-one pick in the draft that year, was going to play one-on-one against Kevin Garnett(!!!), also then an unsigned rookie.[12]
- The game was going to be played at the Trump Taj Mahal in Atlantic City.
- The NBA basically just ignored that any of this was happening.

▶

The very natural reflex to looking at the "Who would've won if Shaq and Hakeem had played one-on-one in 1995?" question is to very quickly and confidently respond with some version of "Oh, Hakeem obviously would've destroyed Shaq, obviously." It's understandable, really, what with the game coming shortly after Olaju-won's Rockets gave O'Neal's Magic the business. Here's the thing of it, though: That matchup would've been way closer than maybe you're assuming. Some numbers:

If we just go all-time matchups, Shaq's teams and Hakeem's teams played against each other 20 times during the regular season and 8 times in the playoffs during their careers. Shaq's teams beat Hakeem's teams 14 of the 20 times during the regular season, and Hakeem's teams beat Shaq's teams 5 of the 8 times in the playoffs.[13] For the regular season, Shaq[14] held statistical advantages in four of the six important categories:

REGULAR SEASON:

	SHAQ		HAKEEM
PPG:	22.1	vs.	18.4
RPG:	12.4	vs.	9.1
APG:	3.6	vs.	2.9
FG%:	54.4	vs.	44.7
BPG:	1.8	vs.	2.4
SPG:	0.9	vs.	1.4

For the playoffs, Shaq held even bigger statistical advantages, this time in five of the six important categories:

PLAYOFFS:

	SHAQ		HAKEEM
PPG:	28.8	vs.	23.0
RPG:	11.4	vs.	9.4
APG:	5.1	vs.	3.0
FG%:	55.6	vs.	46.5
BPG:	3.3	vs.	1.4
SPG:	0.5	vs.	1.6

Now, I don't figure all of this is all that relevant if we're just trying to figure what would've happened had they played their one-on-one game that September in 1995, given that most of their matchups happened well after that, but I just wanted to put their career numbers against each side-by-side because it's interesting to see.

A more accurate measure of things, at least for this particular exercise, would be to look at what was happening only during the 1995 and 1996 seasons.

For Shaq, 1995 was just his third season in the league. He was a baby monster, barely 23 years old, but he'd already proved himself a dynamo. He won his first NBA scoring title that year (29.3 ppg). He was All-NBA Second Team. He finished second in the MVP voting.[15] And his Magic beat Jordan's Bulls in the playoffs, which, I mean, okay, that was the season where Jordan came back from retirement at the very end of it and so of course he wasn't his completely normal self, but still, it's Jordan in the playoffs so we can't completely ignore it.

---

6. The *Orlando Sentinel* wrote a story about Hakeem ducking out of the game. The title: "Hakeem Can't Answer The (taco) Bell Vs. Shaq." The first line of the story: "It will, like some of the contents inside a burrito, forever remain a mystery." The second line in the story: "Now we'll never know for whom the Taco Bell tolls."
7. My favorite one: Shaq plays a two-on-one challenge where it's him versus Muggsy Bogues and Spud Webb together.
8. Gary Payton's second-place take was $50,000.
9. This game was preceded by One on One: Dr. J vs. Larry Bird. I've always preferred the Jordan and Bird version to the Dr. J and Bird version, though. I assume that's because by the time I got around to really enjoying the NBA, Dr. J was gone.
10. The *New York Times* review of it called it a "taint on the game."
11. LeBron would wax Steph. If they played to 15 by ones and twos, it'd be something like 15–4.
12. Garnett, big enough to guard all the big guys but also quick enough to cause problems for the little guys, would be an ideal one-on-one player in an NBA one-on-one tournament.
13. Everyone of course remembers them battling against each other in the 1995 Finals, but most forget that they played in the 1999 playoffs after Shaq joined the Lakers.
14. Interesting sidebar: Shaq has never played an entire season's worth of games. He played 81 games in the 1993 and 1994 seasons.
15. David Robinson won it.

For Olajuwon,[16] 1995 was his eleventh season in the league. He was All-NBA Third Team and he was also All-Defensive Second Team. He turned 32 in January, so he was considerably older than Shaq, but certainly still in his prime. And he'd led his team to a championship in 1994, and so that's a thing we definitely have to take into account because championship pedigree is always important. Here's a bigger thing, though: As good as Olajuwon was in the 1994 season and playoffs, he was even better during the 1995 playoff run. Look at this shit: He averaged 35 points per game against Karl Malone and the Utah Jazz in the first round, 29.6 points per game against Charles Barkley and the Phoenix Suns in the Conference Semis, 35.3 points per game against David Robinson and the San Antonio Spurs in the Conference Finals, and 32.8 points per game against Shaq and the Magic in the NBA Finals.[17] That's a nuts string of games, man. Those four players he knocked off won five of the eight MVP awards from 1993 to 2000.[18]

So when Shaq[19] and Hakeem would've met in September 1995, you'd have had (1) a version of Hakeem who was 32 years old and three months removed from the best basketball of his life (but would never approach that level again), and (2) a 23-year-old Shaq who was also three months removed from the best season of his career to that point (and was still headed toward the best basketball of his career). That's a great game.

If we look at just their matchups from the 1995 season and the 1996 season then it's:

SHAQ: 4 wins (all during the regular season) and 4 losses (all during the 1995 Finals) // 26.5 ppg // 13.9 rpg // 1.9 bpg // 59.7% FG

HAKEEM: 4 wins (all during the 1995 Finals) and 4 losses (all during the regular season) // 30.0 ppg // 10.6 rpg // 2.0 bpg // 46.5% FG

Those, to me, look like just about the same numbers. So really I think all of everything here just turns into a game management situation. That means we're looking at mainly four different things to figure out who wins this game.

FOULS. Originally, the way fouls were going to be handled was the first two fouls of each round were going to be non-shooting fouls, and then everything after that was going to be a shooting foul. Let's assume, given that Hakeem only ever had a sterling reputation in and around basketball, he'd have willfully refrained from doing the Hack-a-Shaq technique. That's a big checkmark in Shaq's favor because if you don't want to send him to the free throw line, then how exactly do you slow him down?[20] Shaq could just pummel his way into the lane, really. And if you want to say that 1995 Shaq was way smaller than, say, 2001 Shaq, who was like if a large building had grown arms and legs, then I'll remind you that it was during the summer of 1995 when Shaq first truly bulked up, gaining over 20 pounds of muscle so he could play *Kazaam*.[21] So he would've shown up to the one-on-one game way bigger than he was even just a few months earlier. That's bad news for Hakeem.

16. This doesn't have to do with the 1995 season but it's a neat stat and I wanted to put it somewhere so here we are: Olajuwon became the first player in NBA history to record at least 200 steals and 200 blocks in a season during 1988–89. As I write this, he's still the only player ever to do it.
17. Shaq was no slouch during the Finals. He averaged 28-13-6-3 for the series.
18. Jordan won two of the other three. Olajuwon won the other.
19. I read a bunch about Shaq and researched a bunch about Shaq to write this chapter. The most egregious quote that I came across: During an interview with ESPN, Shaq, who was answering questions about his own rap career, said, "First time I heard Biggie Smalls was he said my name in a rap. [Biggie] said, 'I'm slamming brothers like Shaquille, shit is real,' and instantly I became a fan." This very much seems like a lie to me. The line is from "Gimme The Loot," a song from Biggie's 1994 album *Ready To Die*. "Gimme The Loot" wasn't one of the singles on RTD. That means Shaq would've somehow had to have not heard "Juicy" or "Big Poppa" or "One More Chance" (all of which were singles) in the lead up to it. We're talking about three of the biggest songs in the country from one of the biggest albums of the year by one of the biggest rap stars in the world. And Shaq never heard it? I'm calling false.
20. Only Wilt Chamberlain missed more free throws (5,805) than Shaq (5,317).
21. This is not a joke. It's a real thing. He really decided he needed to gain 20 pounds of muscle to play a fucking genie.

OUTSIDE THE PAINT. Of course, if we're going to consider the idea that Shaq would've spent most of his time trying to just beat up Hakeem down low, then we have to consider the inverse as well: Shaq would've been a woolly mammoth in the paint, yes, but Hakeem was not only a twisty-twisty demon around the rim, he was also a better shooter and dribbler than Shaq, which are huge assets in this sort of game. How many times do you think he'd have been able to pull Shaq away from the rim? Enough times to cause Shaq a whole bunch of headaches, I'm sure. (A subsequent outcome of this strategy: Long shots usually cause for long rebounds when they're missed, and, all other things being equal, long rebounds usually go to the quicker player, which is another advantage for Hakeem.)

WAY OUTSIDE THE PAINT. You have to fig-ure that either Hakeem or Shaq or both would've at least attempted one or two or three of those 32-foot six-pointers, right? That's a huge bonus if you can con-nect on one of those. Let's say Hakeem chucked up four of them. If he hits even one of them, that's the same as hitting three out of four two-pointers. Could Hakeem have hit 25 percent from 32 feet away from the basket easier than Shaq could've hit 75 percent of his shots near the basket?[22] And if Hakeem does hit one or two, what does Shaq do? Because if he comes all the way out there to guard him, then it's a wrap. Hakeem was just too fast.

OVERALL ENDURANCE. One-on-one is super tax-ing. And that 12-second shot clock would've only made things move faster. I suspect most would be inclined to say that that would favor Hakeem, but there was a part during the *This Magic Moment* documentary about the mid-'90s Magic where they talked about how Hakeem's plan to attack Shaq during the Finals was to just run him to death, only except it ended up no problem for Shaq to keep up with Hakeem because he was nearly a decade younger than him and so Shaq's legs were still

made of rubber.[23] This category probably ends up being somewhere near a draw.

But so those are the main parts of the game that would've determined the winner.

▶

The actual game:

- **Round 1:** Hakeem is surprised by Shaq's new mass. Shaq pounds on him a lot. It's too much for Hakeem. Shaq wins the first round by a score of 12–6.
- **Round 2:** Hakeem, a brilliant tactician, modifies his defense of Shaq. He starts trying to speed the game up. Shaq, who is still upset about the Finals, contin-ues to pummel him. Shaq wins the second round by a score of 10–8.
- **Round 3:** Shaq, feeling proud and hoping to raise the guillotine's blade above Hakeem's neck, attempts an errant six-pointer. It's all the mistake Hakeem needs. He hits three buckets in a row, pulling away. Shaq decides to conserve his energy. Hakeem wins the third round by a score of 14–4.
- **Round 4:** Both players settle in defensively. It's clear that, despite all of the mascot tacos bouncing around the court shouting about some beefy crunch disaster Taco Bell is selling for $0.25 after the game, The War on the Floor has become tense. Neither player scores the entire last minute. They tie, 6–6. The winner of the next round will be awarded points for both that round and this one.
- **Round 5:** Hakeem hits a 19-footer. Shaq creeps out to guard him farther from the rim on the next possession. Hakeem blows by him for an easy layup. Upset, Shaq decides he won't venture any farther than 12 feet away from the basket. Hakeem, testing Shaq's will, dribbles out to the six-point line. Shaq stays firm in the paint, wordlessly daring Hakeem to shoot it. Hakeem does. It swishes through. He wins the round 18–6.

---

22. Shaq only made one three-pointer in his entire NBA career. It was a buzzer beater that he threw up during a game against the Bucks in 1996. He missed the other 21 he took while he was in the NBA. I'm assuming he wouldn't have been very interested in shoot-ing up a bunch of three-pointers and six-pointers during his game against Hakeem.

23. I'm 35 years old. When I go jogging, it feels like my legs are made of if you mixed a bunch of old nails and screws with mud.

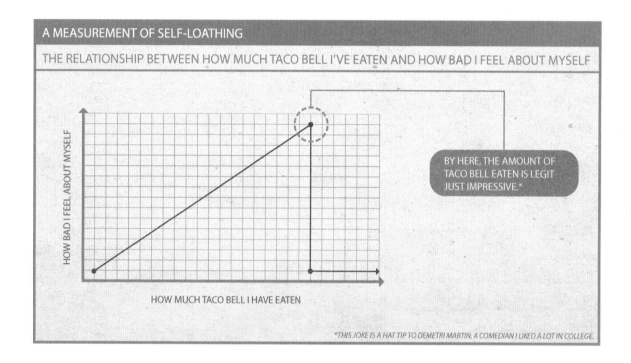

A MEASUREMENT OF SELF-LOATHING

THE RELATIONSHIP BETWEEN HOW MUCH TACO BELL I'VE EATEN AND HOW BAD I FEEL ABOUT MYSELF

HOW BAD I FEEL ABOUT MYSELF

BY HERE, THE AMOUNT OF TACO BELL EATEN IS LEGIT JUST IMPRESSIVE.*

HOW MUCH TACO BELL I HAVE EATEN

*THIS JOKE IS A HAT TIP TO DEMETRI MARTIN, A COMEDIAN I LIKED A LOT IN COLLEGE.

- **Round 6:** Shaq, all the way upset that he's suddenly losing three rounds to two, goes into HULK MODE. He dominates the round, winning by a score of 16–2. They've both won three rounds apiece. Everyone is surprised by how close it is, and how serious both players have become.
- **Round 7:** Shaq hits a jump hook at the buzzer to win the round 10–8.
- **Round 8:** Hakeem puts Shaq in the spin cycle with the Dream Shake. He wins the round 10-8. Both players have won four rounds. It's fucking real.
- **Round 9:** In the game's most intense round, neither player scores. Tie, 0-0. The winner of the final round will be awarded the ninth-round victory as well.
- **Round 10:** Shaq jumps out to an early 4–0 lead, which Hakeem quickly erases with back-to-back up-and-under layups. With just 12 second left on the clock, Hakeem chases down a rebound. He looks at the scoreboard. It's 8–8. He looks at Shaq. He jabs left. Shaq bites. Hakeem jumps right. Shaq tries to

recover. Hakeem raises up to shoot a 9-footer over Shaq's outstretched arm. The ball is in the air. The buzzer sounds. There's perfect peace in the world. The ball drops softly through the rim. Olajuwon wins the round, 10–8, and also the game, six rounds to four. So there you go.

If Shaq and Hakeem *had* played that game, who would've won?

Hakeem, six rounds to four.

The question is not "Which was the best duo in NBA history?" That's too easy to answer because, for most of us, "best" would mean we're talking about "the winningest," in which case all we'd have to do would be to look through the win–loss records of a bunch of different duos and see whose was the best and there you go. For example, Jordan and Pippen won 30 playoff series and six titles during their time together. That's more than any other All-Star duo after the merger.[1] So, were this a thing about "best," then that'd be it. We'd be done. The chapter would be over already.

So, the question isn't that. The question isn't "best." The question is "perfect," because "perfect" is more subtle, more nuanced, more complex. There are layers to it; there are sections of it; there are parts to get lost in and wander around in. Whether or not the duo won games is a part of the answer, sure, but only a part of it. There are other pieces to consider. The full list:

- **Did they win a bunch of games?**[2] This can't be the only thing, but we also can't ignore it.
- **How interesting was the duo's compatibility, both on the court and philosophically?** Any duo who, if you're thinking of them right now and you're saying something like, "I *think* they got along," or "I think they *might*'ve not gotten along," then that's a duo that's scoring poorly here. We need extremes. We need duos that either were cosmically connected and in

love (like Stockton and Malone) or duos that were one or two good arguments away from fistfighting each other during a game (like Wally Szczerbiak and Kevin Garnett[3]).

- **How'd their partnership end?** The most important thing to consider for this category is, "How memorable was the ending?" A good duo has a narrative arc, and a good narrative arc has a strong ending. That being the case, a duo with a forgetful ending to their partnership scores lower here than a duo with a memorable ending, even if it was memorable because it was a plane crash of sorts. Bad endings are fun.
- **Was each member of the duo in his prime during their time together?** The old-player-paired-up-with-a-young-player thing can be fun, as can the two-young-players-on-the-precipice-of-something-great thing, as can the two-older-players-teaming-up-for-a-final-run thing. But for the purposes of this conversation, the closer the two were to being in their primes together, the better. So, as an example, if we're just looking at Shaq-based duos here, then it'd be Shaq and Kobe[4] > Shaq and Penny[5] > Shaq and Dwyane Wade[6] > Shaq and LeBron[7] > Shaq and Nash.[8]
- **Was the duo fun to watch?** This is a big category. What was the watchability of the duo? Like, if they were on TV that night, did you absolutely have to watch their game because maybe they'd both get hot and put up

---

1. Kobe Bryant and Derek Fisher won more playoff series together (32) but less titles (5). Also, Derek Fisher wasn't an All-Star.
2. In March of 2017, I received an email from a guy I'd never met before named Taylor. He said he was in town for the night because he was visiting his best friend, Josh, because Josh's dad was in the hospital. He asked if I had some time to hang out, maybe get dinner. I said sure, and so we three went to dinner that night. While there, we actually brainstormed these duo requirements together. It was great and helpful. The most interesting part of the evening, though, was when we talked about Josh's father, whom he referred to as Beast. The two best Beast stories: (1) One time, while working on a roof, he got into a fight with a man. The man lost his balance during the scuffle and tumbled over the edge of the roof, but Beast, a superhero, caught him by his arm at the last possible moment and prevented him from plummeting down to the ground. Beast didn't catch him just to catch him, though. He caught him because he wasn't done fighting him. He held the man by the wrist with one hand and, as the man dangled helplessly in the air, continued to punch him in the face with the other. (2) One time in high school, Beast, a track runner, ran a four-minute mile during a track meet. Somehow, he still finished last in the race, he said. // I don't know how true either of those stories are, but I'm choosing to believe both of them. I'm very pro-Beast.
3. These two actually got in a confrontation with one another during a Timberwolves practice in 2000.
4. One was definitely in his prime, one was approaching it.
5. Two younger guys.
6. One older guy, one younger guy.
7. One older guy, one younger-ish guy.
8. Both guys are older. (It's very crazy to think about how Shaq has played with Penny, Kobe, Dwyane Wade, LeBron, Steve Nash, and Paul Pierce.)

a combined 95+ points together (like Steph and Klay), or maybe one of them would throw a between-the-legs full-court alley-oop to the other (like Payton and Kemp), or maybe they'd both have life-ending dunks on someone (Moses Malone and Dr. J)?

▶

I propose that we reverse-engineer things for this chapter. Rather than already having a pick for the most perfect duo and then building a case around explaining why they were chosen, I'm going to start out with a big list of memorable duos in NBA history,[9] then go through each of the categories mentioned above and erase names from the list until we get to the final, most perfect pair. Here's who we're starting with:

- **John Stockton and Karl Malone:** Eighteen seasons together on the Jazz (1986–2003).
- **Shaquille O'Neal and Kobe Bryant:** Eight seasons together on the Lakers (1997–2004).
- **Michael Jordan and Scottie Pippen:** Ten seasons together on the Bulls (1988–1993, 1995–1998).
- **Chris Paul and Blake Griffin:** Six seasons[10] together on the Clippers (2012–2017).
- **Magic Johnson and Kareem Abdul-Jabbar:** Ten seasons together on the Lakers (1980–1989).
- **Steve Nash and Amar'e Stoudemire:** Six seasons together on the Suns (2005–2010).
- **Russell Westbrook and Kevin Durant:** Eight seasons together on the Thunder (2009–2016).
- **LeBron James and Dwyane Wade:** Four seasons together on the Heat (2011–2014).
- **Kobe Bryant and Pau Gasol:** Seven seasons together on the Lakers (2008–2014).
- **Shaquille O'Neal and Dwyane Wade:** Three seasons together on the Heat (2005–2007).
- **Magic Johnson and James Worthy:** Nine seasons together on the Lakers (1983–1991).
- **Shaquille O'Neal and Penny Hardaway:** Three seasons together on the Magic (1994–1996).
- **Dirk Nowitzki and Steve Nash:** Six seasons together on the Mavericks (1999–2004).
- **Yao Ming and Tracy McGrady:** Five seasons together on the Rockets (2005–2009).

- **Tim Duncan and David Robinson:**[11] Six seasons together on the Spurs (1998–2003).
- **Charles Barkley and Kevin Johnson:** Four seasons together on the Suns (1993–1996).
- **LeBron James and Kyrie Irving:** Three seasons[12] together on the Cavs (2015–2017).
- **Larry Bird and Kevin McHale:** Twelve seasons together on the Celtics (1981–1992).
- **Deron Williams and Carlos Boozer:** LOL. I apologize.
- **Hakeem Olajuwon and Clyde Drexler:** Four seasons together on the Rockets (1995–1998).
- **Gary Payton and Shawn Kemp:** Seven seasons together on the Sonics (1991–1997).
- **Steph Curry and Klay Thompson:** Six seasons[13] together on the Warriors (2012–2017).
- **Chris Mullin and Tim Hardaway:** Six seasons together on the Warriors. (Hardaway was drafted in 1989. He played on the Warriors until 1996, but one of those seasons was lost to an injury, and he actually finished that 1996 season as a member of the Heat.)
- **Isiah Thomas and Bill Laimbeer:** Thirteen seasons together on the Pistons (1982–1994).
- **Julius Erving and Moses Malone:** Four seasons together on the Sixers (1983–1986).

That's a sample size of 25 different duos. I'm sure that's plenty.

▶

EIGHT ROUNDS OF ELIMINATION

1. Is the duo Deron Williams and Carlos Boozer? If yes, then they're out.
Dang. Okay. So I guess that means we're losing Deron Williams and Carlos Boozer here. Tough break for them.

▶

2. Did they win a bunch of games?
There are three ways to tally things here. We can look at (a) regular season wins, (b) playoff wins, or (c) regular season wins and playoff wins combined. I'm not all the way certain that regular season wins should matter a bunch because the regular season is just the regular season, but I also don't want to disregard them totally

because those wins, if massive, are definitely a version of important. Maybe the best way to handle it is to just look at playoff appearance percentages. What I mean is let's look at the number of seasons a duo was together versus the number of times their team made the play-offs. Any duo whose team made the playoffs less than, say, 75 percent of the time they were together, then we can eliminate them.

With that hurdle in place, it means we're losing Dirk Nowitzki and Steve Nash here. They were together for six seasons and made the playoffs four times, good for 66.7 percent of the time. It also means we're losing Tim Hardaway and Chris Mullin (my dark horse pick).[14] Everyone else on the list was at or above the 75 percent threshold.[15]

REMAINING DUOS: John Stockton and Karl Malone, Shaquille O'Neal and Kobe Bryant, Michael Jordan and Scottie Pippen, Chris Paul and Blake Griffin, Magic Johnson and Kareem Abdul-Jabbar, Steve Nash and Amar'e Stoudemire, Russell Westbrook and Kevin Durant, LeBron James and Dwyane Wade, Kobe Bryant and Pau Gasol, Shaquille O'Neal and Dwyane Wade, Magic Johnson and James Worthy, Shaquille O'Neal and Penny Hardaway, Yao Ming and Tracy McGrady, Tim Duncan and David Robinson, Charles Barkley and Kevin Johnson, LeBron James and Kyrie Irving, Larry Bird and Kevin McHale, Hakeem Olajuwon and Clyde Drexler, Gary Payton and Shawn Kemp, Steph Curry and

Klay Thompson, Isiah Thomas and Bill Laimbeer, Julius Erving and Moses Malone.

▶

3. Did they win a bunch of playoff series together?
I suppose that depends on what we're quantifying as "a bunch" here. Requiring our duos to have won at least 10 playoff series together feels like too big of an ask, given that only 5 of our remaining 23 duos even played together at all for 10 or more seasons.[16] That said, requiring too few series wins here would defeat the purpose of this category, given that, excepting Yao and T-Mac, they all won at least three of them, even Chris Paul and Blake Griffin, if you can even believe that. I say we split the difference and set the requirement for moving past this round of cuts as, "Any duo advancing past this round has to have won at least seven playoff series." That means we're losing Yao and T-Mac (0), Chris and Blake (3), Dr. J and Moses Malone (6; this one hurts), Shaq and Dwyane Wade (6), Charles Barkley and Kevin Johnson (5), Shaq and Penny (5), and Nash and Stoudemire (5).

REMAINING DUOS: John Stockton and Karl Malone, Shaquille O'Neal and Kobe Bryant, Michael Jordan and Scottie Pippen, Magic Johnson and Kareem Abdul-Jab-bar, Russell Westbrook and Kevin Durant, LeBron James and Dwyane Wade, Kobe Bryant and Pau Gasol, Magic Johnson and James Worthy, Tim Duncan and David

---

9. The only duos eligible were ones from after the merger. Apologies to Elgin Baylor and Jerry West, Bill Russell and Bob Cousy, Oscar Robertson and Jerry Lucas, Wilt Chamberlain and Hal Greer, George Mikan and Jim Pollard (the original Shaq and Kobe, except super not), John Havlicek and Dave Cowens, John Havlicek and Bill Russell, Sam Jones and Bill Russell (honestly, you could just stick any name you want with Bill Russell's), Bob Pettit and Slater Martin (I'm sad that we'll never have another big-time NBA player named Bob again), and Willis Reed and Walt Frazier.
10. As of me writing this sentence.
11. Tim Duncan and Tony Parker as a duo actually won 733 regular season games, good for second-place all time among duos, but I just couldn't, in my right mind, separate them from Manu Ginobili. Mostly, I avoided mentioning any of the serious Big Three groups in this chapter. I just didn't want to break them up. The only serious ones I broke up were Bird, Parish, and McHale and also LeBron, Wade, and Chris Bosh. Bird and McHale together as a duo is just too fun of a thing not to talk about, same as LeBron and Wade. All my love and best wishes to Robert Parish and Chris Bosh, though.
12. As of me writing this sentence.
13. As of me writing this sentence.
14. They were together for six seasons and made the playoffs three times.
15. Russell Westbrook and Kevin Durant were at exactly 75 percent. (Six postseason appearances in eight years together.)
16. Stockton and Malone (18), Jordan and Pippen (10), Magic and Kareem (10), Bird and McHale (12), Isiah and Laimbeer (13).

Robinson, LeBron James and Kyrie Irving, Larry Bird and Kevin McHale, Hakeem Olajuwon and Clyde Drexler, Gary Payton and Shawn Kemp, Steph Curry and Klay Thompson, Isiah Thomas and Bill Laimbeer.

▶

4. How interesting was the duo's compatibility, both on the court and philosophically?
This is probably my favorite subsection of all the subsections of this conversation, because this is really what's at the center of what makes duos so much fun and so entertaining. All the very best, most fulfilling duos have some sort of identity attached to their union; they have very set, very easy-to-identify roles and labels and jobs and faults. And more than that: All of those things from one person snap together perfectly when measured up against the ones possessed by the person they're teamed up with.

Stockton and Malone are the easiest and most complete pairing[17] (one was short, one was tall, one was white, one was black, one was unflappable, one was shaky at the worst times, one wanted nothing more on offense than to pass, one wanted nothing more on offense than to shoot, both were iron-tough, etc.), but all the elite duos had a similar pathos, which is to say that they were fundamentally aligned (even when they looked opposite of one another outwardly).

We're making some tough cuts in this category. We just talked about how Stockton and Malone were seamless, so for sure they're safe. And we know we can't cut Shaq and Kobe, given that they were Feuding Gods, and Feuding Gods is always a great angle. And we also know we can't cut Jordan and Pippen, given that Jordan was the perfect overlord and Scottie was the perfect second gun. We also can't cut LeBron and Dwyane Wade (new king + old king), or Magic and Kareem (unburdened love of life savant + ornery savant), or Gary Payton and Shawn Kemp (a true buddy cop movie), or Isiah and Laimbeer (little evil and big evil). I think those are the only ones who make it past this round, though, which is a hard thing for me to type.

We're losing: Russell Westbrook and Kevin Durant (they could never quite get all their pieces sorted);

Kobe Bryant and Pau Gasol (a successful duo, obviously, but not anywhere near as thrilling as Kobe and Shaq); Magic Johnson and James Worthy (just not as cool together as Magic and Kareem, is all); Tim Duncan and David Robinson (my heart is broken); LeBron James and Kyrie Irving (this is a hard cut to make); Larry Bird and Kevin McHale (those Celtics teams always felt a little too much like *teams* for Larry and Kevin to really have a chance here); Hakeem and Clyde (Hakeem probably would've had a better shot if we'd just paired him up with himself, if we're being honest with one another); Steph and Klay (let's you and me have this conversation again in 2021 because Steph and Klay are going to be in a different spot if they stick together through then).

REMAINING DUOS: John Stockton and Karl Malone, Shaquille O'Neal and Kobe Bryant, Michael Jordan and Scottie Pippen, Magic Johnson and Kareem Abdul-Jabbar, LeBron James and Dwyane Wade, Gary Payton and Shawn Kemp, Isiah Thomas and Bill Laimbeer.

5. How'd their partnership end?
The final seven.
- **Shaq and Kobe:** They had a swordfight atop an active volcano. Kobe eventually sliced open Shaq's chest and shoved him in it. Shaq was reborn in Miami a year later.
- **Stockton and Malone:** Stockton ended up retiring in 2003. Malone hung on for one more tumultuous season, chasing a ring with Kobe and Shaq and the Lakers in 2004. He didn't get it.
- **Isiah Thomas and Bill Laimbeer:** Laimbeer retired early in the 1994 season and Isiah's body betrayed him shortly thereafter.
- **Payton and Kemp:** Kemp turned into the real-life version of Vince Vaughn's *Delivery Man*. Payton, like Malone, attempted chasing a ring down after his and Kemp's partnership ended. (He was even on that same 2004 Lakers team as Malone, Kobe, and Shaq.) He caught up to his in Miami in 2006 on a team led by Shaq and Dwyane Wade.

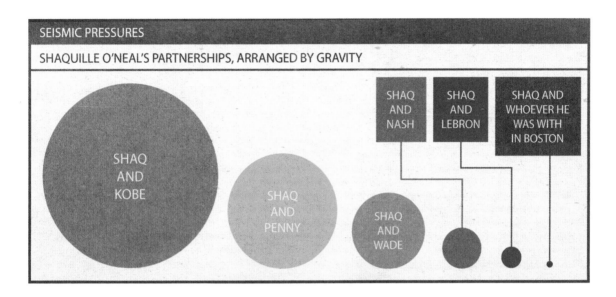

SEISMIC PRESSURES

SHAQUILLE O'NEAL'S PARTNERSHIPS, ARRANGED BY GRAVITY

SHAQ AND KOBE

SHAQ AND PENNY

SHAQ AND WADE

SHAQ AND NASH

SHAQ AND LEBRON

SHAQ AND WHOEVER HE WAS WITH IN BOSTON

- **Jordan and Pippen:** Jordan retired in 1998 (for the second of three times). Pippen left on a solo journey of self-examination.
- **Magic and Kareem:** Kareem retired in 1989. Two years later, Magic was forced to retire after finding out he'd contracted HIV.
- **LeBron and Wade:** LeBron left for home in Cleveland. Wade left for home in Chicago.

This one seems like a tricky round of cuts because minus Shaq and Kobe's ending, easily the best and most gigantic of all the endings, all the rest land within a pretty close proximity of one another. It's actually an easy cut, though. There are two duos we're losing. We're losing Isiah and Laimbeer, mostly because that ending felt very lackluster when it happened, and also we're losing LeBron and Dwyane. They get cut because they're the only one duo of the remaining non-Shaq-and-Kobe duos where one of the members still had bigger, more substantial days ahead of him.

REMAINING DUOS: John Stockton and Karl Malone, Shaquille O'Neal and Kobe Bryant, Michael Jordan and Scottie Pippen, Magic Johnson and Kareem Abdul-Jabbar, Gary Payton and Shawn Kemp.

6. Was each member of the duo in his prime during their time together?
This is a simple fill-in-the-blank category.
- **Stockton and Malone:** Duh. They played their whole goddamn lives together. (A fun thing: Stockton and Malone won a total of 906 regular season games together. Only three other guys in the whole history of the NBA ever won more.)[18]
- **Shaq and Kobe:** Nope. Shaq was the fully realized version of Shaq, but we were still four or five years from the fully realized version of Kobe.
- **Payton and Kemp:** Yes. (Here's a thing to think about: Jordan retired in 1998, officially ending that era of basketball. If we look at the final half-dozen years

---

17. While working on this book, I had a person whose name I refuse to say argue that Steve Nash and Amar'e Stoudemire were a better duo than John Stockton and Karl Malone. And while I acknowledge that they were masters of the uptempo game, I mean, *come on*. When you line them up against Stockton and Malone, they were like when you'd ask for an iPhone for Christmas and your mom would buy you an ePhone she saw at the grocery store that "looked like the one you wanted."

of that period, which is when Payton and Kemp were dynamos, the Sonics won 357 games, second only to the Bulls [362]. That's an average of almost 60 wins a season for six straight seasons. That's what Payton and Kemp did. It's incredible. And yet history barely remembers them.)

- **Jordan and Pippen:** Yes.
- **Magic and Kareem:** They overlapped primes, but certainly not as perfectly as the others.

We lose Shaq and Kobe and Magic and Kareem here.

REMAINING DUOS: John Stockton and Karl Malone, Michael Jordan and Scottie Pippen, Gary Payton and Shawn Kemp.

▶

7. Was the duo fun to watch?

When I was in middle school—this was something like seventh grade, maybe eighth—I spent the night at a friend's house. That evening, right around dinnertime, his mom hollered back toward his room that dinner was ready. We quit whatever it was we were doing (probably playing video games, but possibly ignoring each other while we looked at separate issues of *Playboy*) and walked to the kitchen. When I got to the table, I could barely believe what I saw. His mom, who, to the best of my knowledge to that point, was not an insane person, had set our dinner out for us, and guess what it was? Hand to God, it was a single piece of ham between two pieces of white bread. That's it. That's all. There was no mustard, no mayonnaise, no lettuce, no tomatoes, no nothing. There weren't even any chips on the plate, or fruit on the plate, or anything else on the table. The only thing there was bread, ham, bread, plate, top to bottom, in that exact order.

Now, to be sure, we ate it, of course. And it was fine, of course. And we felt full afterward, of course. It was sustenance, of course. We could've survived a week or month or year or entire lifetime on just that bread, ham, bread, plate, over and over again, forever, of course. But

why would we want to, and why would anyone ever want to, when there are more enjoyable foods out there, you know what I'm saying?

We're losing Stockton and Malone here.

REMAINING DUOS: Michael Jordan and Scottie Pippen, Gary Payton and Shawn Kemp.

▶

8. Tiebreaker.

We're at a tie here.

Both of our final two duos won games (though MJ and Pippen won far more). Both duos were wonderfully compatible (if we're picking sides, though, I prefer my duos to be one big guy and one small guy, so Payton and Kemp get the nod here). Both duos had narrative endings that were okay-but-not-super. Both duos featured two guys in their prime. And both duos were exceptionally fun to watch play together.

So, I say again: We're at a tie here.

I don't want to end things on a tie, though, because ties are for cowards. And I also don't want to end things by just looking at championships won, because too many basketball conversations end that way, and it's rarely ever fun. And so that means we need a different tiebreaker micro-category to tilt things one way or the other. I'm going with nicknames.

For an exceptional duo (which both of these are) to be a perfect duo (which only one of these are), both of the guys in it need to have their own very great, very neat, very dope, very wonderful nicknames. It might seem like a tiny thing, or a dumb thing, or a sidebar thing, but it's not. It's vital when you're rubbing your fingers across the texture of perfection; you have to feel that part; it has to be there.

And so, with that final benchmark in place, I say with certainty that the most perfect duo in NBA history was Gary Payton, otherwise known as The Glove, and Shawn Kemp, otherwise known as The Reign Man.

THE WINNING DUO: Gary Payton and Shawn Kemp.

---

18. Kareem won 1074, Robert Parish won 1014, and Tim Duncan won 1001.

A scenario: If you could dunk on any figure in time, past or present, basketball-related or otherwise, who would you pick? Someone famous? Someone giant? A renowned physicist? A person from your work you secretly hate? Would you dunk on James Naismith? That would be a delicious slice of irony. Would you dunk on the Pope? Anne Hathaway? Usher?

We should put at least a few rules in place here for who you can and can't pick for your Dream Dunk:

- **YOU GET ONE DUNK.** That's it. It's guaranteed to go in and it's guaranteed to be monstrous—something like Baron Davis booming on Andrei Kirilenko in Game 3 of the 2007 Western Conference Semifinals—but it's just the one. So don't waste it.[1]
- **TIME TRAVEL IS PARTIALLY ALLOWED.** We're treating this like a *Timecop* situation. Do you remember *Timecop*? It was a movie about a tiny government agency that policed time travel. One of the main parts of the time travel in that movie was, okay, you can travel through time, sure, but you can only go backward. You can't go forward in time because the future hasn't happened yet. We're doing that here, too. So if you want to pick a person from any moment in time prior to you reading this sentence at this exact moment, that's cool. Go for it. But nobody from the future is eligible.
- **JESUS CHRIST IS OUT.** It'd for sure be a lot of fun to bang one home against The Redeemer. I mean, if for nothing else than just because there'd be so many incredible things you could say to him as you were dunking on him or immediately after you dunked on him. ("Resurrect yourself from this!" "And on the eighth day God created the windmill dunk!" "You just got baptized!" "Let he without sin get yammed on!") Ultimately, though, it's just too easy

of an answer. So he's out. You can't pick him. (FYI, my number-one Dream Dunk if we were able to pick both the dunker and the dunkee: 1988 Dominique Wilkins dunking on 32 CE Jesus Christ. The Human Highlight Film vs. The Captain of Salvation. That's first-class billing.)

- **NO FICTIONAL CHARACTERS ARE ALLOWED.** Let's keep this at least a tiny bit based in reality. Your pick has to be someone real. You want to dunk on Ishmael from *Moby-Dick*? Sorry, he's out. Coach Eric Taylor from *Friday Night Lights*? He's out, too. Clarice Starling from *The Silence of the Lambs*? Nope, sorry.[2] (This one hurts. She'd be a top tier pick were this rule not in place.) Has to be an actual, real person.

So those are the four rules for this particular exercise. As long as your pick meets those requirements, he or she is eligible to get dunked on in your Dream Dunk.

▶

When I was growing up, my friends and I would play basketball at an elementary school near my house in San Antonio. There were other courts that were closer (it was about a mile walk to get to the school), and there were other courts that were more accessible (there was a tall chain-link fence that wrapped around the perimeter of the whole school that was supposed to keep people out), and there were certainly courts that posed fewer risks for playing at them (the police would show up to run us off every so often). But none of that mattered, because none of the other courts in the area offered what that particular one could: 8-foot rims.[3]

I have a very real jealousy in my bones for anyone who's able to dunk on a regulation-size rim. I've never done so, and I never will be able to do so. I have accepted this as fact, hard as it may be. Imagine that.

---

1. It'll happen during a game that you for some reason both ended up playing in.
2. You can, however, dunk on Jodie Foster if you so choose.
3. Better still: There were several courts set up around the edge of the play area. Two of the goals happened to be parallel to one another, which meant that you could play full court on them if you wanted to. This was not their intention, FYI. The two goals just happened to be positioned opposite each other by chance. A proper NBA court is 94 feet long. The distance between the goals at the school was at least 130 feet. There was also a big dip in the middle if you were running from one side to the other. And the pavement had loose rubble on it and also a few divots that could grab ahold of your foot if you stepped in them the right way. It was like playing in Boston Garden, but with fewer white people.

Imagine being born loving a thing only to grow up and realize that your body is the opposite of what's required to excel at the thing. Imagine a catfish wanting to ride a motorcycle, or a horse wanting to rock climb.[4] That was me, or *is* me, rather. That's my conundrum. I love basketball, a sport where size and strength are coveted, and yet every morning I wake up and look in the mirror and remember that I am not that. But so that's why I remember those days of trespassing onto that school's court and playing basketball there so fondly. For those hours we were there, the unreachable parts of the game were made accessible.

The first time I dunked on someone there was an exhilarating feeling. We were playing 3-on-3 and someone had driven into the lane and then passed it out to me. The guy guarding me was caught off guard by the pass, and so I was able to gain a step on him as he spun around to try and stay close to me. I jumped and he jumped, too, but he was just enough out of position that I knew he wasn't going to be able to block me. So I cocked the ball back, then rammed it through the rim as hard as I could, Zeus claiming his position as ruler of the gods. I let out a yell, slapped my own chest, then collected my high-fives from my teammates.

The best part, though: Turned out, when I'd dunked the ball, it'd hit the back part of the rim as it was going through, causing it to ricochet downward right the fuck into the guy's face who'd tried to block the dunk. So not only had I dunked my first dunk, but I'd dunked it with such ferocity that the guy who was defending me started bleeding. Dunking it so hard that your opponent starts to bleed is just about the most impressive nonsexual thing a 14-year-old boy can do. It was great. I never forgot that day, or that feeling, or that blood.

▶

Some questions to ask yourself when considering who to choose as your dunkee for your Dream Dunk:

"DO I WANT A DUNK THAT'S INTERESTING AS ITS OWN THING?"

A dunk story can be interesting for three different reasons, the first of which being the dunk itself. The story I just told earlier about the guy getting hit in the face with the ball—that's an example of this. Dunks are cool enough things that they can stand as their own story arcs if they need to. Dunks featuring feats of unusual athleticism typically fall into this category. They get specific names that live on in history as their own things. Dr. J's Rock the Baby cradle dunk, for example. Or MJ's Free Throw Line dunk. Or the Shea Serrano Bloody Nose dunk.[5] Things like that.

"DO I WANT A DUNK THAT'S INTERESTING BECAUSE I HAVE SOME SORT OF RELATIONSHIP WITH THE PERSON GETTING DUNKED ON?"

The second way a dunk story can be interesting is because of the intimate nature of the dunk: with this version what I mean is you dunk on someone that you have a personal relationship with, so that's why it's interesting. ("Oh fuck, you dunked on your grandma!?" "Oh fuck, you dunked on your principal!?") These dunks mostly exist to serve as a self actualization-type thing. You do a dunk like this because you want to carry it around in your chest, not necessarily because you want to tell other people about it. Your dad walked out on your family when you were four. You happen across him at the park when you're 19. You drop a two-handed hammer on him in the lane then burst into tears about it later when you're in your room in private. That's this dunk.

"DO I WANT A DUNK THAT'S INTERESTING BECAUSE OF HOW FAMOUS THE PERSON ON THE OTHER END OF THE DUNK IS?"

The third way a dunk story is interesting is because of the big-name recognition involved in the dunk. This kind of dunk is the story you tell at the cocktail party

---

4. I legit had an Animals Wanting To Do Things They Can't Do list of, like, 15 different things for this part and the catfish on the motorcycle and the horse rock climber were my two favorites. Some of the other ones that ended up getting cut: an elephant that wants to be a skier (he's too big); a pig that wants to be an archer (his little arms wouldn't be able to pull the arrow back far enough); a mouse that wants to be a lawyer (mice can't read); a great white shark that wants to work for the UN (great white sharks are racist).
5. I'm really trying to usher this into the dunk canon.

EXECUTIVE JUSTICE

PRESIDENTS, ARRANGED BY HOW DIFFICULT THEY (PROBABLY) WOULD BE TO DUNK ON

ABRAHAM LINCOLN
94 PERCENT DIFFICULT

GEORGE WASHINGTON
87 PERCENT DIFFICULT

BARACK OBAMA
81 PERCENT DIFFICULT

BILL CLINTON
68 PERCENT DIFFICULT

THEODORE ROOSEVELT
61 PERCENT DIFFICULT

FRANKLIN ROOSEVELT
54 PERCENT DIFFICULT

6. Abraham Lincoln would be the first best president to dunk on. Second would be Obama. Third would be Kennedy. Last would be Roosevelt after he was in the wheelchair.

7. They were especially stodgy in the 1800s. I have to believe that getting dunked on could've derailed someone's entire life back then.

8. Regarding scientists, I wouldn't mind dunking on Charles Darwin just to make some sort of "survival of the fittest" joke to him afterward. Or maybe Thomas Edison or Isaac Newton because they're the most recognizable scientist names to people who aren't scientists. I've never been a big fan of the structure of atoms so dunking on Niels Bohr could be fulfilling. I don't know. It's a hard decision. There are a lot of dunk-worthy scientists. I know one thing: Louis Pasteur is safe from catching this dunk hammer because I have a lot of respect for his work in pasteurization. Pasteurization makes milk delicious and safe. Shoutout pasteurization.

9. More blocks than anyone else in the history of the league (3,830).

10. Do you think it would be harder to dunk on Martin Luther King Jr. or Malcolm X? I bet there's no way you get that dunk off on Malcolm X. Malcolm X seems like the type who would for sure hit you with a flagrant foul before he let you dunk on him. "By any means necessary," he'd shout, as he undercut you on your way up like they did Shep in the championship game in *Above the Rim*. If you get a dunk off on Malcolm X, you really earned that shit.

and everyone wants to hear about it because everyone knows the person you dunked on. Picture you walk into a room and then someone grabs you around the shoulder and then shouts across the room, "Aye, Steve! Steve! This is the guy I was telling you about! . . . What? . . . Yeah! This is him! The guy who dunked on Beyoncé!" That's this.

"COULD THIS DUNK POSSIBLY AFFECT THE COURSE OF HISTORY IN A PROFOUND WAY?"

Maybe there's a chance World War I never happens if you dunk on Archduke Franz Ferdinand, you know what I'm saying. Or maybe you dunk on John Wilkes Booth and he never gets around to assassinating Abraham Lincoln. Ooh, or maybe you go straight to the source and dunk on Abraham Lincoln[6] instead. Who knows how that plays out? Maybe it inspires him to be an even better president.

Oh shit. Or maybe it crushes him? What if he never even gets elected president because he's never able to outrun the shame that comes along with getting posterized?[7] You dunk on Honest Abe and then hop back in your time machine to head home thinking everything is great and then you get back to today and find out that slavery is still around because you dunked Lincoln right the fuck out of the White House.

"COULD THIS DUNK POSSIBLY AFFECT THE COURSE OF HISTORY IN A POSITIVE WAY?"

I feel like maybe if you went back in time and dunked on Marie Curie she'd have been so driven to get a revenge dunk in on you that she'd have spent a little more time outside getting some fresh air and away from all that radioactive matter. You could save Marie Curie's life with a tomahawk dunk. *That's* real heroism.[8]

▶

I'm not sure who to pick for my Dream Dunk. There are so many options. I wouldn't mind dunking on 1999 Brad Pitt. The only thing I'd worry about there is my boner catching him in the eye on my way up because he was so beautiful. Ernest Hemingway seems like a good pick. (For sale: basketball shoes, once worn.) Will Smith

has been an important part of my pop culture life for a long time so crushing one on him would be especially satisfying. Bruce Willis would be high up the list for me. ("I fucking dunked on John McClane at the gym today.") It'd be cool to dunk on Mariah Carey or, if they come as a package, all four of the guys in Boyz II Men.

I just realized we've gone all this way and zero basketball names have been brought up for contention. You'd do well to go with any of the great shot blockers— Hakeem,[9] Dikembe (anybody nicknamed after a mountain is a good choice), Bill Russell, Mark Eaton (he's listed at 7'4" but I'm fairly confident he's somewhere closer to 9'6"), Tim Duncan, etc. Ben Wallace always seemed very ferocious so cramming it in against him would be pretty gratifying. Dwight Howard won Defensive Player of the Year from 2009 to 2011 so he'd be a good pick. (Bonus reason: *HE'S DWIGHT HOWARD* and Dwight Howard has been annoying since, like, 2008).

Maybe James Harden. Maybe Xavier McDaniel. Maybe Bill Laimbeer. Maybe Gregg Popovich. Maybe Aaron Rodgers. Walt Disney. George Washington Carver. One of the Kardashians. All of the Kardashians. Kanye. Tupac.

Channing Tatum? Pre-2002 Ginuwine? Audrey Hepburn? Carmen Electra? Antonio Banderas? Arnold Schwarzenegger? Jean-Claude Van Damme? Selena? Leonardo DiCaprio? Montell Jordan?

Oh snap.

I got it.

I know who my Dream Dunk is on.

I got it.

It's perfect.

It's so perfect.

Are you ready for this?

Okay.

I'm dunking on . . .

. . . wait for it . . .

. . . wait . . .

. . . hold on . . .

. . . here it comes . . .

Martin Luther King Jr.[10]

I'm dunking on MLK.

That's my Dream Dunk.

That's my dream.

WHICH NBA PLAYER'S LEGACY
IS THE MOST GREATLY AFFECTED
IF WE GIVE HIM THE
CHAMPIONSHIP HE NEVER WON?

This is a list of 13 very great NBA players who never won a championship.[1] Included with each person's name is a number. That number represents that player's placement in ESPN's All-Time Best NBA Player Rankings conversation:[2] Karl Malone (16th), Charles Barkley (18th), John Stockton (19th), Steve Nash (30th), Patrick Ewing (32nd), Dominique Wilkins (44th), Allen Iverson (46th), Reggie Miller (51st), Carmelo Anthony (59th; he's still playing as I write this but I'm guessing he's never going to win one[3]), Shea Serrano[4] (62nd[5]), Tracy McGrady (63rd), Chris Webber (66th), Vince Carter (69th), and Dikembe Mutombo (73rd).

I mention their ranks because we need them for the thing we're going to figure out here, which is: Pretend we can go back in time. Pretend, while on our way to back in time, we tinker with some of the universe's inner gears and spin some of its knobs the opposite direction. Pretend that by doing so we change the results of some key playoff games and key playoff series. Pretend that some people we know to have won championships in our lifetimes actually lost those championships, and pretend that some people we know to have lost championships in our lifetimes actually won those championships. If we do that for each of the players mentioned in the above paragraph, if we give each person the championship he missed out on, then whose legacy is the most greatly affected?

▶

Let's go player by player through those 13, and for each one I'm going to list three things:

1. HIS ALL-TIME BEST NBA PLAYER RANK.

I would like to mention here that I don't necessarily agree with the placement of each player on ESPN's list.[6] (Steph Curry, for example, who is for sure a darling and obviously great, is already listed as the 23rd greatest NBA player of all time, which is preposterous.) We just needed a list to use to keep things in order and theirs seemed solid enough.

2. THE PLAYOFF GAME CHANGES WE'RE RIGGING IN HIS FAVOR.

I think a good way to handle this one is, okay, if we have to change a whole bunch of stuff in history to get a player his championship, then that player's legacy gets pumped up less than someone for whom we only need to change one or two things to get him his title. So think on it like: Patrick Ewing came within one game of winning a championship. (His Knicks lost in Game 7 of the Finals to the Rockets in 1994.) He only needs for us to make some very minor changes to history for him to get a ring. Meanwhile, Tracy McGrady never made it out of the first round of the playoffs while he was a key player on a team.[7] We have to rearrange planets to get him his ring. As such, Patrick's legacy would get a greater bump by him winning a title than McGrady's would by him winning one. It's one of those "You have to help me help you" situations.

3. THE POTENTIAL RAMIFICATIONS OF THE CHANGES MADE.

In addition to looking at what winning a championship would mean for someone, we have to talk about what happens when we start taking away championships from other players. It's an equally interesting and important thing because within the mythology of sports, things that don't happen are often as impactful as things that do happen.

---

1. I didn't include Elgin Baylor. I'm not sure why, I just didn't. Sorry.
2. They made the ranking in 2016.
3. This part made me sad to write.
4. This part made me happy to write. It's not true, though. I did not really play in the NBA.
5. They actually have Alex English at 62nd. I didn't include him either. Sorry. Consider this my formal apology to Alex, to the entire English family, to anyone who speaks English, to anyone named Alex.
6. The first 25: 1. Jordan, 2. Kareem, 3. LeBron, 4. Magic, 5. Wilt, 6. Bird, 7. Bill Russell, 8. Timmy, 9. Shaq, 10. Hakeem, 11. The Big O, 12. Kobe, 13. Jerry West, 14. Dr. J, 15. Moses Malone, 16. Karl, 17. Dirk, 18. Barkley, 19. Stockton, 20. The Admiral, 21. KG, 22. Durant, 23. Steph Curry, 24. Elgin Baylor, 25. Scottie Pippen.
7. He went to the Finals with the Spurs in 2013 as a bit player.

▶

I lied.

Sort of. I'm not going to do a longform version of an answer for each player I listed earlier because it's already pretty clear which ones are serious contenders for having their legacies impacted the greatest amounts and which ones are not. As such, I'm just going to burn through the five non-contenders here before we get to the eight actual real contenders.

JOHN STOCKTON (19TH): The NBA's all-time leader in assists and also the all-time leader in steals, so of course he is a force. But he also played his entire career with Karl Malone,[8] which, I mean, come on. Let's say we give the Jazz the 1997 title over the Bulls. Most of the credit and acclaim will go to Malone if that happens, even if Stockton was the whole entire reason they won. His legacy is nearly the same with or without a title. // He gets his ring and he jumps from 19th to 17th, still one spot behind Malone.

REGGIE MILLER (51ST): My heart is telling me that if Reggie wins that 2000 Finals (where his Pacers lost to the Lakers, 4–2), he jumps from 51st all the way to 1st. My brain, however, is telling me that it's actually probably something like he jumps from 51st to 32nd, and that even despite that big move, it doesn't do a whole, whole bunch for his legacy beyond enhancing his reputation as a deadly late-game performer, which is already airtight.

CARMELO ANTHONY[9] (59TH): The closest Carmelo ever got to winning a title was when his Nuggets made it to Game 6 of the Western Conference Finals in 2009. They lost to the Lakers there, and then the Lakers beat Dwight Howard and the Magic in the Finals. Let's swap that. The Nuggets beat the Lakers in the Conference Finals and then beat the Magic in the Finals. Is anyone really excited by that? // He jumps from 59th to 54th.

CHRIS WEBBER (66TH): Love. We get to give Webber and his maniac Kings the 2002 title.[10] And since we're making things up, let's also go ahead and make up that he dominates in the Finals. Check this out: For his first five seasons in Sacramento (1999–2003),

Webber averaged 24.1 points per game, 10.9 rebounds per game, 4.7 assists per game, 1.6 blocks per game, and 1.5 steals per game. That's such a tough stat line. Let's say that Webber upped all of those numbers a tick in the Pretend Finals. He gets his ring, he gets to take down the Lakers while doing so, and he gets to wash away the "choker" label that chased him around. All great things for Webber. That said, all his championship likely does is end up legitimizing his cult hero status. // He jumps from 66th to 51st.

DIKEMBE MUTOMBO (73RD): Same as what happened with Stockton, if we give a title to Dikembe— like, say we give him a ring for 2001 when his Sixers made it to the Finals and got smashed by the Lakers— all the credit is going to end up going to Allen Iverson, that team's supernova. // If Dikembe gets a ring, he jumps from 73rd to 70th.

THE EIGHT CONTENDERS

PLAYER:	Karl Malone
RANKING:	16th
YEAR HE'S WINNING THE CHAMPIONSHIP:	1997 (His Jazz lost to the Bulls in the Finals, 4–2.)

I'm picking this year over giving him the 1998 championship for a couple of reasons.

First, and this is the most important thing here: I don't want to erase Michael Jordan's last shot as a Chicago Bull being a swish that wins the Bulls a championship. Sorry.

Second, this was the year John Stockton buried the Rockets with a three at the buzzer in Game 6 of the Western Conference Finals to send the Jazz to the Finals. Those kinds of moments are always great to look back on and say, "That was it. That was when we knew the Jazz were winning the title that year."

Third, Malone won the league MVP that season. It just makes sense for us to juice the Finals so he also gets the Finals MVP trophy, too.

And fourth, Malone missed two gigantic free throws at the end of Game 1 of the Finals that year that would've given the Jazz a two-point lead with 9.2 seconds to go. Jordan hit the walk-off jumper at the buzzer after that to win the game for the Bulls, which super magnified the "Malone shrinks in the biggest moments" criticisms. So we're going to take that and just flip-flop those results: Malone hits the free throws, Jordan misses, the Jazz steal Game 1, and all of a sudden Karl Malone is clutch.

Games 2, 3, and 4 all play out in our fake scenario like they did in the real scenario (Bulls win Game 2, Jazz win Games 3 and 4), which puts them up 3–1 now. The Flu Game still happens in Game 5, except this time we're draining just a tiny bit of juice from Jordan's legs so that he misses the three he hit to give the Bulls the lead in the final minute. In our fake version, it rims out, Malone gets the rebound, he's fouled, he hits the free throws to give the Jazz a two-point lead, the Bulls miss their next shot, and that's that.

How Do Things Look Different Afterward? Malone, like Webber, gets to shed the "choker" tag, which is huge. Bigger than that, though, is that all of his other accolades (among them: 2-time league MVP, 14-time All-Star, 11-time All-NBA First Team, second in the history of the league in scoring) all of a sudden start to look way, way, way shinier. Winning that ring in 1997 would jump him at least up to the 13th spot, overtaking Julius Erving and Jerry West along the way (but still leaving him behind Jordan, Kareem, LeBron, Magic, Wilt, Larry, Russell, Timmy, Shaq, Hakeem, Oscar, and Kobe).

PLAYER:	Steve Nash
RANKING:	30th
YEAR HE'S WINNING THE CHAMPIONSHIP:	2007 (His Suns lost to the Spurs in the Western Conference Semifinals, 4–2.)

Nash never made a Finals, so it'd seem like getting there would mean we'd have to change a whole bunch of stuff. That's not the case, though. It's an easy fix because at the end of Game 4 of the 2007 Western Conference Semifinals (a game the Suns would go on to win), Robert Horry hip-checked Steve Nash into the scorer's table as he tried to dribble the ball up the court. When it happened, Amar'e Stoudemire and Boris Diaw jumped off the bench and ran onto the floor, which led to their suspensions for Game 5, which the Spurs won, then closed out the series in six. Let's make it so that those two dummies don't come off the bench, the Suns win Game 5 at home, lose Game 6 in San Antonio like they did in the real scenario, then win Game 7 to go to the Conference Finals. Once there, they blow out the ultra mismatched Jazz, and then in the Finals they also blow out the ultra mismatched Cavs. Nash gets his ring.

How Do Things Look Different Afterward? It's a big jump for Nash. There are only 14 players in the history of the NBA who have won two or more MVP trophies. Steve Nash is one of them. He's also one of only two players in that group to not have a title, though.[11] If he gets one, it becomes basically impossible to keep him out of the Top 20, which is wild to think about. What

---

8. Technically, Stockton entered the NBA one year earlier than Malone, but the general point stands.

9. If I'm being all the way honest, Chris Paul should be included in this chapter. I don't think he'll ever win a championship either. It's very sad, too, because he's incredible. As I write this, he's first in Offensive Rating, third in Win Shares per 48 Minutes, third in Offensive Box Plus/Minus, sixth in PER, second in Assist Percentage, ninth in Steal Percentage, sixth in Playoff PER, second in Playoff Assist Percentage, fifth in Playoff Steal Percentage, seventh in Playoff Offensive Rating, fifth in Playoff Win Shares per 48 Minutes, and third in Playoffs Box Plus/Minus. You don't even have to know what all that shit means, really. All you have to know is that if there's a stat important to point guards, Paul is somewhere near the top. His ring turns him from a stat darling into a champion stat darling. Without a title he's 29th on ESPN's rankings. With one, I think he jumps all the way to 17th, at the very least.

10. It feels like I've been trying to give that team a title for this entire book.

11. Karl Malone is the other.

also happens is that the Suns' speedball version of basketball, where they were just really running teams to
death, becomes legitimized, like what we saw happen
when the 2015 Warriors won the title. All big things for
Nash. He jumps from 30th to 20th.

PLAYER:	Charles Barkley
RANKING:	18th
YEAR HE'S WINNING THE CHAMPIONSHIP:	1993 (His Suns lost to the Bulls in the Finals, 4–2.)

We don't have to change very much here to help Barkley get his ring. The Suns were down 103–106 in the
final minute of Game 2 of the 1993 Finals. Danny
Ainge, who'd just hit a three and then a layup, had a
chance to tie the game on a three-point attempt but
Scottie Pippen, that fucking beautiful shark, he managed to block the shot. The Suns ended up losing the
game 111–108. Let's take that Pippen play and make
it so that rather than him blocking the shot, Ainge not
only is able to get it off, but he also makes it while
being fouled and then makes the free throw, too, giving
the Suns a 107–106 lead that they hold on to. So now
the series is tied, 1–1.

In the real scenario, the Suns won that iconic triple
overtime game in Game 3. We'll obviously keep that the
same, so now the Suns are up 2–1. The Bulls won Game
4 in the real scenario. We'll keep that the same, too, so
now it's 2–2. The Suns won Game 5 in the real scenario,
so that stays the same, which has us at 3–2. And the
Bulls won Game 6 in the real scenario (that's the game
where John Paxson hit the three to put the Bulls up
one with 3.9 seconds left). In our fake scenario, Paxson
misses, Barkley gets the rebound, makes the free
throws, and there you go: Sir Charles wins his championship. All we had to do was get an and-one on Scottie
Pippen in Game 2 and a brick from John Paxson at the
end of Game 6. Easy work.

How Do Things Look Different Afterward? Very different. Consider this: This was the season after the Dream

Team was a global phenomenon, and Barkley was the
runaway best basketball player during that Olympics.
So you have that, *plus* he won the league MVP in 1993,
plus he won his first championship by beating the
wildly competitive Jordan. Is there any way that
Jordan retires that season after that string of events? It
doesn't seem likely, does it? So we're stealing Jordan's
1993 championship, but does that mean he sticks
around for the 1994 season and also the 1995 season?
And if so, do we get five straight titles from the Bulls
from 1994 to 1998? And while all of that is going on with
Jordan, what's going on with Barkley? Does he rate as
a Top 10 player of all time if he retires with that 1993
ring? It feels a lot like he does.

PLAYER:	Dominique Wilkins and Vince Carter
RANKING:	44th and 69th, respectively
YEAR HE'S WINNING THE CHAMPIONSHIP:	Dominique wins the 1988 title and Vince wins the 2001.

Dominique, a mega-force dunk-monster, dueled with
Larry Bird in a wonderful series in the second round of
the playoffs in 1988. His team lost by a bucket in Game
7. Vince, a mega-force dunk-monster, dueled with Allen
Iverson in a wonderful series in the second round of the
playoffs in 2001. His team lost by a bucket in Game 7.

For Dominique, we're letting him hit a three at the
buzzer to get his Hawks past the Celtics in Game 7.
Then he gets them past the Pistons in the Conference
Finals. Then, in a miraculous showing, he out-guns the
Showtime Lakers to win the 1988 championship. For
Vince, we're letting him hit a two at the buzzer to get
his Raptors past the Sixers in Game 7. Then he gets
them past the Bucks in the Conference Finals. Then, in
a miraculous showing, he out-guns the New Showtime
Lakers to win the 2001 championship.

How Do Things Look Different Afterward? They probably
don't look all that different for Vince—at least, not if

we're talking about big picture stuff. He was never a serious MVP contender[12] and never even made an All-NBA First Team. If we give him the 2001 title—which, to be sure, would've been monumental because it means he'd have had to beat the best version of the Shaq-Kobe Lakers we ever saw—it'd probably end up being seen as an aberration of sorts. He certainly makes a jump in the rankings, but it's probably just him going from 69th all-time to 59th all-time, putting him one spot above Carmelo.

For Dominique, his title has a much bigger effect on his legacy. He was left off the Dream Team in 1992, but if he beats Magic for a ring in 1988 then he almost certainly gets on there,[13] and that does wonders for his everything. He makes the NBA's Top 50 list in 1996, which he was also somehow left off of. And so even with just those two accomplishments on his resume, we're talking about him less as just a boutique talent from the '80s and more of a massive, important figure. He jumps from 44th to 32nd, knocking Patrick Ewing back a spot to take his position.

PLAYER:	Patrick Ewing
RANKING:	32nd
YEAR HE'S WINNING THE CHAMPIONSHIP:	1994 (His Knicks lost to the Rockets in the Finals, 4—3.)

John Starks goes 5–18 instead of 2–18. The Knicks win Game 7 by one, 91–90, instead of losing it by six.[14]

How Do Things Look Different Afterward? Possibly very different. Hakeem's two championships (particularly grabbing them back-to-back) are a decent-sized part of the reason he's regularly considered one of the 10 greatest basketball players ever.[15] If he only has one, how far back does he fall? And if he loses in the Finals to Ewing, that means Ewing holds an NCAA Championship game over Hakeem and also an NBA championship over him, too. Do people start arguing that Ewing is better than Hakeem? Does that happen? Let me know if that pretend happens during these pretend conversations so I can fucking pretend fight everyone. Thank you.

PLAYER:	Tracy McGrady
RANKING:	63rd
YEAR HE'S WINNING THE CHAMPIONSHIP:	I don't know. It doesn't matter. Pick whatever one you want. 2003? Do you want that one? Let's use that one since that's the season he averaged over 32.1 points per game.

How Do Things Look Different Afterward? I actually hadn't intended on including Tracy McGrady in this. While I was working on this chapter, though, my researcher, Mike Lynch, sent me this note: "Tracy McGrady would be a super interesting case. He could be like the Sandy Koufax or Gale Sayers of the NBA if he had a ring. Koufax and Sayers get talked about among the best at their position in the history of each of their games despite their short careers. (Or maybe Bill Walton is already the NBA's version of this?) T-Mac had a shorter prime than most due to injuries, but holy shit, his peak was about as good as any wing has ever been. At 23, he led the NBA in PER, Offensive Win Shares, Win Shares per 48 Minutes, and Box Plus/Minus. From 2001 to 2007, he had a 6.5 Box Plus/Minus. For context, during that span Kobe was 5.2, Vince was 4.5, Ray Allen was 4.1, and Paul Pierce was 3.8. We might be talking about if he would have been the best ever without the injuries if he had won a ring as a young player before his demise."

T-Mac gets his 2003 ring, he's jumping from 63rd to 38th.

PLAYER:	Allen Iverson
RANKING:	46th
YEAR HE'S WINNING THE CHAMPIONSHIP:	2001 (His Sixers lost to the Lakers in the Finals, 4—1.)

Chris Paul, a master facilitator willing to be a slithering snake when necessary, is on one side of the point guard spectrum. Allen Iverson, a righteous warrior who scored

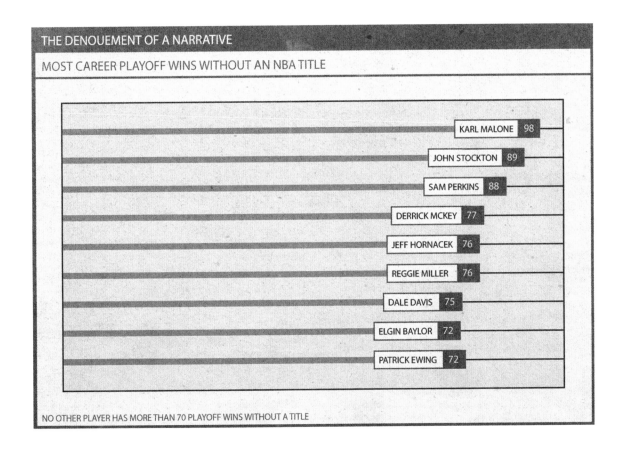

THE DENOUEMENT OF A NARRATIVE

MOST CAREER PLAYOFF WINS WITHOUT AN NBA TITLE

KARL MALONE	98
JOHN STOCKTON	89
SAM PERKINS	88
DERRICK MCKEY	77
JEFF HORNACEK	76
REGGIE MILLER	76
DALE DAVIS	75
ELGIN BAYLOR	72
PATRICK EWING	72

NO OTHER PLAYER HAS MORE THAN 70 PLAYOFF WINS WITHOUT A TITLE

the way those 50-caliber machine guns shoot bullets in old war movies,[16] is on the exact opposite side. Giving him a championship ring for 2001 is my favorite thing to daydream about. It's half the reason I wanted to write the book. I just wanted to write the sentence "Allen Iverson wins the 2001 championship." Imagine that.

How Do Things Look Different Afterward? I never ever stop crying. Iverson jumps from 46th to 25th.

So, which NBA player's legacy is the most greatly affected if we give him the championship he never won? I think it's Barkley. It has to be Barkley. We have to change just a tiny amount to get him his ring, and him getting his ring ends up with him jumping up into the ultra elite level of iconography. After him, it's Malone. After that, it's probably Ewing. And then after that, it's a toss-up, the same as all of this, really.

---

12. Vince's best-ever finish in MVP voting was when he finished 10th in the 2000 season.
13. I hate to do it, but he can have Chris Mullin's spot.
14. In this pretend scenario, Starks makes two 15-footers and hits a late three he otherwise missed.
15. ESPN has him in their All-Time Rankings as 10th.
16. Iverson has three 50-point playoff games. Only MJ (8) and Wilt (4) have more. And his 29.7 points per game average for his playoff career is second-best in NBA history to Jordan (33.5).

ACKNOWLEDGMENTS

There are a lot of people I need to thank.

Thank you to Samantha Weiner. You are a far more patient and understanding editor than I have any right to expect. I appreciate the way you let me roam around in outer space while I'm writing these books we work on together, and I also appreciate the way you keep me tethered to the planet so I don't float too far away and get myself killed. You deserve everything good that happens to you.

Thank you to Arturo. The artwork you did here is the most interesting and auspicious you've done yet. You're the best at drawing. I'm a big fan of yours. You're also the worst at deadlines. So sometimes I want to fight. Sorry about any of the times I cussed you out while we were working on this book.

Thank you to Mike Lynch. I am so glad I found you and that you agreed to fact-check the book and also to help me research for the book. This book would be a floppy, floppy mess without you. Thank you to Cole Mickelson, who also helped me research for the book. I can't even say how thankful I am that you were there to answer all of the emails I sent you because I don't know big enough words. You're a gem and the best.

Thank you to Sebit Min for designing this book, to Devin Grosz, my design manager, and thank you to Annalea Manalili, Margaret Moore, Shauna Rossano, and Tim Stobierski for copyediting and proofreading this book. I appreciate it a great deal. I hope that it was not too terrible fixing all of my mistakes.

Thank you to all of the talented and exceptional people who contributed a blurb to the Memory Heroes chapter of this book. That means Bill Simmons, Sean Fennessey, Ramona Shelburne, Seerat Sohi, Chris Ryan, Rembert Browne, Candace Buckner, Jonathan Abrams, Zach Lowe, Doris Burke, Jason Concepcion, Mike Lynch, and Kristen Ledlow. I wish you all knew how much it means to me that you were willing to participate. Please let me know if I can ever help any of you with anything. (Except you, Rembert.)

Since we're here, let me send an extra thank you to Kristen Ledlow, who, in addition to writing a blurb, was the person who arranged for Reggie Miller to write the foreword. I sent her one email outlining what I was hoping to have happen; she responded with something like, "Don't worry. I got you," and then two days later I was on the phone with Reggie.

Thank you to Reggie. I remember being in high school and *Sports Illustrated* had this promo CD that they sent to people (this was back in the early days of the Internet when there wasn't streaming video). The CD was clips of a bunch of sporting events they'd determined to be excellent. One of those was that 25-point fourth quarter you had against the Knicks in the playoffs. I must've watched that thing about 500 times. I still watch it today (on YouTube now). I feel like I have a hundred tiny anecdotes like that about you. You'll likely never know how important you were to my basketball fandom (and the basketball fandom of so many others), but I'll never stop trying to explain it.

Oh, let me do some extra thank yous to Sean Fennessey and Bill Simmons right here, too. Thank you for letting me come work for you at *The Ringer*. I never told you all (or anyone) this, but I was standing in the backyard with Larami and the baby when we were going back and forth on the phone during the pre-hiring stuff. When we got everything nailed down, I hung up the phone, looked at Larami, smiled, looked at the sky, screamed as loud as I could, then grabbed the ball the baby was playing with out of his hands and kicked it a million miles into the sky.

Thank you to the FOH ARMY. I am rooting for every single person in it. I desperately want to see all of you win so many times that you get tired of winning, at which point you win a trophy for being the first ever to get tired of winning. Even if those Ws come few and far between, though, just know that I am here and I will always protect you and love you and shield you from the ugliness of the world.

Thank you to everyone I leaned on, either directly or indirectly, for some kind of basketball insight while I was working on this book, including but not limited to all of the people I mentioned who wrote blurbs, Jade Hoye, Dan Devine, Amin Elhassan, Henry Abbott, Tony Parker, Kirk Goldsberry, Gregg Popovich, Manu Ginóbili, the cast of *Pitch Perfect*, the cast of *Blood In Blood Out*, each of *The Starters*, anyone who's ever participated on NBA TV's *Open Court*, Evan Auerbach, Kevin Pelton, Kevin Arnovitz, Kevin O'Connor, Jonathan Tjarks, Bill Barnwell, Clinton Yates, Michelle Beadle, Rachel Nichols, the Super Secret Basketball Email Chain, Twitter, Paul Cantor, all of the Slack channels I belong to, Chaz and Larry Culbertson, Alfred Young, my dad, my uncles, my cousin Gary and my cousin Jesse, and probably a bunch of other people I'm accidentally leaving out because I'm an idiot.

Thank you to Basketball-Reference for existing. I love you so, so much. I hope that you are around forever because life without you would be awful.

Thank you to James Naismith for inventing basketball, and thank you to Barry Tuttle's dad for installing the first basketball goal on our street when we were in middle school and letting us all play on it, and thank you to Tim Duncan for the championships you brought to San Antonio and also for wearing a leg brace that had The Punisher on it.

Thank you to my sisters, Yasminda and Nastasja and Marie. I have enjoyed watching all three grow up into women and two of you grow into loving, caring mothers. (Marie, don't have a baby with that idiot.)

Thank you to my dog. You know all of my secrets and will never tell anyone. I respect you so much.

Thank you to my mom for being my mom and to my dad for taking me to so many Spurs games growing up. It always meant a lot to me that that was our thing we did together, and I am very excited and happy to be doing the same thing with my sons now. I'll make sure they see and pay attention to all the things you would make sure I saw and paid attention to when we'd go.

Thank you to my sons, Caleb and Braxton and Parker. You three are the biggest dorks of all and I just love you so much for it. The only thing I care about is hugging you and kissing you and talking to you and going into your bedrooms while you're sleeping and looking at your perfect, perfect, dorky faces. Please never grow up.

And thank you to my wife, Larami. As I write this, you are lying in the bed next to me asleep, looking perfect and being perfect. It's 1 A.M. and you just went to bed about 20 minutes ago. You were up for 19 hours today, and you were taking care of either me or the boys or the dog for about 18 of those hours. I don't know how you do it. I honestly don't. Everything would be a disaster without you. You're the center of it all—of my life, of my love, of my happiness, of the family. Thank you. I love you. I don't deserve you, but I am glad that I have you.

Editor: Samantha Weiner
Designer: Sebit Min
Production Manager: Alex Cameron

Library of Congress Control Number:
2017930301

ISBN: 978-1-4197-2647-7

ABRAMS The Art of Books
195 Broadway, New York, NY 10007
abramsbooks.com

WILL
SMITH
GUARD
FLEER '18

MONICA
WRIGHT
GUARD
FLEER '18

JIM
HALPERT
FORWARD
FLEER '18

CLARENCE
WITHERS
GUARD
FLEER '18

NO. 22 PICK — Monica Wright

HEIGHT: 5'7"

WEIGHT: approximately 130 pounds

POSITION: point guard

Most Memorable On-Court Moment: Winning a one-on-one matchup against Quincy McCall in college.

Monica was a star player in high school, a star player in college, and a star player on the team that won the championship in a women's professional league overseas. There is no fear in her. She would make a fine pick for any team looking to strengthen their guard play for the upcoming season.

NO. 11 PICK — Will Smith

HEIGHT: 6'2"

WEIGHT: approximately 180 pounds

POSITION: guard

Most Memorable On-Court Moment: Demolishing Isiah Thomas in a game of one-on-one in a dream.

Smith, a high-school-to-the-NBA prodigy, averaged 61.5 points per game during his high school career.* Best case scenario, he ends up being the new Kobe. Worst case scenario, he ends up washing out of the league and becoming an actor, though, to be all the way honest, both of those options sound like good things to me.

*In the two games we see him play, I mean.

NO. 17 PICK — Clarence Withers

HEIGHT: 5'10"

WEIGHT: approximately 160 pounds

POSITION: guard

Most Memorable On-Court Moment: Executing the first-ever alley-oop.

Clarence was, to be sure, the most talented of any of the basketball players in *Semi-Pro*, but mostly he's getting drafted at the 17th spot because he was played by André 3000, and André 3000's verse on 2007's "Walk It Out (Remix)" was so good and perfect that I feel like he'd have little to no problem at all playing in the NBA, even though I'm not entirely sure how those two things are related.

NO. 26 PICK — James Duncan "Jim" Halpert

HEIGHT: 6'3"

WEIGHT: approximately 190 pounds

POSITION: small forward

Most Memorable On-Court Moment: Giving a Michael Jordan shrug to another man's fiancée after scoring a basket.

There are only six minutes of footage of Jim Halpert playing basketball in all nine seasons of *The Office*, but in that tiny amount of time he displayed fearlessness, tenacity, intelligence, savvy, a firm allegiance to team, assertiveness, toughness, and a willingness to obliterate a man in front of the woman that man's supposed to marry. Jim Halpert is a winner.